Autodesk Inventor 2016
Learn by doing

Tutorial Books

Copyright © 2015 Kishore

This book may not be duplicated in any way without the express written consent of the publisher, except in the form of brief excerpts or quotations for the purpose of review. The information contained herein is for the personal use of the reader and may not be incorporated in any commercial programs, other books, database, or any kind of software without written consent of the publisher. Making copies of this book or any portion for purpose other than your own is a violation of copyright laws.

Limit of Liability/Disclaimer of Warranty:
The author and publisher make no representations or warranties with respect to the accuracy or completeness of the contents of this work and specifically disclaim all warranties, including without limitation warranties of fitness for a particular purpose. The advice and strategies contained herein may not be suitable for every situation. Neither the publisher nor the author shall be liable for damages arising here from.

Trademarks:
All brand names and product names used in this book are trademarks, registered trademarks, or trade names of their respective holders. The author and publisher is not associated with any product or vendor mentioned in this book.

Download Resource Files from:

www.tutorialbook.info

Contents

Chapter 1: Getting Started with Inventor 2016 1

   Starting Autodesk Inventor 2

   User Interface 3

      Ribbon 3

      Application Menu 5

      Quick Access Toolbar 6

      Browser window 6

      Status bar 6

      Navigation Bar 7

      ViewCube 7

      Shortcut Menus and Marking Menus 7

      Dialogs 8

      Customizing the Ribbon, Shortcut Keys, and Marking Menus 9

      Color Settings 10

Chapter 2: Part Modeling Basics 1

   TUTORIAL 1 1

      Creating a New Project 1

      Starting a New Part File 12

      Starting a Sketch 12

      Adding Dimensions 12

      Creating the Base Feature 13

      Adding an Extruded Feature 16

      Adding another Extruded Feature 17

      Saving the Part 18

   TUTORIAL 2 19

      Starting a New Part File 19

      Sketching a Revolve Profile 19

      Creating the Revolved Feature 20

      Creating the Cut feature 21

Contents

    Creating another Cut feature 22

    Adding a Fillet 23

    Saving the Part 23

  TUTORIAL 3 23

    Starting a New Part File 24

    Creating the Cylindrical Feature 24

    Creating Cut feature 24

    Saving the Part 25

  TUTORIAL 4 25

    Start Extruded feature 25

    Applying Draft 25

    Saving the Part 26

Chapter 3: Assembly Basics 27

  TUTORIAL 1 27

    Top-Down Approach 28

    Bottom-Up Approach 28

    Starting a New Assembly File 28

    Inserting the Base Component 28

    Adding the second component 28

    Applying Constraints 28

    Adding the Third Component 33

    Checking the Interference 35

    Saving the Assembly 35

    Starting the Main assembly 35

    Adding Disc to the Assembly 35

    Placing the Sub-assembly 36

    Adding Constraints 36

    Placing the second instance of the Sub-assembly 37

    Saving the Assembly 37

  TUTORIAL 2 37

    Starting a New Presentation File 37

v

Contents

Creating the Exploded View 37
Animating the Explosion 39

Chapter 4: Creating Drawings **41**

TUTORIAL 1 41
    Starting a New Drawing File 41
    Editing the Drawing Sheet 42
    Generating the Base View 42
    Generating the Section View 43
    Creating the Detailed View 44
    Creating Centermarks and Centerlines 44
    Retrieving Dimensions 45
    Adding additional dimensions 46
    Populating the Title Block 47
    Saving the Drawing 48

TUTORIAL 2 48
    Creating New Sheet Format 48
    Creating a Custom Template 50
    Starting a Drawing using the Custom template 52
    Adding Dimensions 52

TUTORIAL 3 .... **53**
    Creating a New Drawing File 53
    Generating Base View 53
    Generating the Exploded View 54
    Configuring the Parts list settings 54
    Creating the Parts list 54
    Creating Balloons 55
    Saving the Drawing 55

Chapter 5: Additional Modeling Tools **57**

TUTORIAL 1 57
    Creating the First Feature 57
    Adding the Second feature 60

Contents

    Creating a Counterbore Hole 60

    Creating a Threaded hole 61

    Creating a Circular Pattern 62

    Creating Chamfers 63

TUTORIAL 2 63

    Creating the first feature 64

    Creating the Shell feature 65

    Creating the Third feature 66

    Creating a Cut Feature 67

    Creating the Rib Feature 67

TUTORIAL 3 69

    Creating the Coil 69

TUTORIAL 4 70

    Creating First Section and Rails 71

    Creating the second section 72

    Creating the Loft feature 73

    Creating the Extruded feature 73

    Creating the Emboss feature 74

    Mirroring the Emboss feature 74

    Creating Fillets 75

    Shelling the Model 75

    Adding Threads 75

TUTORIAL 5 77

    Creating a 3D Sketch 77

    Creating the Sweep feature 81

    Creating the Along Curve pattern 82

    Editing the Freeform Shape 85

    Create another Freeform box 86

TUTORIAL 6 87

    Start a new part file 87

    Creating the second feature 87

Contents

    Adding Threads 88

    Creating iParts 89

  TUTORIAL 7 92

    Creating the First Feature 92

    Creating the Extruded surface 92

    Replacing the top face of the model with the surface 93

    Creating a Face fillet 93

    Creating a Variable Radius fillet 94

    Shelling the Model 95

    Creating the Boss Features 95

    Creating the Lip feature 97

    Creating the Grill Feature 98

Chapter 6: Sheet Metal Modeling **101**

  TUTORIAL 1 101

    Starting a New Sheet metal File 101

    Setting the Parameters of the Sheet Metal part 101

    Creating the Base Feature 102

    Creating the flange 103

    Creating the Contour Flange 103

    Creating the Corner Seam 105

    Creating a Sheet Metal Punch iFeature 105

    Creating a Punched feature 108

    Creating the Rectangular Pattern 109

    Creating the Bend Feature 111

    Applying a corner round 112

    Creating Countersink holes 112

    Creating Hem features 113

    Mirroring the Features 114

    Creating the Flat Pattern 115

    Creating 2D Drawing of the sheet metal part 116

Chapter 7: Top-Down Assembly and Motion Simulation **119**

Contents

TUTORIAL 1 119
Creating a New Assembly File 119
Creating a component in the Assembly 119
Creating the Second Component of the Assembly 121
Creating the third Component of the Assembly 122
Adding Bolt Connections to the assembly 124
Applying the constraint to the components 126

TUTORIAL 2 127
Creating the Slider Joint 128
Creating the Rotational Joint 130
Creating the Rigid Joint 131
Driving the joints 132

Chapter 8: Dimensions and Annotations **135**

TUTORIAL 1 135
Creating Centerlines and Centered Patterns 136
Editing the Hatch Pattern 138
Applying Dimensions 138
Placing the Datum Feature 142
Placing the Feature Control Frame 143
Placing the Surface Texture Symbols 144
Modifying the Title Block Information 145

Additional Exercises **146**

Exercise 1 146
Exercise 2 147
Exercise 3 148
Exercise 4 149
Exercise 5 150
Exercise 6 151

Contents

INTRODUCTION

Autodesk Inventor as a topic of learning is vast, and having a wide scope. It is package of many modules delivering a great value to enterprises. It offers a set of tools, which are easy-to-use to design, document and simulate 3D models. Using this software, you can speed up the design process and reduce the product development costs.

This book provides a step-by-step approach for users to learn Autodesk Inventor. It is aimed for those with no previous experience with Inventor. However, users of previous versions of Inventor may also find this book useful for them to learn the new enhancements. The user will be guided from starting an Autodesk Inventor 2016 session to creating parts, assemblies, and drawings. Each chapter has components explained with the help of real world models.

Scope of this book

This book is written for students and engineers who are interested to learn Autodesk Inventor 2016 for designing mechanical components and assemblies, and then create drawings.

This book provides a step-by-step approach for learning Autodesk Inventor 2016. The topics include Getting Started with Autodesk Inventor 2016, Basic Part Modeling, Creating Assemblies, Creating Drawings, Additional Modeling Tools, and Sheet Metal Modeling, Assembly Tools, Dimensions and Annotations.

Chapter 1 introduces Autodesk Inventor. The user interface and terminology are discussed in this chapter.

Chapter 2 takes you through the creation of your first Inventor model. You create simple parts.

Chapter 3 teaches you to create assemblies. It explains the Top-down and Bottom-up approaches for designing an assembly. You create an assembly using the Bottom-up approach.

Chapter 4 teaches you to create drawings of the models created in the earlier chapters. You will also learn to place exploded views, and part list of an assembly.

Chapter 5: In this chapter, you will learn additional modeling tools to create complex models.

Chapter 6 introduces you to Sheet Metal modeling. You will create a sheet metal part using the tools available in the Sheet Metal environment.

Chapter 7 teaches you create Top-down assemblies. It also introduces you create mechanisms by applying joints between the parts.

Chapter 8: teaches you to apply dimensions and annotations to a 2D drawing.

Chapter 1: Getting Started with Autodesk Inventor 2016

This tutorial book brings in the most commonly used features of the Autodesk Inventor.

In this chapter, you will:

- Understand the Inventor terminology
- Start a new file
- Understand the User Interface
- Understand different environments in Inventor

In this chapter, you will learn some of the most commonly used features of Autodesk Inventor. In addition, you will learn about the user interface.

In Autodesk Inventor, you create 3D parts and use them to create 2D drawings and 3D assemblies.

Inventor is Feature Based. Features are shapes that are combined to build a part. You can modify these shapes individually.

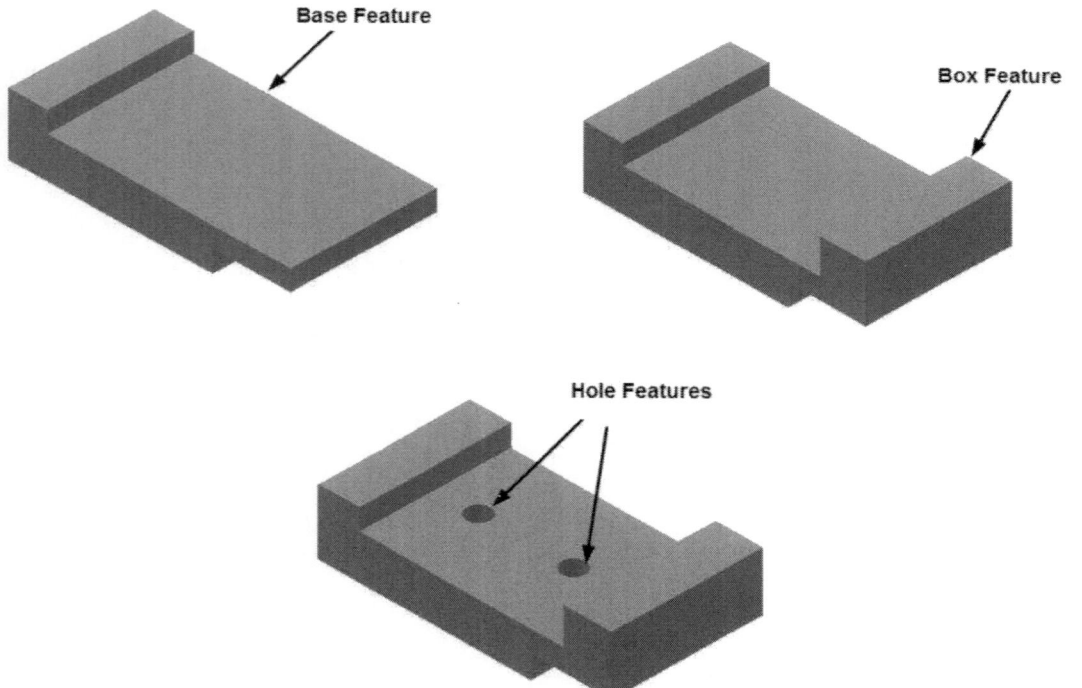

Most of the features are sketch-based. A sketch is a 2D profile and can be extruded, revolved, or swept along a path to create features.

Getting Started with Inventor 2016

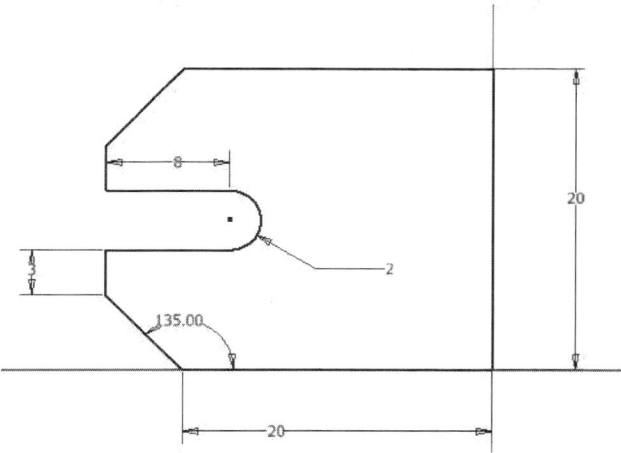

Inventor is parametric in nature. You can specify standard parameters between the elements. Changing these parameters changes the size and shape of the part. For example, see the design of the body of a flange before and after modifying the parameters of its features.

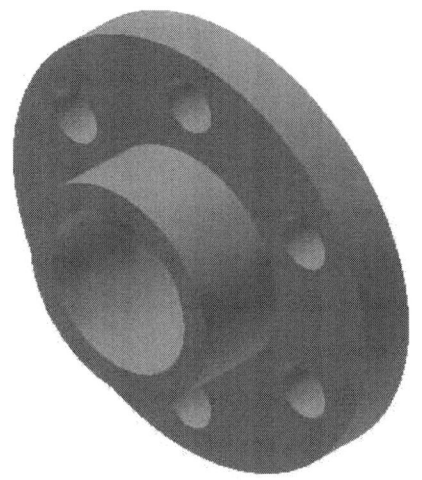
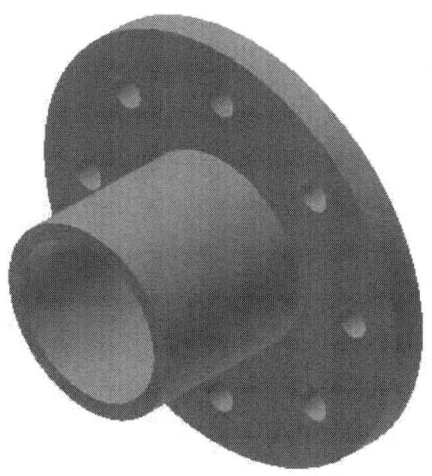

Starting Autodesk Inventor

- Click the **Start** button on the Windows taskbar.
- Click **All Programs**.
- Click **Autodesk > Autodesk Inventor 2016 > Autodesk Inventor 2016**.
- On the ribbon, click **Get Started > Launch > New**.
- On the **Create New File** dialog, click the Templates folder located at the top left corner. You can also select the **Metric** folder to view various metric templates.
- In the **Part – Create 2D and 3D objects** section, click the **Standard.ipt** icon. You can also select the
- Click **Create** to start a new part file.

Notice these important features of the Inventor window.

Getting Started with Inventor 2016

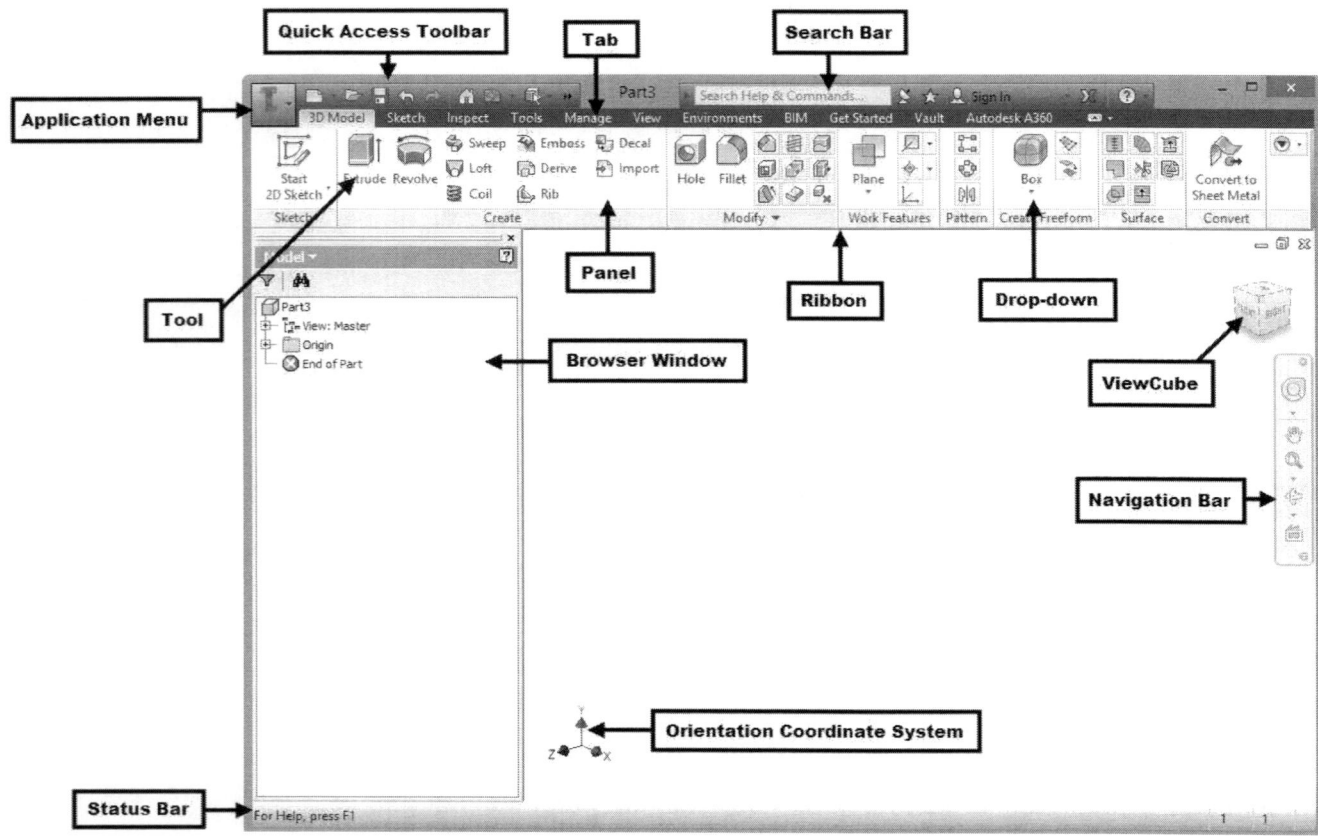

User Interface
Various components of the user interface are discussed next.

Ribbon
Ribbon is located at the top of the window. It consists of various tabs. When you click on a tab, a set of tools appear. These tools are arranged in panels. You can select the required tool from this panel. The following sections explain the various tabs of the ribbon available in Autodesk Inventor.

The Get Started ribbon tab
This ribbon tab contains the tools such as **New**, **Open**, **Projects** and so on.

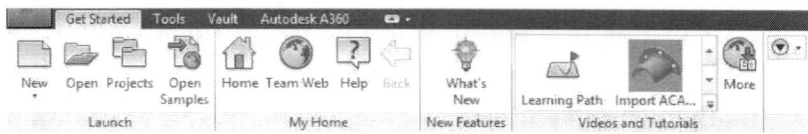

The 3D Model ribbon tab
This ribbon tab contains the tools to create 3D features, planes, surfaces, and so on.

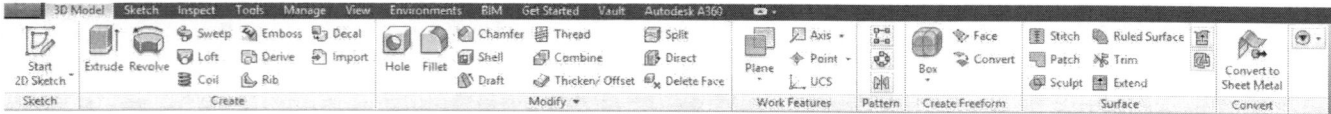

Getting Started with Inventor 2016

The View ribbon tab
This ribbon tab contains the tools to modify the display of the model and user interface.

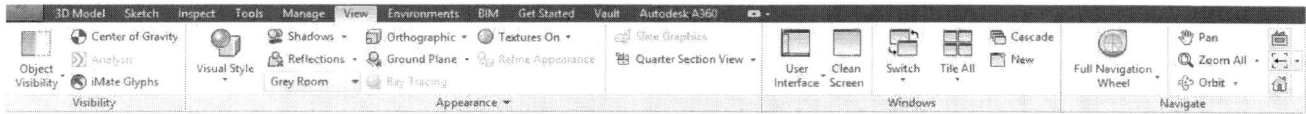

This Inspect ribbon tab
This ribbon tab has tools to measure the objects. It also has analysis tools to analyze the draft, curvature, surface and so on.

Sketch ribbon tab
This ribbon tab contains all the sketch tools.

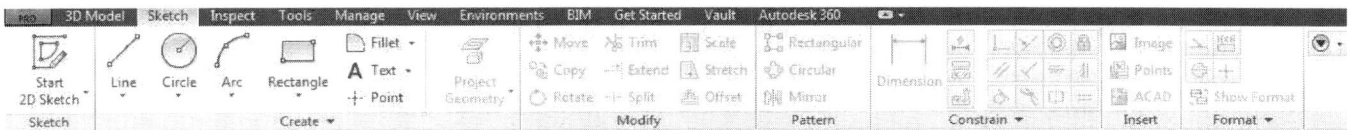

Assemble ribbon tab
This ribbon tab contains the tools to create an assembly. It is available in an assembly file.

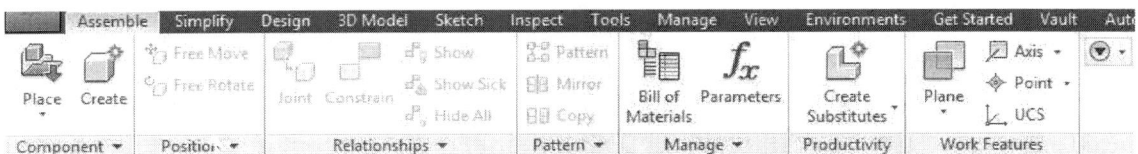

Presentation ribbon tab
This tab contains the tools to create the exploded views of an assembly. It also has the tools to create presentations, assembly instructions, and animation of an assembly.

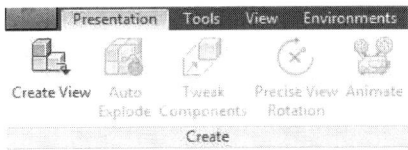

Drawing Environment ribbon tabs
In the Drawing Environment, you can create print-ready drawings of a 3D model. The ribbon tabs in this environment contain tools to create 2D drawings.

Getting Started with Inventor 2016

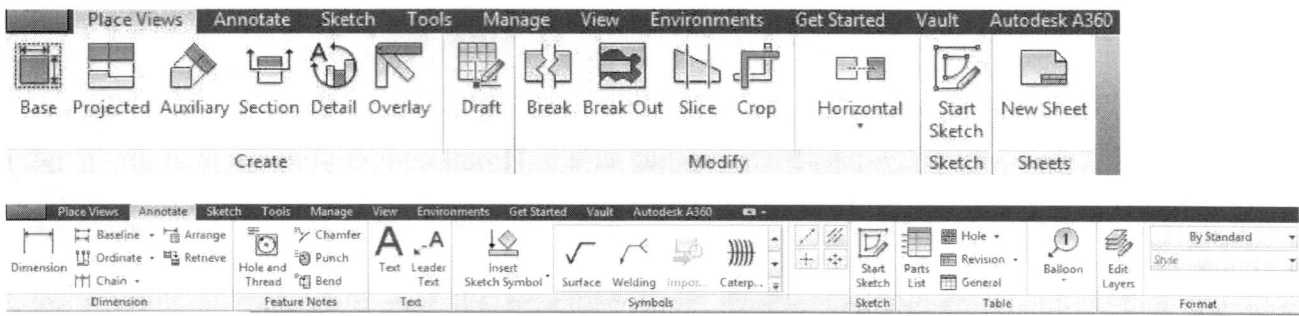

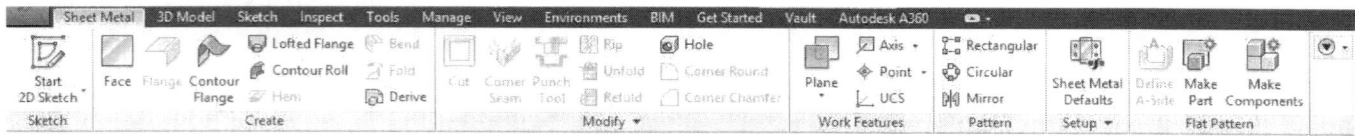

The Sheet Metal ribbon tab
The tools in this tab are used to create sheet metal components.

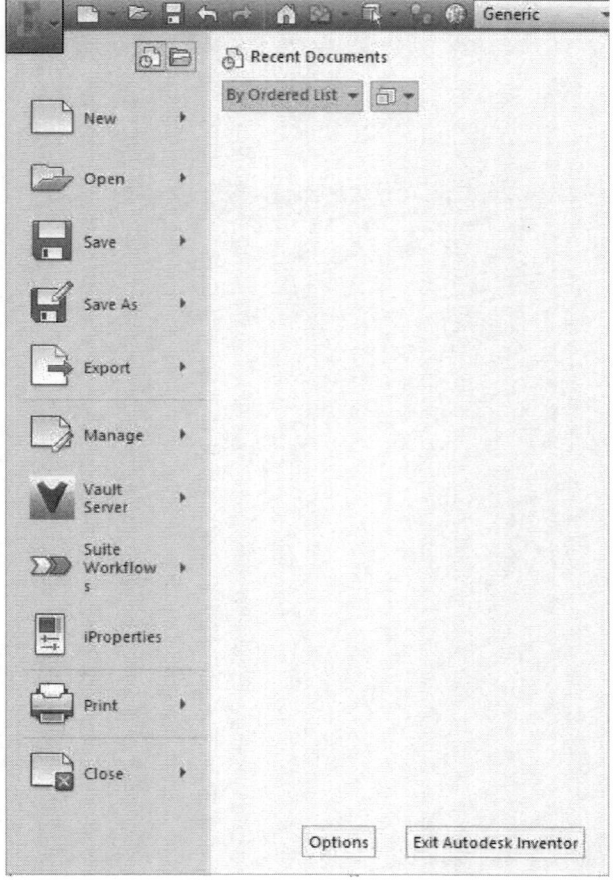

Application Menu
This appears when you click on the icon located at the top left corner. This menu contains the options to open, print, export, manage, save, and close a file.

Getting Started with Inventor 2016

Quick Access Toolbar
This is available at the top left of the window. It contains the tools such as **New**, **Save**, **Open,** and so on.

You can customize this toolbar by clicking the down arrow at the right side of this toolbar.

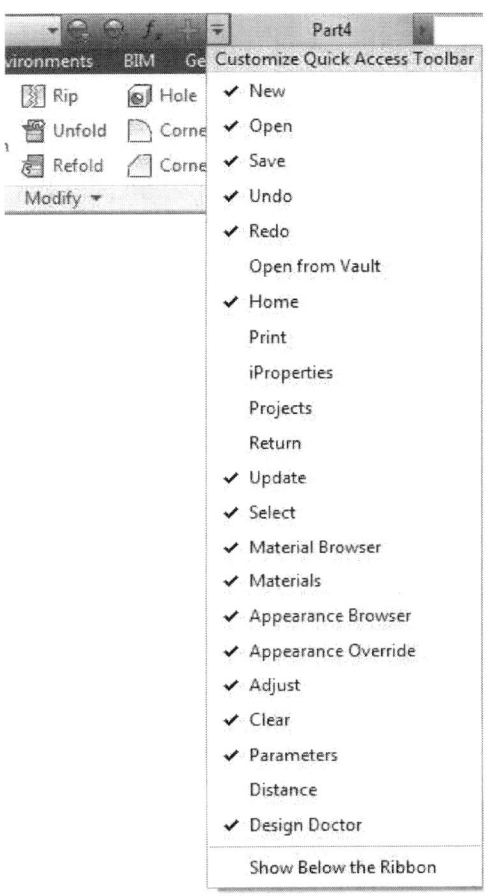

Browser window
This is located at the left side of the window. It contains the list of operations carried in an Autodesk Inventor file.

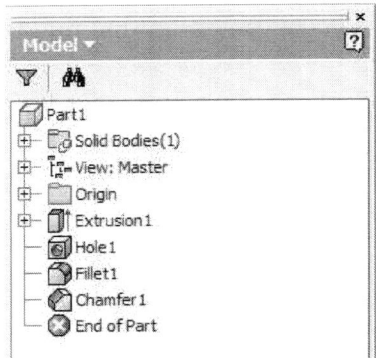

Status bar

Getting Started with Inventor 2016

This is available below the Browser window. It displays the prompts and the actions taken while using the tools.

Navigation Bar
This is located at the right side of the window. It contains the tools to zoom, rotate, pan, or look at a face of the model.

ViewCube
It is located at the top right corner of the graphics window. It is used to set the view orientation of the model.

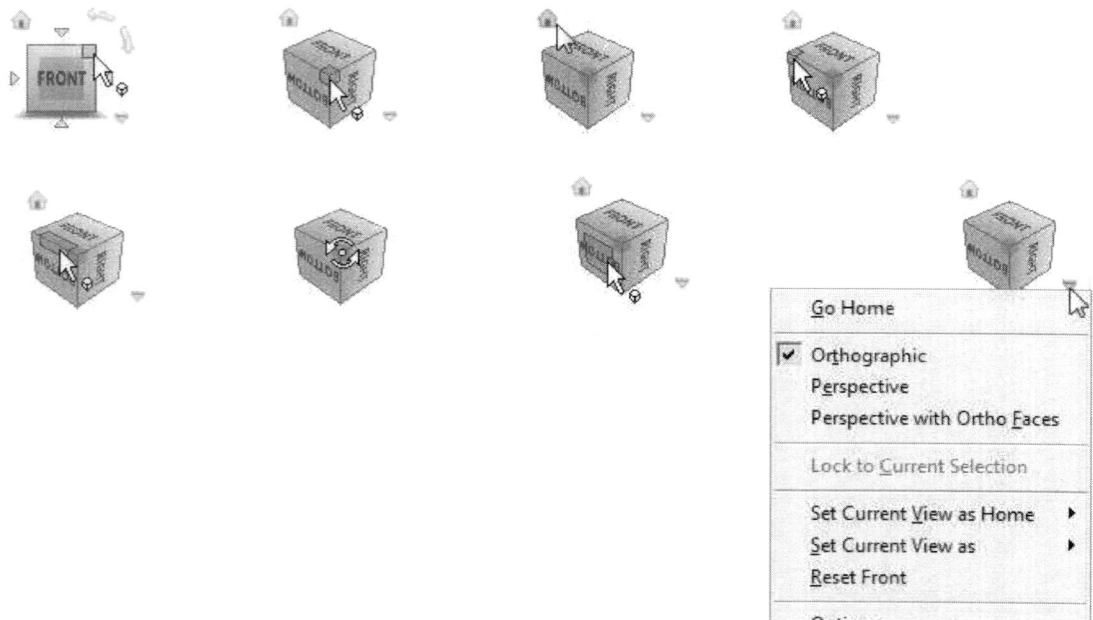

Shortcut Menus and Marking Menus
When you click the right mouse button, a shortcut menu along with a marking menu appears. A shortcut menu contains a list of some important options. The marking menu contains important tools. It allows you to access the tools quickly. You can customize the marking menu (add or remove tools).

Getting Started with Inventor 2016

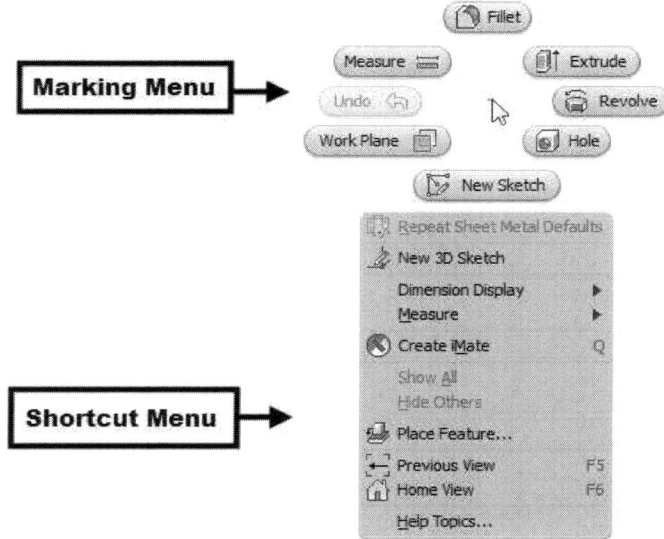

Dialogs

When you activate any tool in Autodesk Inventor, the dialog related to it appears. It consists of various options, which help you to complete the operation. The following figure shows the components of the dialog.

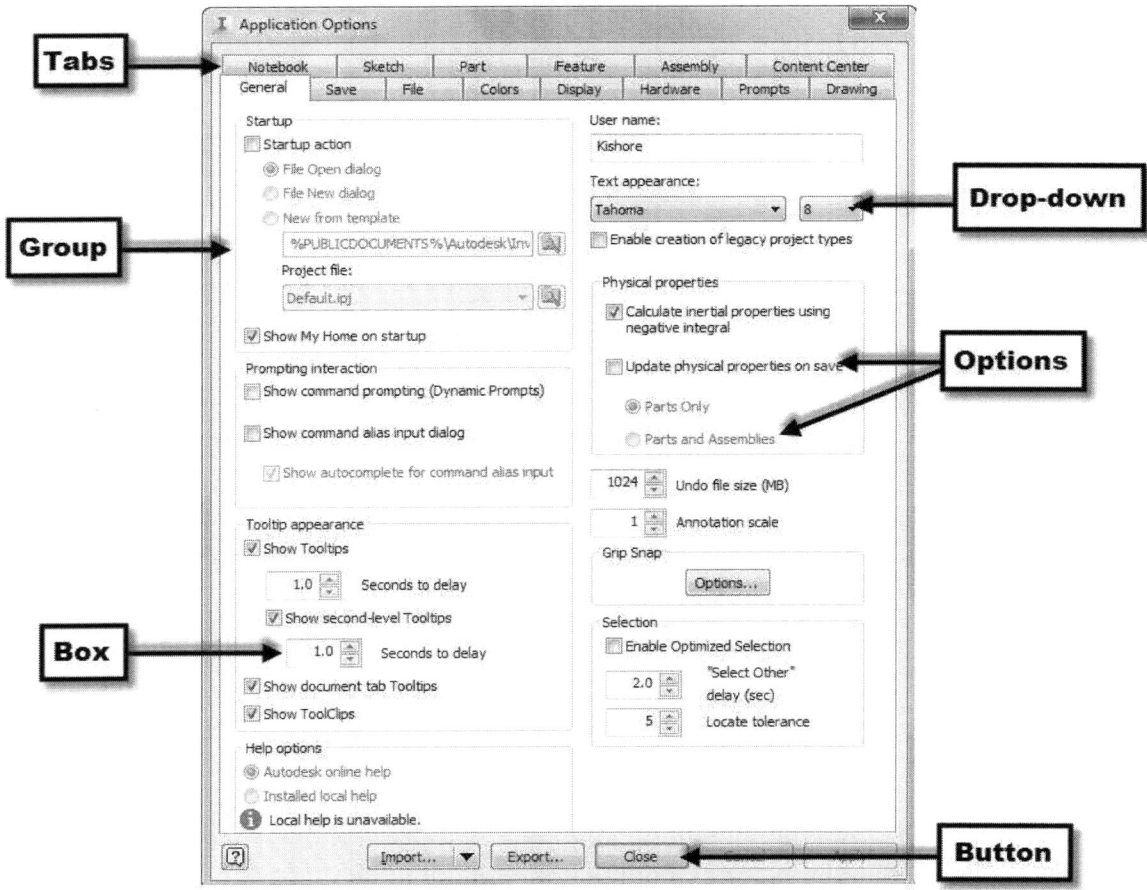

8

Getting Started with Inventor 2016

Customizing the Ribbon, Shortcut Keys, and Marking Menus

To customize the ribbon, shortcut keys, or marking menu, click **Tools > Options > Customize** on the ribbon. On the **Customize** dialog, use the tabs to customize the ribbon or marking menu, or shortcut keys.

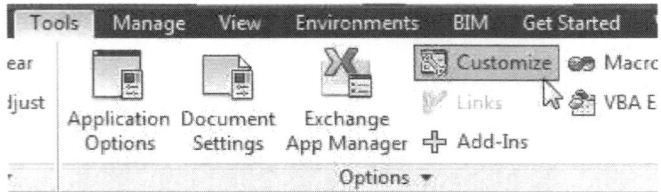

For example, to add a command to the ribbon, select the command from the list on the left side of the dialog and click the **Add** >> button. If you want to remove a command from the ribbon, then select it from the right-side list and click the **Remove** << button. Click **OK** to make the changes to effect.

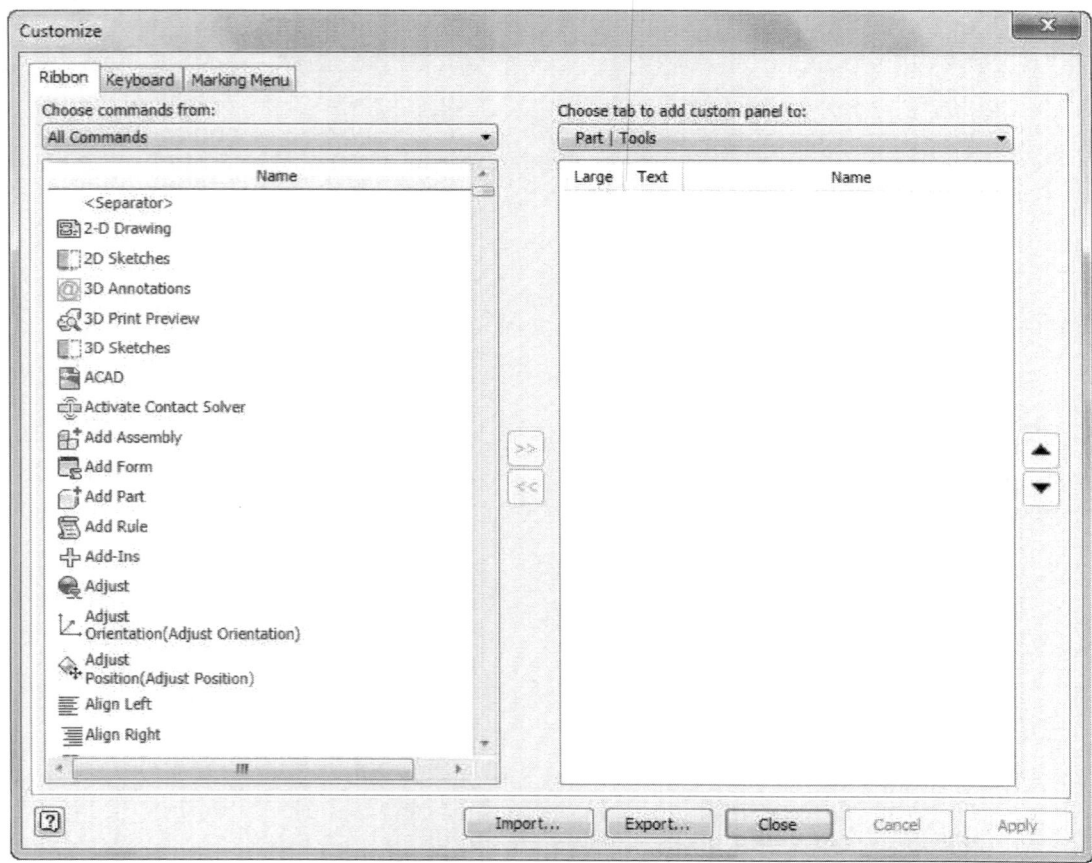

To add or remove panels from the ribbon, click the **Show Panels** icon located at the right-side of the ribbon and check/uncheck the options on the flyout.

Getting Started with Inventor 2016

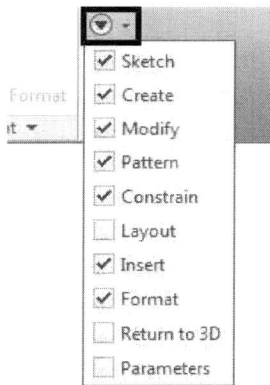

Color Settings

To change the background color of the window, click **Tools > Options > Application Options** on the ribbon. On the **Application Options** dialog, click the **Colors** tab on the dialog. Set the **Background** value to **1 Color** to change the background to plain. Select the required color scheme from the **Color Scheme** group. Click **OK**.

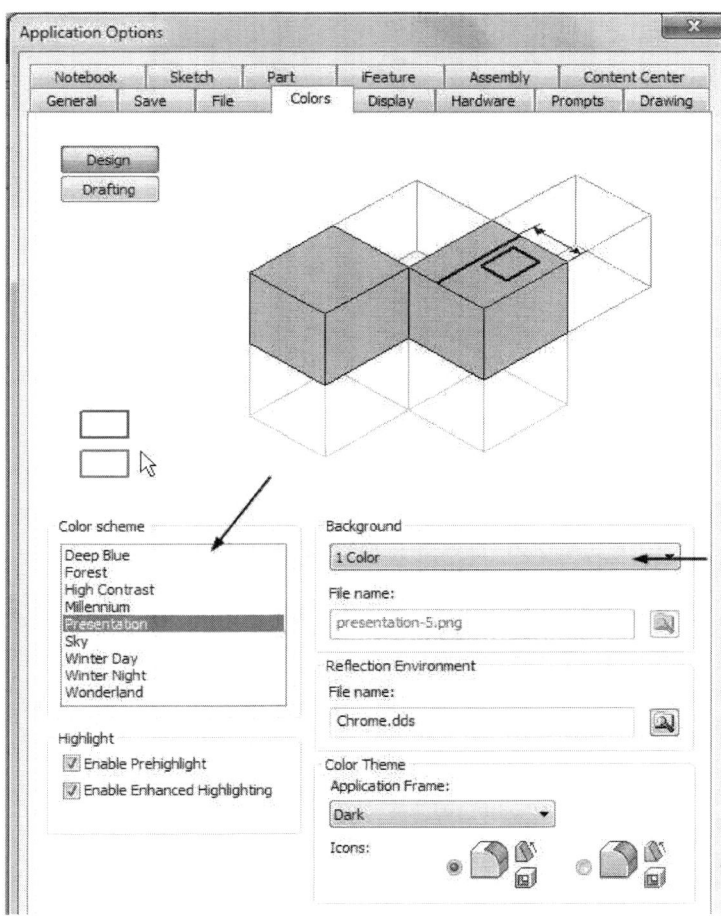

10

Chapter 2: Part Modeling Basics

This chapter takes you through the creation of your first Inventor model. You create simple parts:

In this chapter, you will:

- Create Sketches
- Create a base feature
- Add another feature to it
- Create revolved features
- Create cylindrical features
- Create box features
- Apply draft

TUTORIAL 1

This tutorial takes you through the creation of your first Inventor model. You will create the Disc of an Old ham coupling:

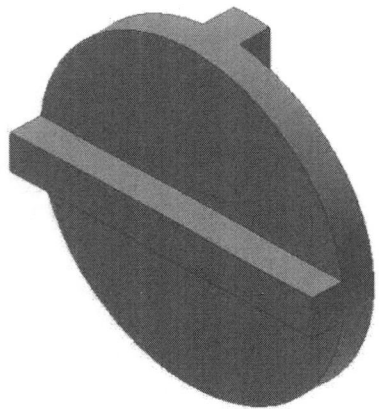

Creating a New Project
1. Start **Autodesk Inventor 2015** by clicking the **Autodesk Inventor 2015** icon on your desktop.

2. To create a new project, click **Get Started > Launch > Projects** on the ribbon.

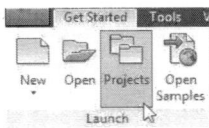

3. Click the **New** button on the **Projects** dialog.

4. On the **Inventor project wizard** dialog, select **New Single User Project** and click the **Next** button.

5. Enter **Oldham Coupling** in the **Name** field.

6. Set **Project(Workspace) Folder** to **C:\Users\Username\Documents\Inventor\Oldham Coupling** and click **Next**.

7. Click **Finish**.

8. Click **OK** on the **Inventor Project Editor** dialog.

Part Modeling Basics

9. Click **Save**.

10. On the **Inventor Project Editor** dialog, click **Yes**.

11. Click **Done**.

Starting a New Part File
1. To start a new part file, click **Get Started > Launch > New** on the ribbon.

2. On the **Create New File** dialog, click the Templates folder located the top right corner.

3. Click the **Standard.ipt** icon.

4. Click the **Create** button on the **Create New File** dialog.

A new model window appears.

Starting a Sketch
1. To start a new sketch, click **3D Model > Sketch > Start 2D Sketch** on the ribbon.

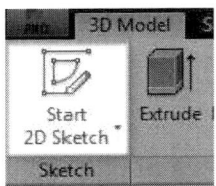

5. Click on the **XY Plane**. The sketch starts.

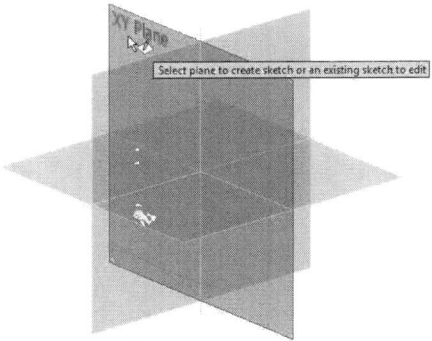

The first feature is an extruded feature from a sketched circular profile. You will begin by sketching the circle.

6. On the ribbon click **Sketch > Create > Circle > Circle Center Point**.

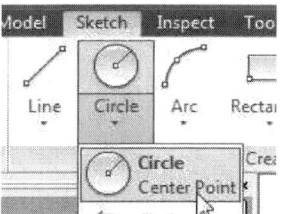

7. Move the cursor to the sketch origin, and then click on it.

8. Drag the cursor and click to create a circle.

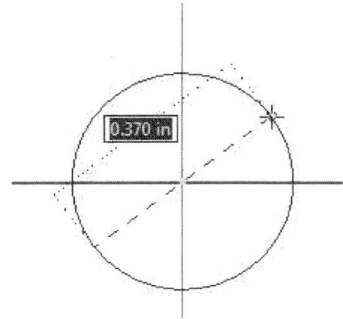

9. Press **ESC** to deactivate the tool.

Adding Dimensions
In this section, you will specify the size of the sketched circle by adding dimensions. As you add dimensions, the sketch can attain any one of the following states:

Fully Constrained sketch: In a fully constrained sketch, the positions of all the entities are fully described by dimensions, constraints, or both. In a fully constrained sketch, all the entities are dark blue color.

Under Constrained sketch: Additional dimensions, constraints, or both are needed to completely specify the geometry. In this state, you can drag under constrained sketch entities to modify the sketch. An under constrained sketch entity is in black color.

If you add any more dimensions to a fully constrained sketch, a message box will appear showing that dimension over constraints the sketch. In addition, it prompts you to convert the dimension into a driven dimension. Click **Accept** to convert the unwanted dimension into a driven dimension.

Part Modeling Basics

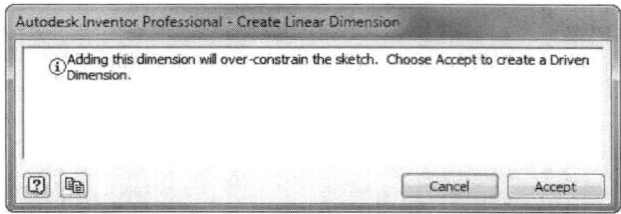

1. On the ribbon, click **Sketch > Constrain > Dimension**.

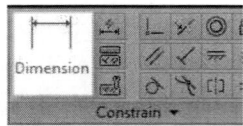

2. Select the circle and click; the **Edit Dimension** box appears.

3. Enter **4** in the **Edit Dimension** box and click the green check.

4. Press **Esc** to deactivate the **Dimension** tool.

You can also create dimensions while creating the sketch objects. To do this, enter the dimension values in the boxes displayed while sketching.

5. To display the entire circle at full size and to center it in the graphics area, use one of the following methods:

   - Click **Zoom All** on the **Navigate Bar**.
   - Click **View > Navigate > Zoom All** on the ribbon.

6. Click **Finish Sketch** on the **Exit** panel.

7. Click **Zoom All** on the **Navigate Bar**.

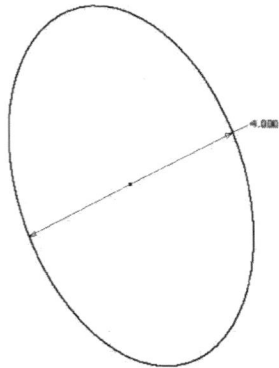

Creating the Base Feature

The first feature in any part is called a base feature. You now create this feature by extruding the sketched circle.

1. On the ribbon, click **3D Model > Create > Extrude.**

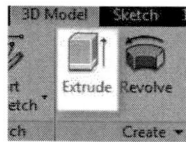

2. Type-in 0.4 in the **Distance** box attached to extrusion.

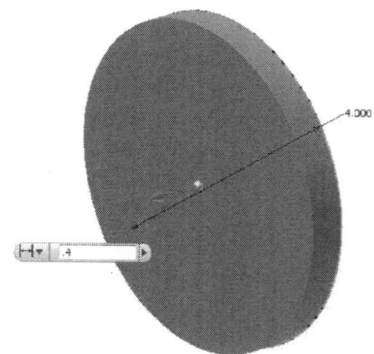

3. Place the pointer on the handle attached to the extruded feature.
4. Click **OK** to create the extrusion.

13

Part Modeling Basics

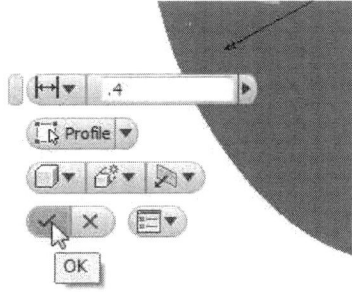

Notice the new feature, **Extrude 1**, in the **Browser window**.

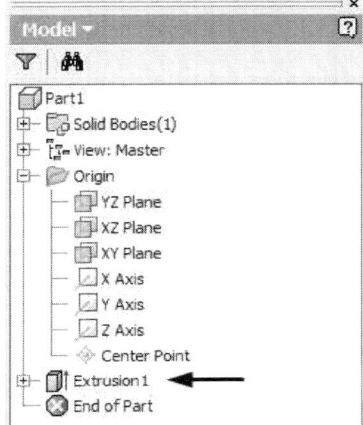

To magnify a model in the graphics area, you can use the zoom tools available on the **Zoom** drop-down in the **Navigate** panel of the **View** tab.

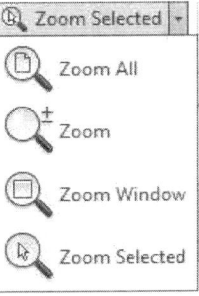

Click **Zoom All** to display the part full size in the current window.

Click **Zoom Window**, and then drag the pointer to create a rectangle; the area in the rectangle zooms to fill the window.

Click **Zoom**, and then drag the pointer. Dragging up zooms out; dragging down zooms in.

Click on a vertex, an edge, or a feature, and then click **Zoom Selected**; the selected item zooms to fill the window.

To display the part in different modes, select the options in the **View Style** drop-down on the **Appearance** panel of the **View** tab.

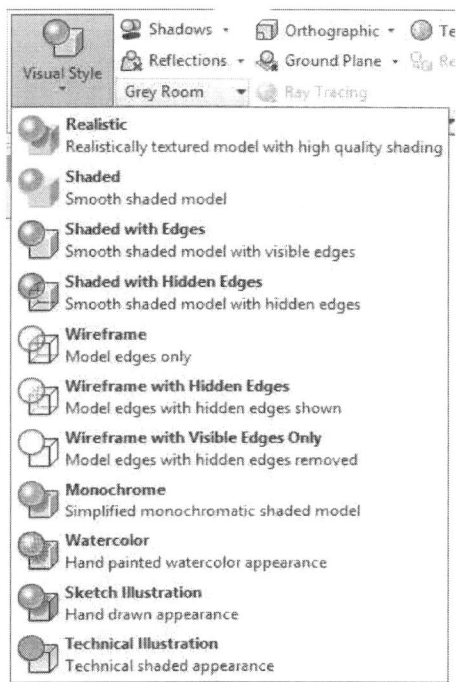

Realistic

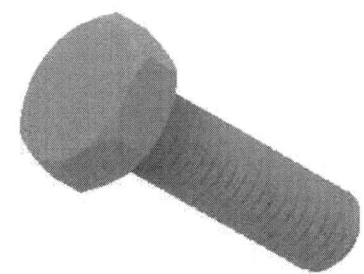

Shaded

14

Part Modeling Basics

Shaded With Edges

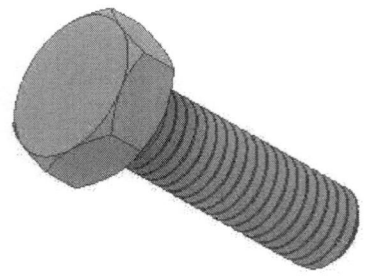

Shaded with Hidden Edges

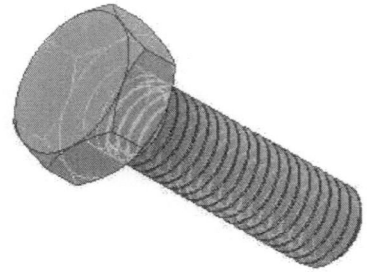

Wireframe

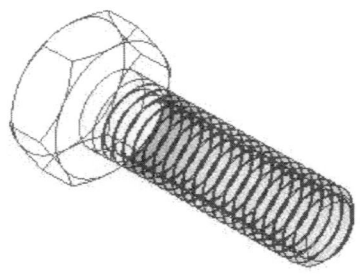

Wireframe with Hidden Edges

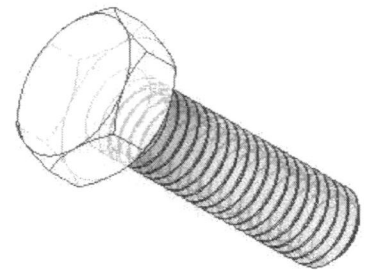

Wireframe with Visible Edges Only

Monochrome

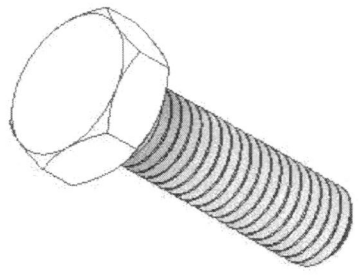

Watercolor

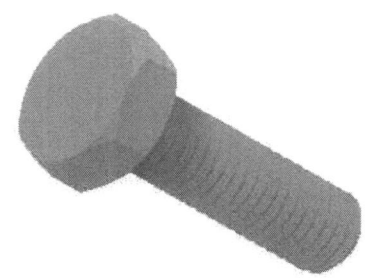

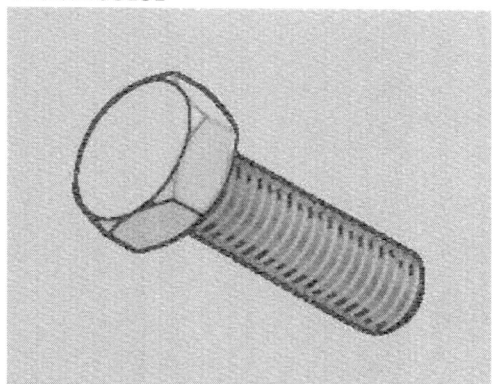

Sketch Illustration

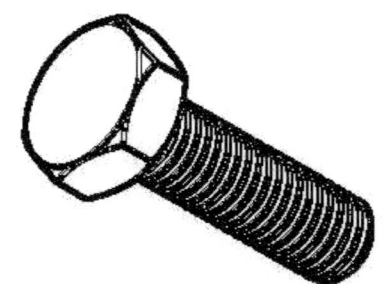

Technical Illustration

Part Modeling Basics

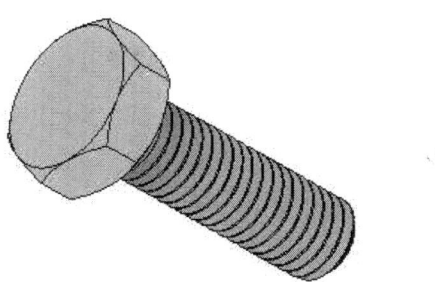

The default display mode for parts and assemblies is **Shaded**. You may change the display mode whenever you want.

Adding an Extruded Feature

To create additional features on the part, you need to draw sketches on the model faces or planes, and then extrude them.

1. On the ribbon, click **View > Appearance > View Style > Wireframe**.

2. On the ribbon, click **3D Model > Sketch > Start 2D Sketch**.

3. Click on the front face of the part.

4. Click **Line** on the **Create** panel.

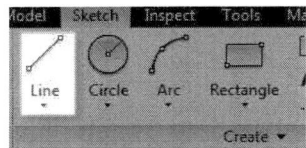

5. Click on the circular edge to specify the first point of the line.

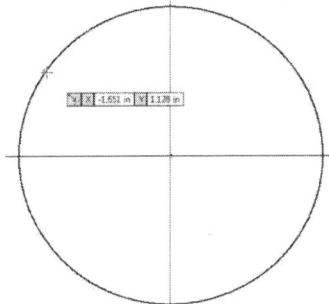

6. Move the cursor towards right.

7. Click on the other side of the circular edge; a line is drawn.

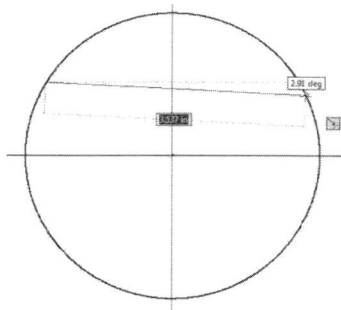

8. Draw another line below the previous line.

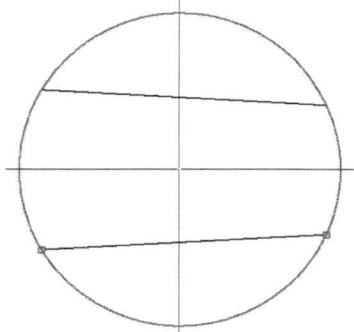

9. On the ribbon, click **Sketch > Constrain > Horizontal Constraint**.

10. Select the two lines to make them horizontal.

11. On the ribbon, click **Sketch > Constrain > Equal**.

12. Select the two horizontal lines to make them equal.

13. Click **Dimension** on the **Constrain** panel.

14. Select the two horizontal lines.

15. Move the cursor toward right and click to locate the dimension; the **Edit Dimension** box appears.

16. Enter **0.472** in the **Edit Dimension** box and click the green check.

Part Modeling Basics

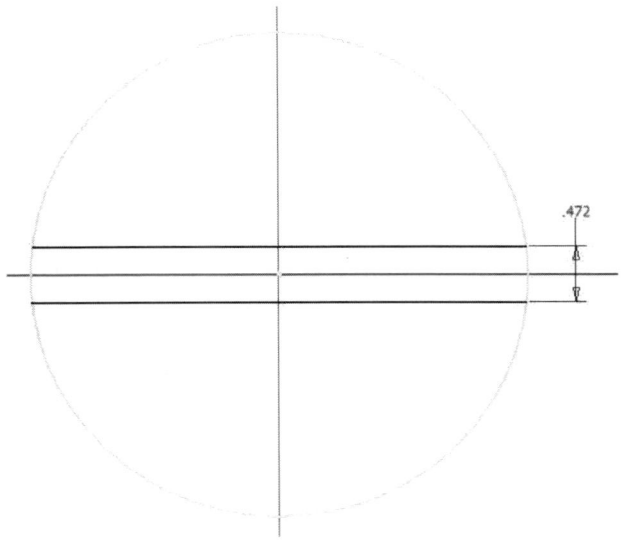

17. Click **Finish Sketch** on the **Exit** panel.

18. Click on the sketch, and then click **Create Extrude** on the **Mini Toolbar**; the **Extrude** dialog appears.

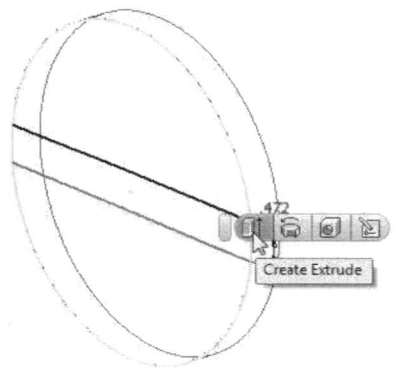

19. Click in the region bounded by the two horizontal lines.

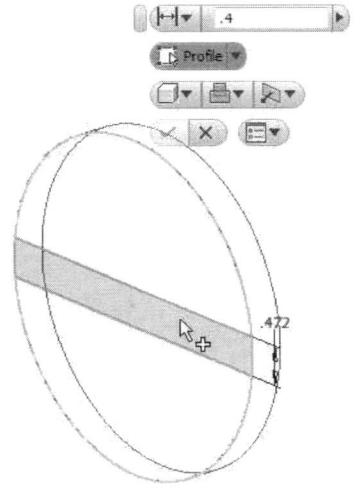

20. Enter **0.4** in the **Distance1** box.

21. Click **OK** ✓ to create the extrusion.

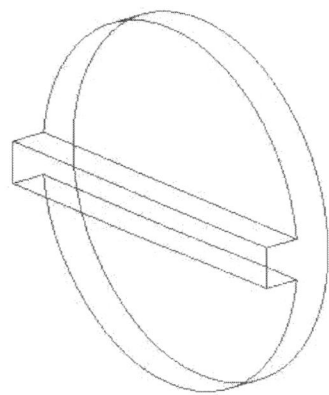

📝 *You can reuse the sketch of an already existing feature. To do this, expand the feature in the Browser Window, right click on the sketch, and select **Share Sketch** from the shortcut menu. You will notice that the sketch is visible in the graphics window. You can also unshare the sketch by right clicking on it and selecting **Unshare**.*

Adding another Extruded Feature

1. Click **Start 2D Sketch** on the **Sketch** panel.

2. Use the **Free Orbit** button from the **Navigate Bar** to rotate the model such that the back face of the part is visible.

3. Right click and select **OK**.

Part Modeling Basics

4. Click on the back face of the part.

5. Click **Line** on the **Create** panel.

6. Draw two lines, as shown below.

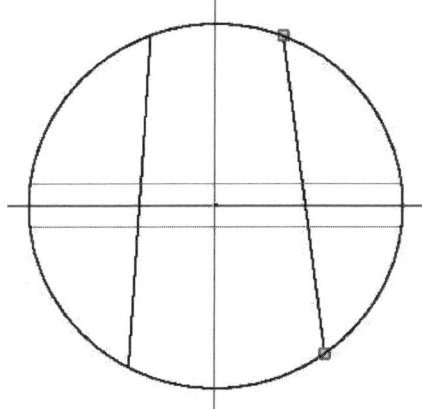

📝 *You can specify a point using various point snap options. To do this, activate a sketching tool, right click and select **Point Snaps**; a list of point snaps appears. Now, you can select only the specified point snap.*

7. On the ribbon, click **Sketch > Constrain > Vertical Constraint**.

8. Select the two lines to make them vertical.

9. On the ribbon, click **Sketch > Constrain > Equal**.

10. Select the two vertical lines to make them equal.

11. Create a dimension of 0.472in between the vertical lines.

Note: Ensure that the end points of the lines coincide with the circular edge. You can use the Coincident constraint to make them coincident with each other.

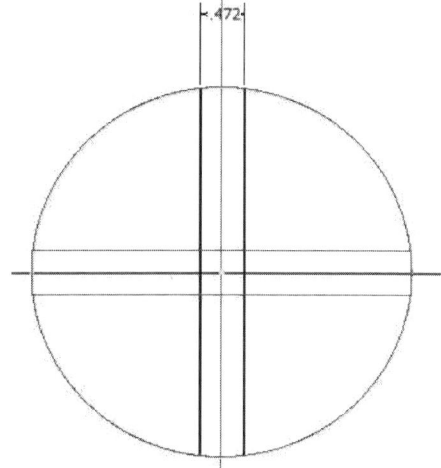

12. Click **Finish Sketch**.

13. Extrude the sketch up to 0.4in distance.

    To move the part view, click **Pan** on **Navigate Bar**, and then drag the part to move it in the graphics area.

14. On the ribbon, click **View > Appearance > View Style > Shaded with Edges**.

15. On the ribbon, click **View > Navigation > Home View**.

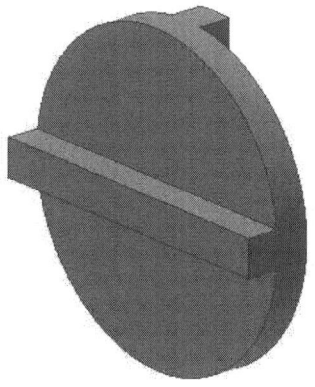

Saving the Part

1. Click **Save** on the **Quick Access Toolbar**.

2. On the **Save As** dialog, type-in **Disc** in the **File name** box.

3. Click **Save** to save the file.

Part Modeling Basics

4. Click **Application Menu > Close**.

Note:
*.ipt is the file extension for all the files that you create in the Part environment of Autodesk Inventor.

TUTORIAL 2

In this tutorial, you create a flange by performing the following:

- Creating a revolved feature
- Creating a cut features
- Adding fillets

Starting a New Part File

1. To start a new part file, click the **Part** icon on the welcome screen.

Sketching a Revolve Profile

You create the base feature of the flange by revolving a profile around a centerline.

1. Click **3D Model > Sketch > Start 2D Sketch** on the ribbon.

2. Select the YZ plane.

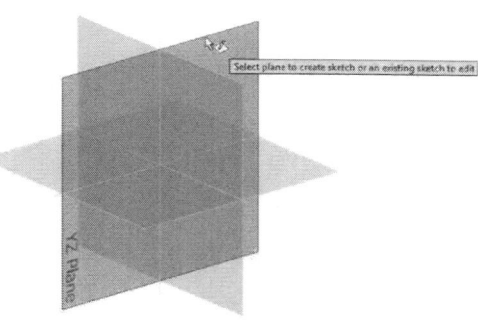

3. Click **Line** on the **Create** panel.

4. Create a sketch similar to that shown in figure.

Part Modeling Basics

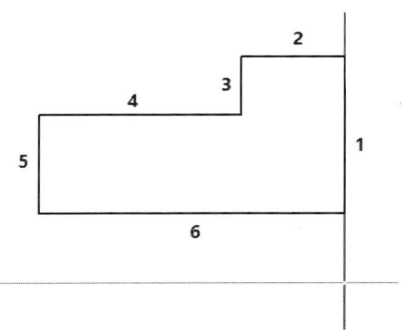

5. On the ribbon, click **Sketch > Format > Centerline** .

6. Click **Line** on the **Create** panel.

7. Create a centerline, as shown below.

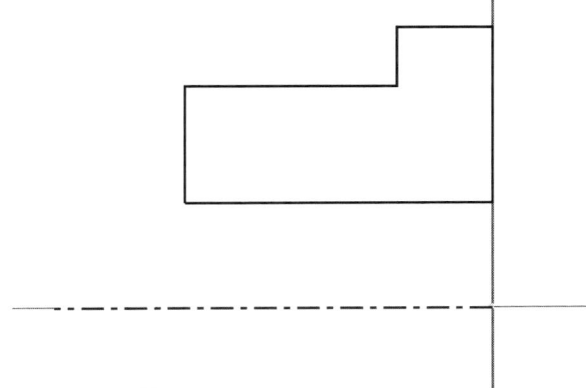

8. Click **Fix** on the **Constrain** panel.

9. Select the Line 1.

10. Click **Dimension** on the **Constrain** panel.

11. Select the centerline and Line 2; a dimension appears.

12. Place the dimension and enter **4** in the **Edit Dimension** box.

13. Click the green check.

14. Select the centerline and Line 4; a dimension appears.

15. Set the dimension to 2.4in.

16. Select the centerline and Line 6; a dimension appears.

17. Set the dimension to 1.2in.

18. Create a dimension between Line 1 and Line 3.

19. Set the dimension to 0.8in.

20. Create a dimension of 2 in between Line 1 and Line 5.

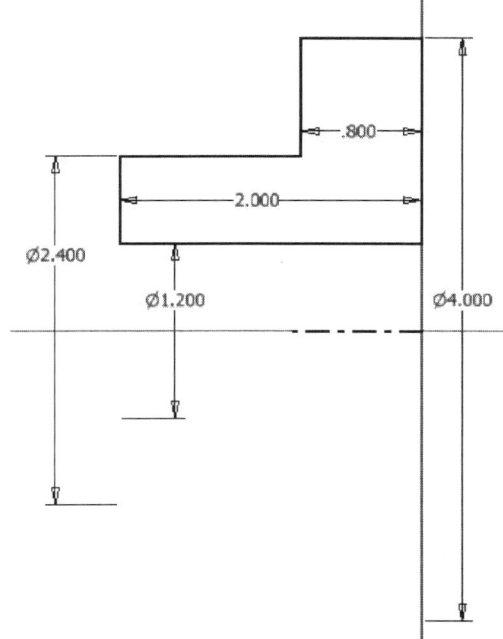

*You can display all the constraints by right clicking and selecting **Show All Constraints** option. You can hide all the constraints by right clicking and selecting the **Hide All Constraints** option.*

21. Right-click and select **Finish 2D Sketch**.

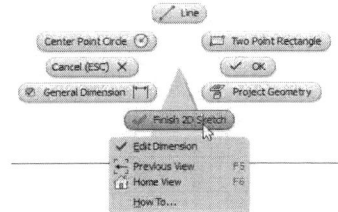

Creating the Revolved Feature

1. On the ribbon, click **3D Model > Create > Revolve** (or) right-click and select **Revolve** from the Marking menu.

20

Part Modeling Basics

2. Set **Extents** to **Full** on the Mini toolbar.

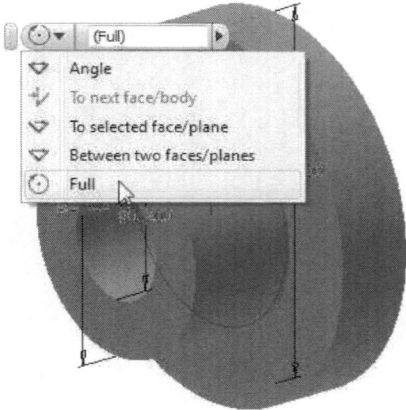

3. Click **OK** to create the revolved feature.

Creating the Cut feature

1. On the ribbon, click the **Show Panels** icon located at the right corner, and then check the **Primitives** option from the drop-down.

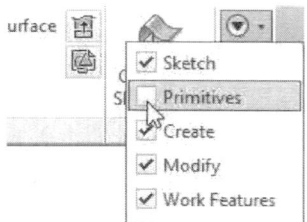

The **Primitives** panel is added to the ribbon.

2. On the ribbon, click **3D Model > Primitives > Primitive drop-down > Box** on the **Primitives** panel.

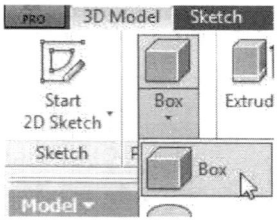

3. Rotate the model such that its back face is visible.

4. Click the back face of the part; the sketch starts.

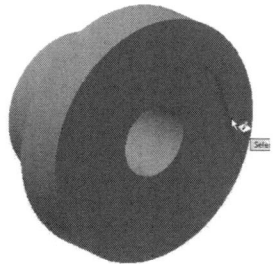

5. Select the origin to define the center point.

6. Move the cursor diagonally toward right.

7. Enter 4.1 in the horizontal box.

8. Press Tab key and enter 0.472 in the vertical box.

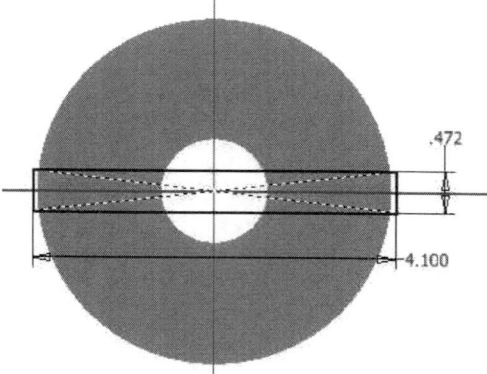

9. Press the Enter key; the **Extrude** dialog appears.

10. Expand the **Extrude** dialog by clicking the down arrow ▼ button.

11. Click the **Cut** button on the **Extrude** dialog.

Part Modeling Basics

12. Enter 0.4 in the **Distance** box.
13. Click **OK** to create the cut feature.

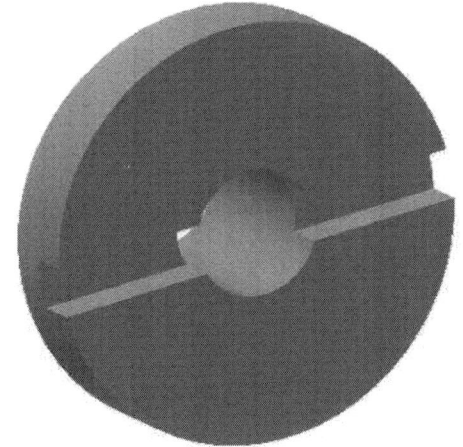

Creating another Cut feature

1. Create a sketch on the front face of the base feature.

- Draw three lines and the circle, as shown in figure.

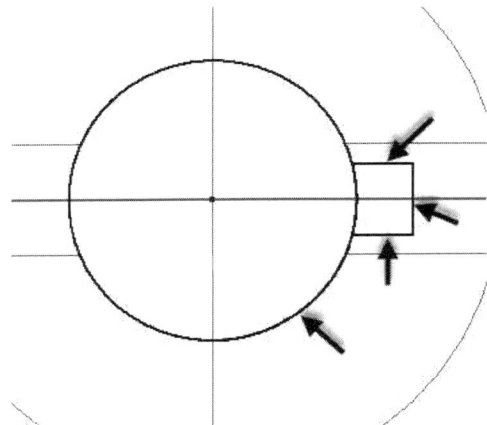

- Apply the **Horizontal** constraint to the horizontal lines.
- Apply the **Equal** constraint between the horizontal lines.
- Ensure that the endpoints of the horizontal line coincide with the circle.
- Apply dimension of 0.236 to the vertical line.
- Apply dimension of 0.118 to horizontal line.
- Apply dimension of the 1.2 diameter to the circle.

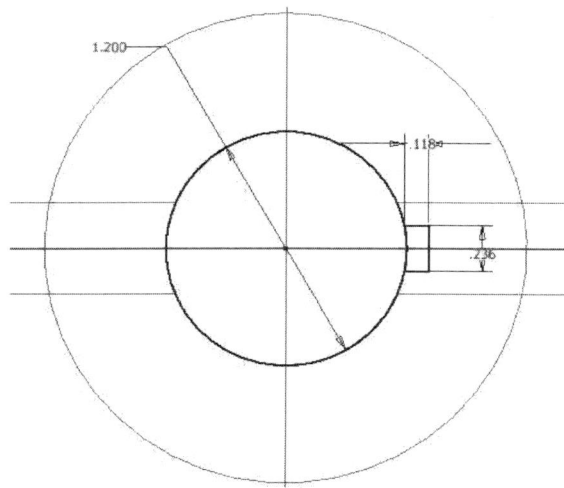

- On the ribbon, click **Sketch > Modify > Trim**.
- Click on the circle to trim it.

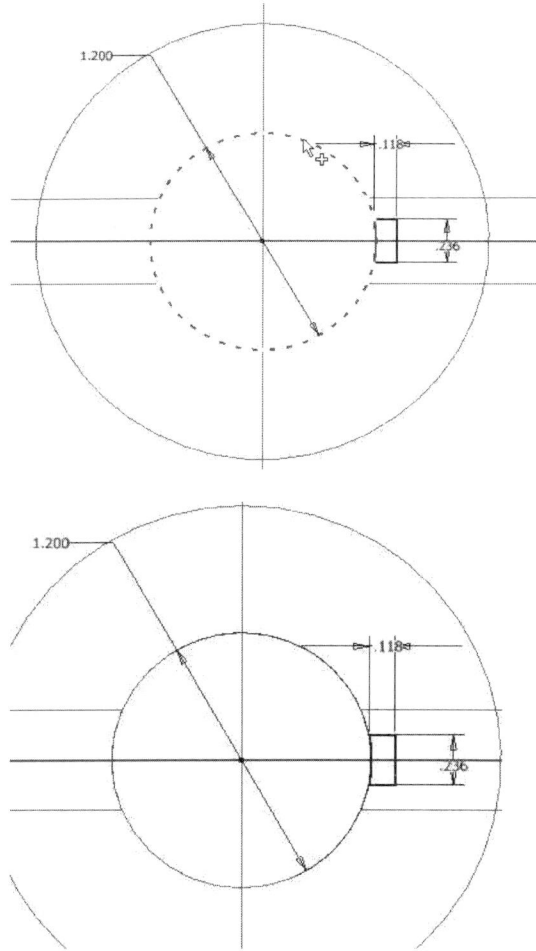

2. Finish the sketch.

22

Part Modeling Basics

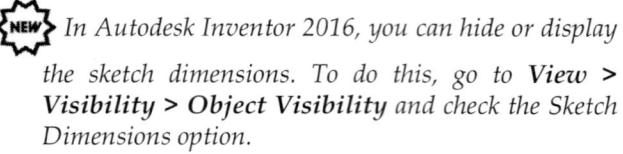 *In Autodesk Inventor 2016, you can hide or display the sketch dimensions. To do this, go to **View > Visibility > Object Visibility** and check the Sketch Dimensions option.*

3. Click **Extrude** on the **Create** panel.

4. Click in the region enclosed by the three lines and the arc.

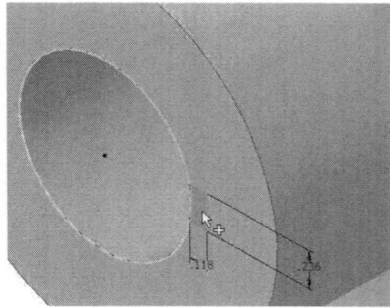

5. Select **All** from the **Extents** drop-down.

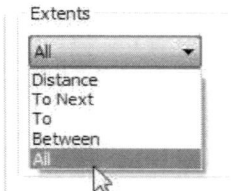

6. Click the **Cut** button on the **Extrude** dialog.

7. Click **OK** to create the cut feature.

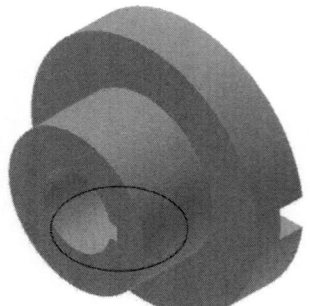

Adding a Fillet

1. On the ribbon, click **3D Model > Modify > Fillet** (or) right-click and select **Fillet** from the Marking menu.

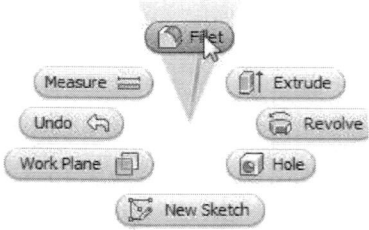

2. Click on the inner circular edge and set **Radius** as 0.2.

3. Click **OK** to add the fillet.

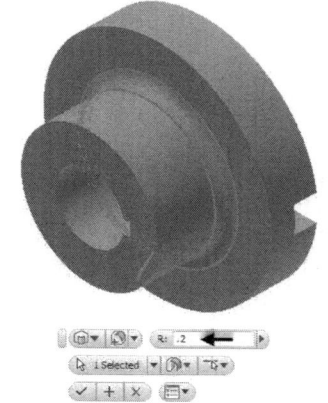

Saving the Part
1. Click **Save** on the **Quick Access Toolbar**.

2. On the **Save As** dialog, type-in **Flange** in the **File name** box.

3. Click **Save** to save the file.

4. Click **Application Menu > Close**.

TUTORIAL 3
In this tutorial, you create the Shaft by performing the following:

- Creating a cylindrical feature
- Creating a cut feature

Part Modeling Basics

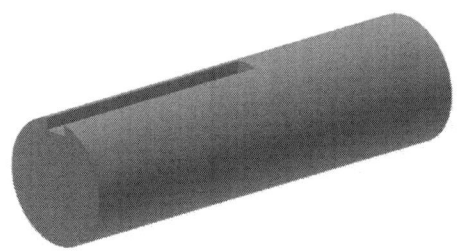

Starting a New Part File

1. On the ribbon, click **Get Started > Launch > New**.

2. On the **Create New File** dialog, select **Standard.ipt**.

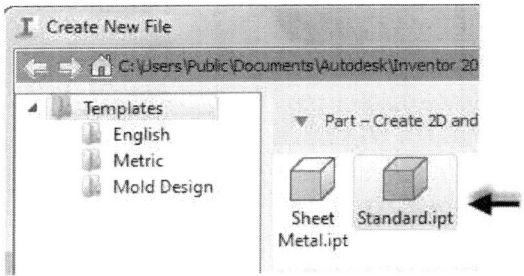

3. Click **Create**.

Creating the Cylindrical Feature

1. On the ribbon, click **Primitives > Primitive drop-down > Cylinder**.

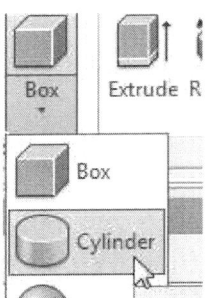

2. Click on the XY plane to select it; the sketch starts.

3. Click at the origin and move the cursor outward.

4. Enter 1.2 in the box attached to the circle.

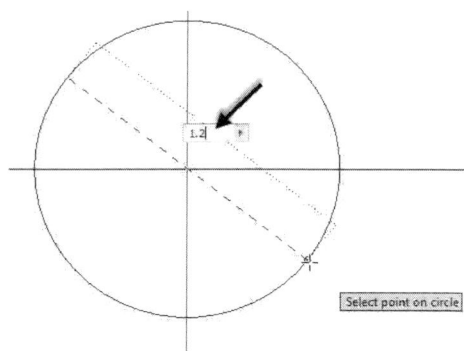

5. Press Enter key; the **Extrude** dialog appears.

6. Enter **4** in the **Distance** box.

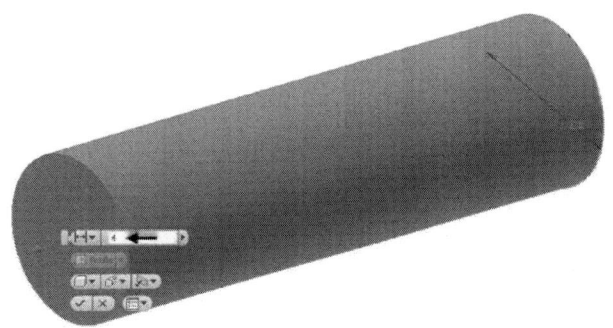

7. Click **OK** to create the cylinder.

Creating Cut feature

1. Create a sketch on the front face of the base feature.

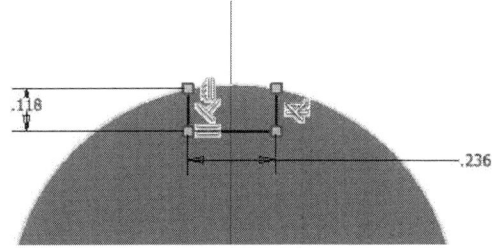

2. Finish the sketch.

3. Click **Extrude** on the **Create** panel.

4. Click in the region enclosed by the sketch.

5. Click the **Cut** button on the **Extrude** dialog.

6. Set **Distance** to **2.165**.

Part Modeling Basics

7. Click **OK** to create the cut feature.

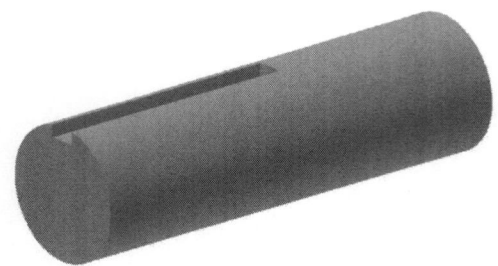

Saving the Part
1. Click **Save** on the **Quick Access Toolbar**; the **Save As** dialog appears.

2. Type-in **Shaft** in the **File name** box.

3. Click **Save** to save the file.

4. Click **Application Menu > Close**.

TUTORIAL 4
In this tutorial, you create a Key by performing the following:

- Creating an Extruded feature
- Applying draft

Start Extruded feature
1. Start a new part file using the **Standard.ipt** template.

2. On the ribbon, **Primitives > Primitive** drop-down **> Box**.

3. Select the XY plane.

4. Create the sketch, as shown in figure.

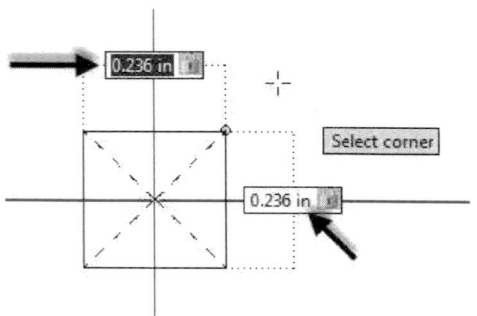

5. Press ENTER.

6. Enter 2 in the **Distance** box.

7. Click **OK** to create the extrusion.

Applying Draft
1. On the ribbon, click **3D Model > Modify > Draft**.

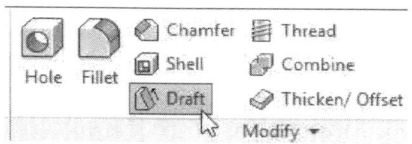

2. Select the **Fixed Plane** option.

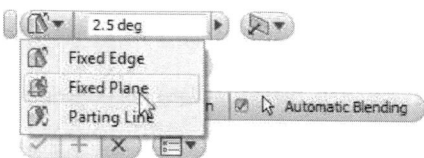

3. Select front face as the fixed face.

Part Modeling Basics

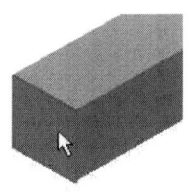

4. Select the top face as the face to be draft.

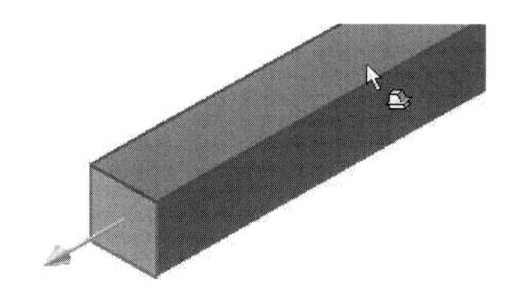

5. Set **Draft Angle** to **1**.

6. Click the **Flip pull direction** button on the **Face Draft** dialog.

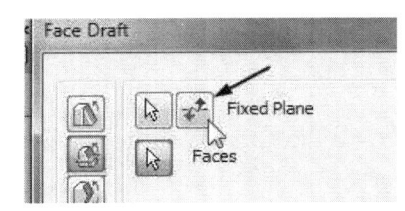

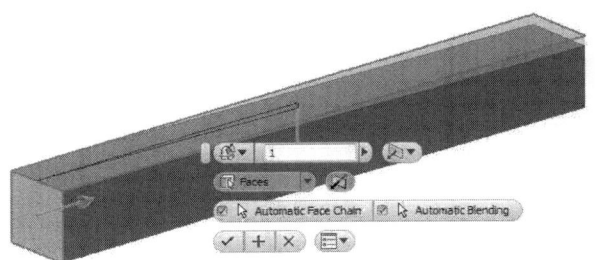

7. Click **OK** to create the draft.

Saving the Part

1. Click **Save** on the **Quick Access Toolbar**; the **Save As** dialog appears.

2. Type-in **Key** in the **File name** box.

3. Click **Save** to save the file.

4. Click **Application Menu > Close**.

Assembly Basics

Chapter 3: Assembly Basics

In this chapter, you will:

- Add Components to assembly
- Apply constraints between components
- Check Degrees of Freedom
- Check Interference
- Create exploded view of the assembly

TUTORIAL 1

This tutorial takes you through the creation of your first assembly. You create the Oldham coupling assembly:

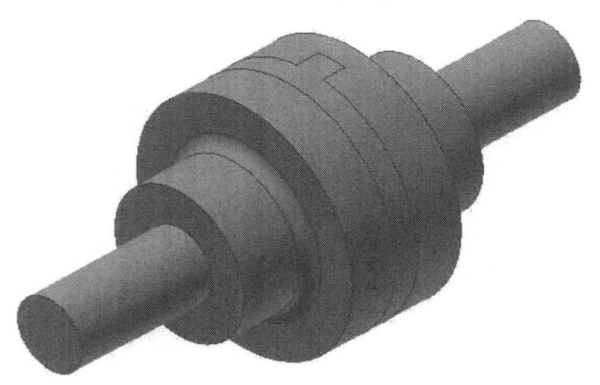

PARTS LIST		
ITEM	PART NUMBER	QTY
1	Disc	1
2	Flange	2
3	Shaft	2
4	Key	2

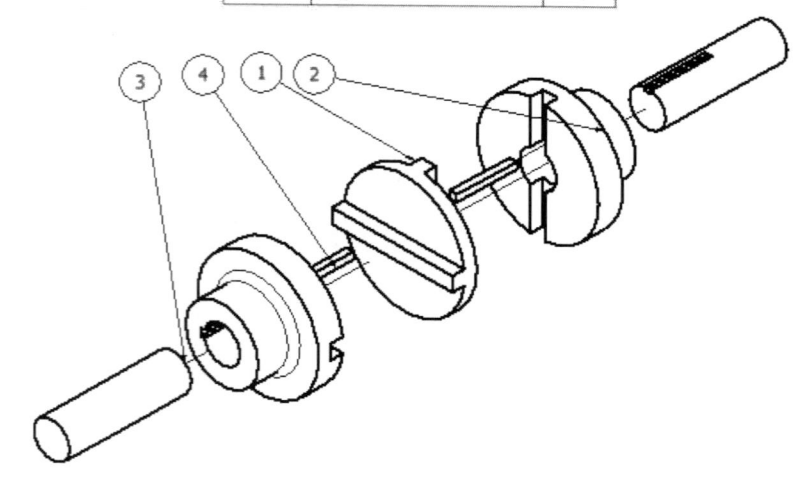

27

Assembly Basics

There are two ways of creating any assembly model.

- Top-Down Approach
- Bottom-Up Approach

Top-Down Approach
The assembly file is created first and components are created in that file.

Bottom-Up Approach
The components are created first, and then added to the assembly file. In this tutorial, you will create the assembly using this approach.

Starting a New Assembly File

1. To start a new assembly file, click the **Assembly** icon on the welcome screen.

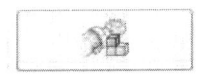

Inserting the Base Component

1. To insert the base component, click **Assemble > Component > Place** on the ribbon.

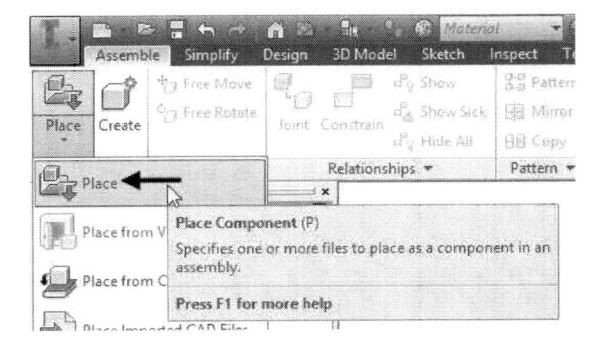

2. Browse to the project folder and double-click on **Flange.ipt**.

3. Right-click and select **Place Grounded at Origin**; the component is placed at the origin.

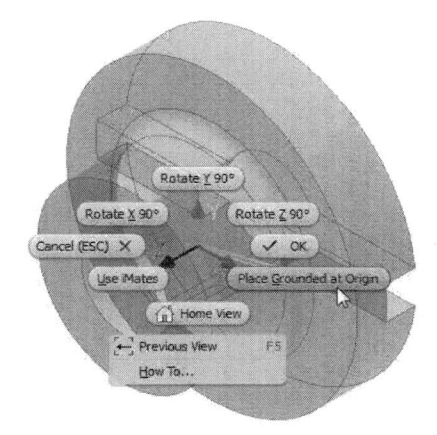

4. Right-click and select **OK**.

Adding the second component

1. To insert the second component, right-click and select **Place Component**; the **Place Component** dialog appears.

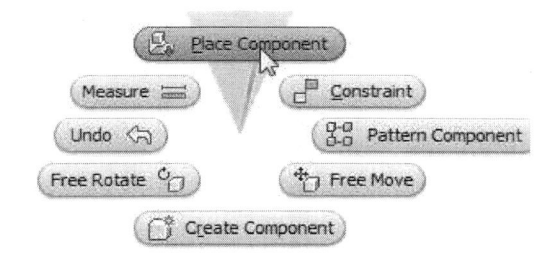

2. Browse to the project folder and double-click on **Shaft.ipt**.

3. Click in the window to place the component.

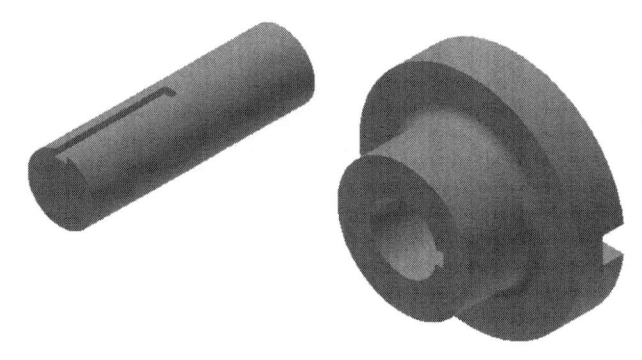

4. Right-click and select **OK**.

Applying Constraints

After adding the components to the assembly environment, you need to apply constraints between

Assembly Basics

them. By applying constraints, you establish relationships between components.

1. To apply constraints, click **Assemble > Relationships > Constrain** on the ribbon

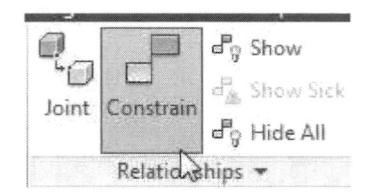

The **Place Constraint** dialog appears on the screen.

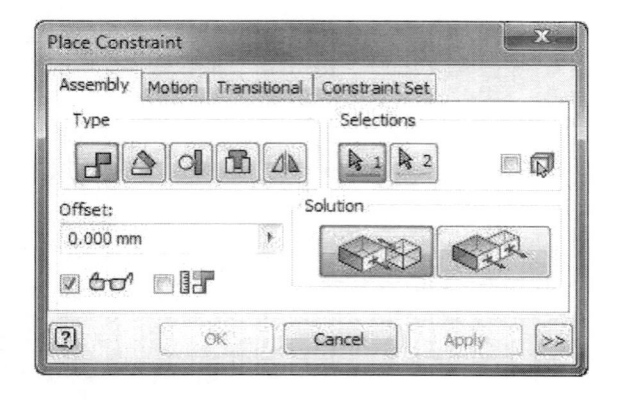

Different assembly constraints that can be applied using this dialog are given next.

Mate: Using this constraint, you can make two planar faces coplanar to each other.

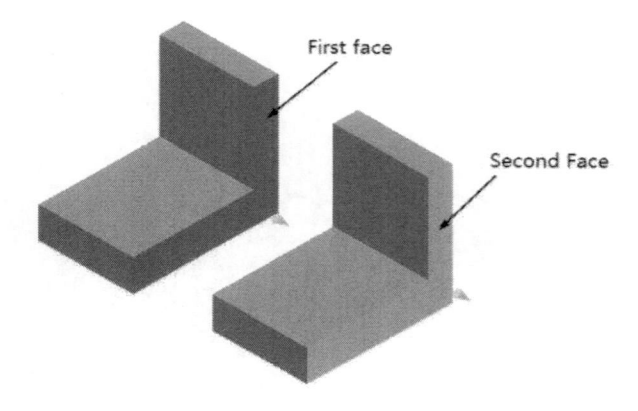

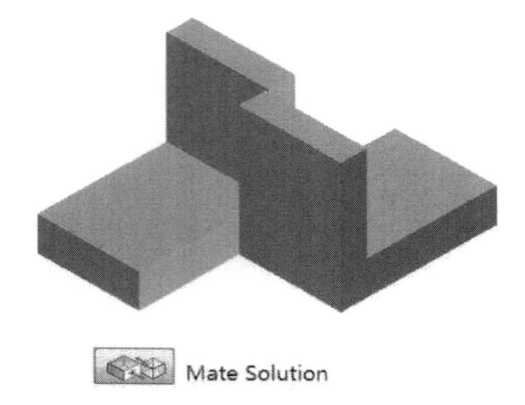

Mate Solution

Note that if you set the **Solution** to **Flush**, the faces will point in the same direction.

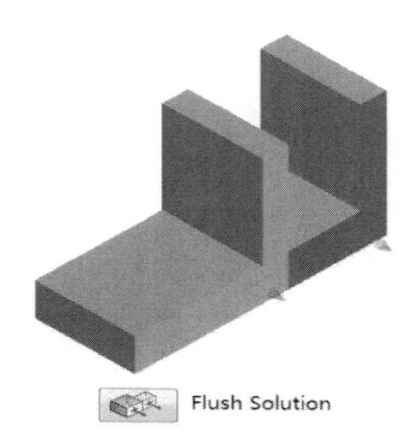

Flush Solution

You can also align the centerlines of the cylindrical faces.

29

Assembly Basics

Angle: Applies the angle constraint between two components.

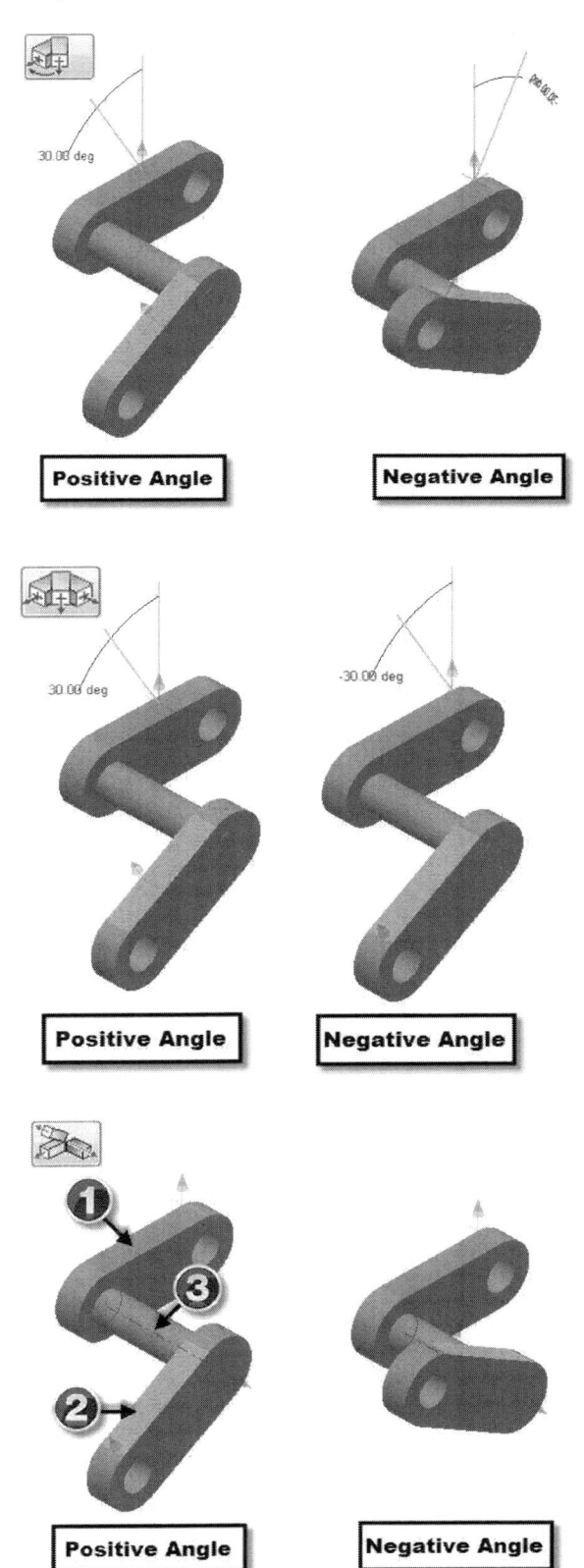

Positive Angle / Negative Angle

Positive Angle / Negative Angle

Positive Angle / Negative Angle

Tangent: This constraint is used to apply a tangent relation between two faces.

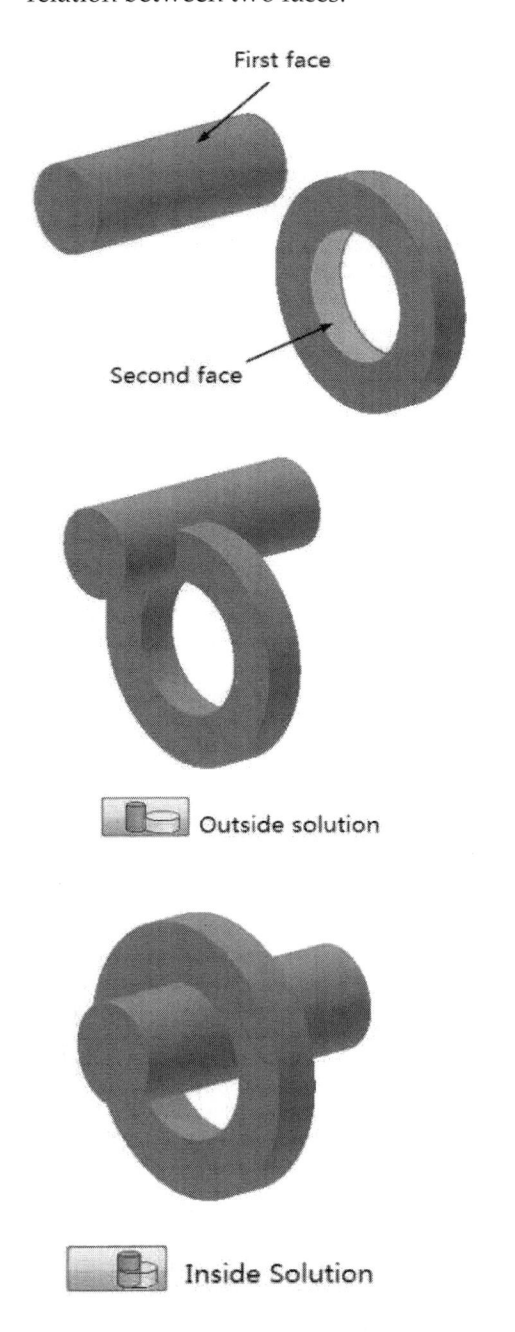

First face
Second face

Outside solution

Inside Solution

Insert: This constraint is used to make two cylindrical faces coaxial. In addition, the planar faces of the cylindrical components will be on the same plane.

30

Assembly Basics

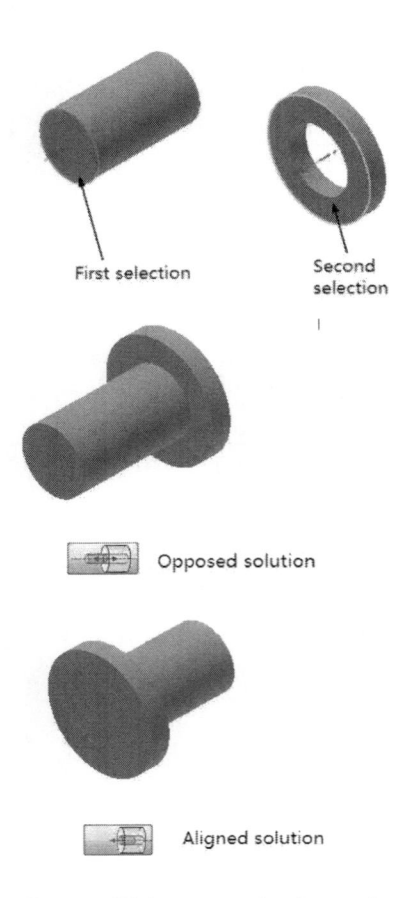

Center: This constraint is used to position the two components symmetrically about a plane.

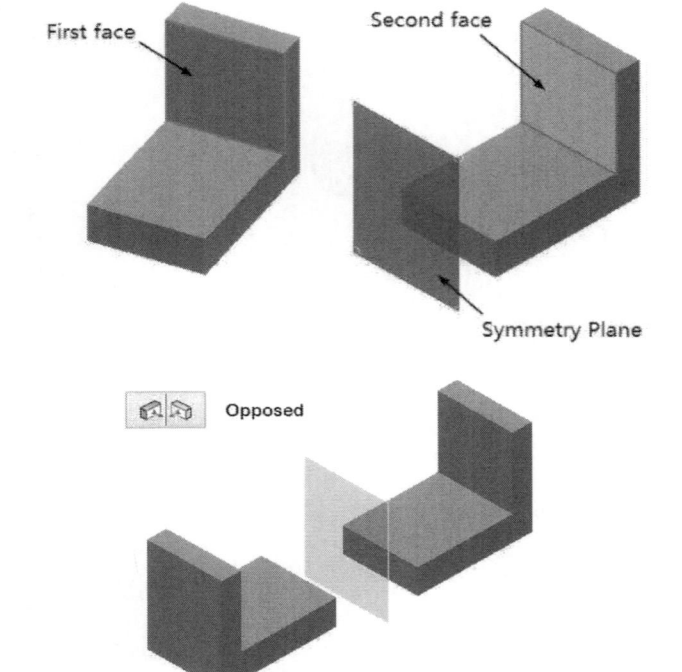

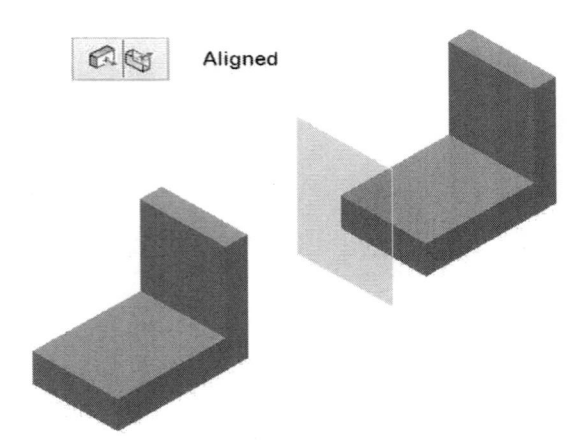

2. On the **Place Constraints** dialog, under the **Type** group, click the **Mate** icon.

3. Click on the cylindrical face of the Shaft.

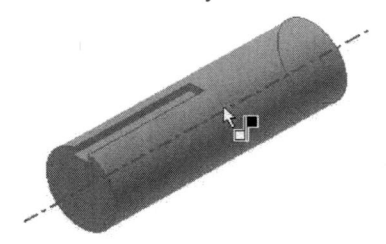

4. Click on the inner cylindrical face of the Flange.

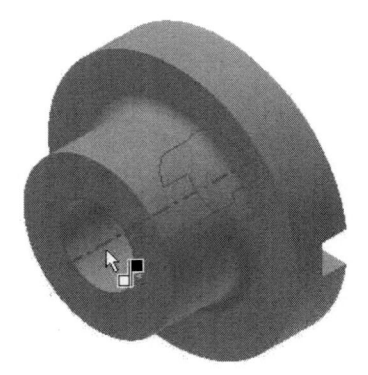

5. Click the **Apply** button.

6. Ensure that the **Mate** icon is selected in the **Type** group.

7. Click on the front face of the shaft.

31

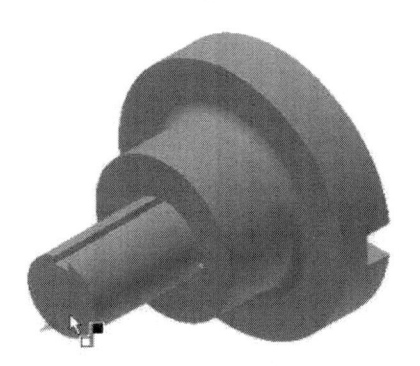

Assembly Basics

8. Rotate the model

9. Click on the slot face of the flange, as shown in figure.

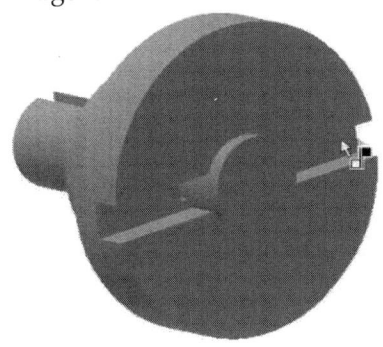

10. Click the **Flush** button on the **Place Constraint** dialog.

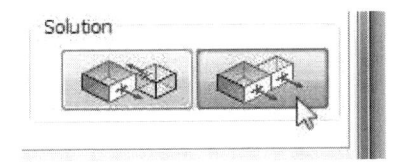

11. Click **Apply**. The front face of the Shaft and the slot face of the Flange are aligned.

12. Ensure that the **Mate** button is selected in the **Type** group.

13. Expand **Flange: 1** in the Browser window.

14. Select the XZ Plane of the Flange.

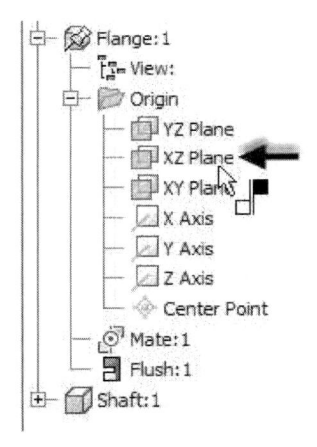

15. Expand **Shaft: 1** and select the YZ plane of the Shaft.

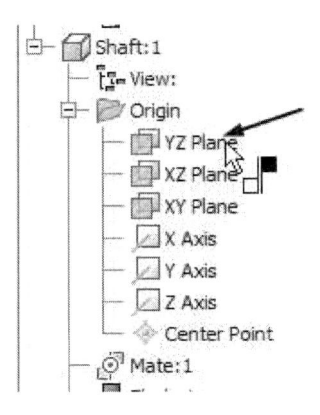

16. Click the **Flush** button on the **Place Constraint** dialog.

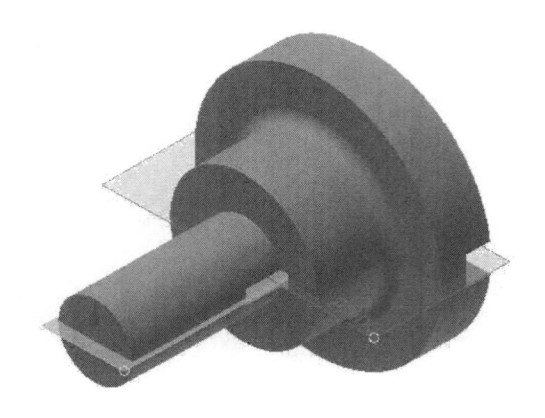

Assembly Basics

17. Click **OK** to assemble the components.

Adding the Third Component

1. To insert the third component, click **Assemble > Component > Place** on the ribbon.

2. Go to the project folder and double-click on **Key.ipt**.

3. Click in the window to place the key.

4. Right-click and click **OK**.

5. Right-click on **Flange: 1** in the Browser window.

6. Click **Visibility** on the shortcut menu; the Flange will be hidden.

7. Click **Constrain** on the **Relationships** panel.

8. Click **Mate** on the **Place Constraint** dialog.

9. Select **Mate** from the **Solution** group.

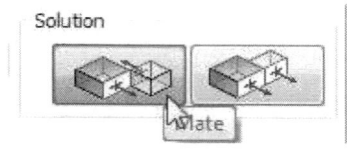

10. Click the right mouse button on the side face of the key and click **Select Other** on the shortcut menu.

11. Select the bottom face of the Key from the flyout.

12. Select the flat face of the slot.

Face to be selected

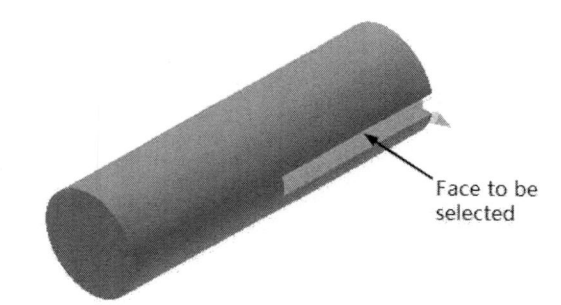

13. Click the **Apply** button. The bottom face of the key is aligned with the flat face of the slot.

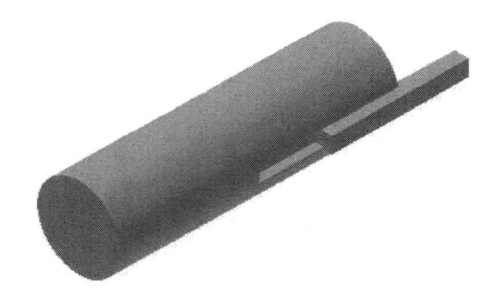

14. Click the **Mate** icon on the **Place Constraint** dialog.

15. Select **Flush** from the **Solution** group.

16. Select the front face of the Key and back face of the Shaft, as shown.

33

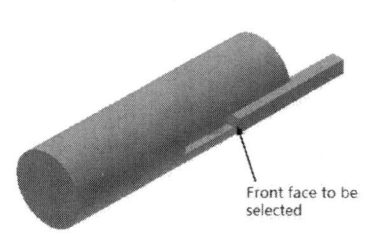

Assembly Basics

Front face to be selected

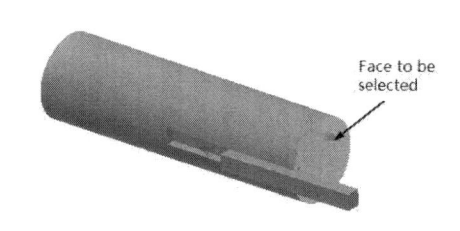

Face to be selected

17. Click **Apply** on the dialog; the mate is applied.

    Now, you need to check whether the parts are fully constrained or not.

18. Click **View > Visibility > Degrees of Freedom** on the ribbon.

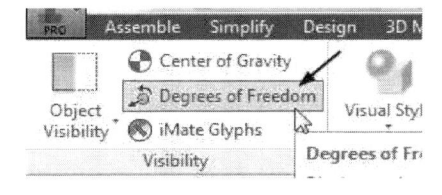

You will notice that an arrow appears pointing in the upward (or downward) direction. This means that the Key is not constrained in the Z-direction.

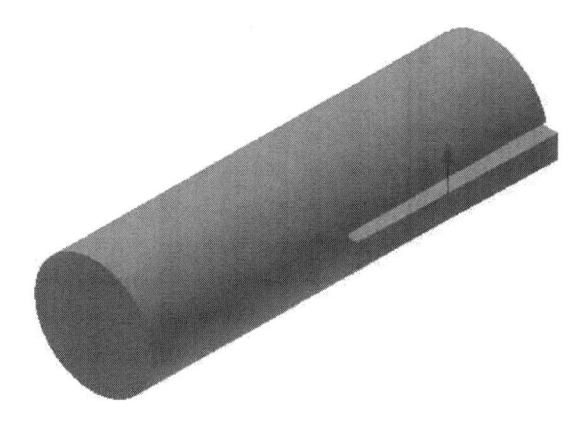

You must apply one more constraint to constrain the key.

19. Click **Constrain** on the **Relationships** panel.

20. Click the **Mate**  icon the dialog.

21. Select **Flush** from the **Solution** group.

22. Expand the **Origin** node of the **Assembly** in the **Browser window** and select **XZ Plane**.

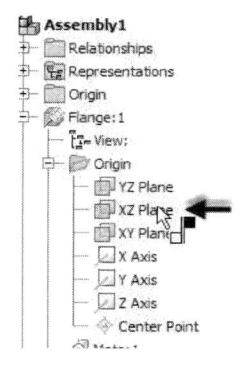

23. Expand the **Key: 1** node in the **Browser window** and select **YZ Plane**.

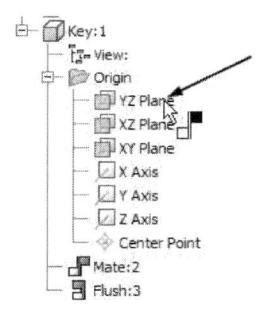

24. Click **OK**. The mate is applied between the two planes.

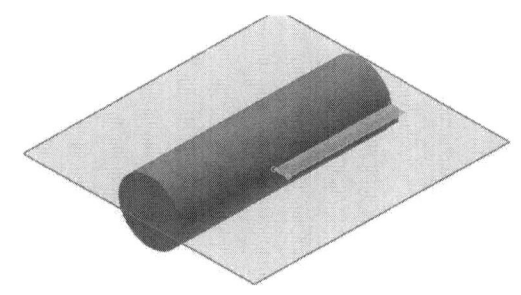

Now, you need to turn-on the display of the Flange.

34

Assembly Basics

25. Right-click on the **Flange** in the **Browser window** and select **Visibility**; the **Flange** appears.

Checking the Interference
1. Click **Inspect > Interference > Analyze Interference** on the Ribbon. The **Interference Analysis** dialog appears.

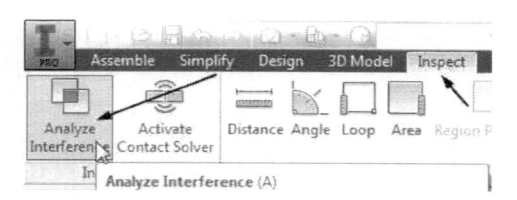

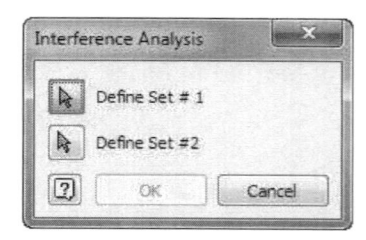

2. Select the Flange and Shaft as **Set #1**.

3. Click the **Define Set #2** button.

4. Select the Key as **Set # 2**.

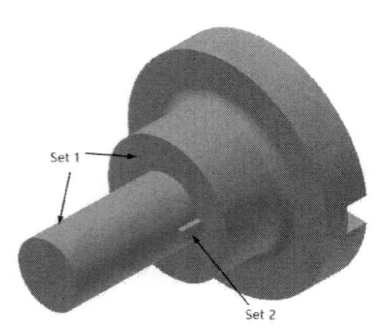

5. Click **OK**; the message box appears showing that there are no interferences.

Saving the Assembly
1. Click **Save** on the **Quick Access Toolbar**; the **Save As** dialog appears.

2. Type-in **Flange_subassembly** in the **File name** box.

3. Go to the project folder.

4. Click **Save** to save the file.

5. Click **Application Menu > Close**.

Starting the Main assembly
1. On the ribbon, click **Get Started > Launch > New**.
2. On the **Create New File** dialog, click the **Standard.iam** icon.

3. Click **Create** to start a new assembly.

Adding Disc to the Assembly
1. Click **Assemble > Component > Place** on the ribbon.

2. Go to the project folder and double-click on **Disc.ipt**.

3. Right-click and select **Place Grounded at Origin**; the component is placed at the origin.

4. Right-click and select **OK**.

35

Assembly Basics

Placing the Sub-assembly

1. To insert the sub-assembly, click the **Place** button on the **Component** panel of the ribbon.

2. Go to the project folder and double-click on **Flange_subassembly.iam**.

3. Click in the window to place the flange sub assembly.

4. Right-click and click **OK**.

Adding Constraints

1. Click **Constrain** on the **Relationships** panel of the **Assemble** ribbon.

2. Click the **Insert** button on the **Place Constraint** dialog.

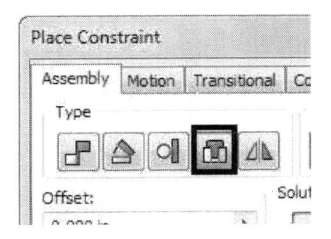

3. Select **Opposed** from the **Solution** group.

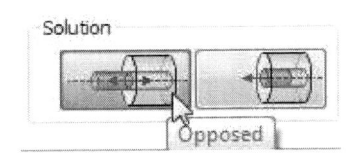

4. Click on the circular edge of the Flange.

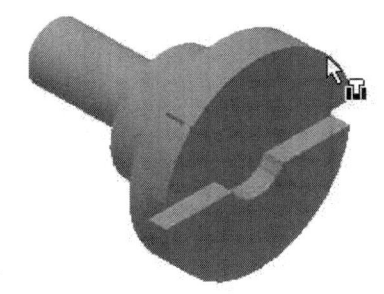

5. Click on the circular edge of the Disc.

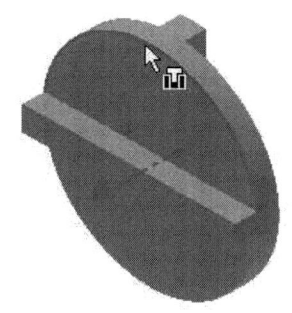

6. Click **OK** on the dialog.

Next, you have to move the subassembly away from the Disc to apply other constraints.

7. Click **Free Move** on the **Position** panel.

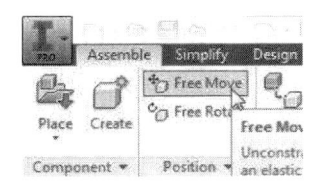

8. Select the flange subassembly and move it.

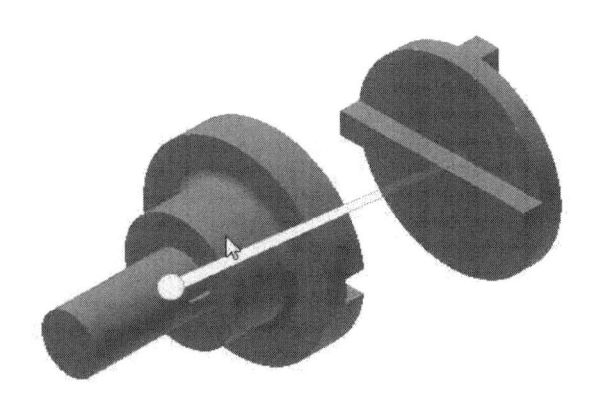

9. Click the **Constrain** button on the **Relationships** panel.

10. Click **Mate** on the **Place Constraints** dialog.

11. Select **Mate** from the **Solution** group.

12. Click on the face on the Flange, as shown in figure.

36

Assembly Basics

13. Click on the face on the Disc as shown in figure.

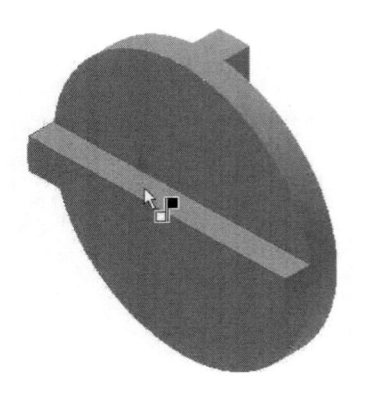

14. Click **OK** on the dialog.

Placing the second instance of the Sub-assembly

1. Insert another instance of the Flange subassembly.

2. Apply the **Insert** and **Mate** constraints.

Saving the Assembly

1. Click **Save** on the **Quick Access Toolbar**; the **Save As** dialog appears.

2. Type-in **Oldham_coupling** in the **File name** box.

3. Click **Save** to save the file.

4. Click **Application Menu > Close**.

TUTORIAL 2

In this tutorial, you create the exploded view of the assembly:

Starting a New Presentation File

1. On the welcome screen, click the **Presentation** icon.

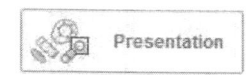

Creating the Exploded View

1. To create the exploded view, click the **Create View** button on the **Presentation** ribbon.

37

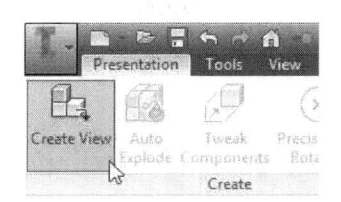

Assembly Basics

2. Click **Open existing file** button on the **Select Assembly** dialog.

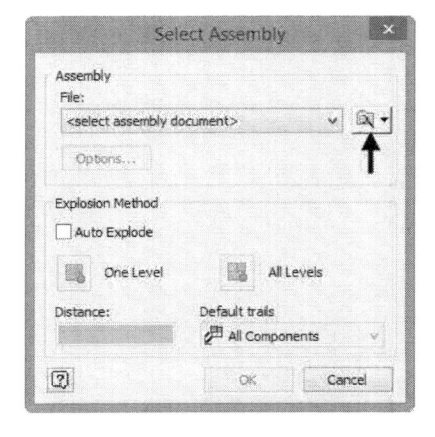

3. Go to the project folder.

4. Check the **Auto Explode** option. This will explode the assembly automatically.

5. Select the **One Level** option. This will explode the upper levels (sub-assemblies) of the main assembly.

6. Select the **Default trails > All Components**. This will create tracelines of all exploded components.

7. Type **4** in the **Distance** box to specify the explosion distance.

8. Click **OK** to create the exploded view of the assembly.

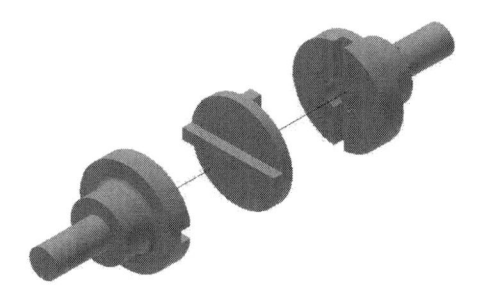

9. Click the **Tweak Components** button on the **Presentation** ribbon.

Now, you must specify the direction along which the parts will be exploded.

5. On the Mini Toolbar, select **Part** from the drop-down, as shown.

6. Click **Locate** on the Mini Toolbar.

7. Click on the shaft and ensure that the Z-axis points in the direction, as shown in figure below.

8. Click on the Z axis of the manipulator.

9. Type 4 in the box attached to the manipulator, and then press Enter.

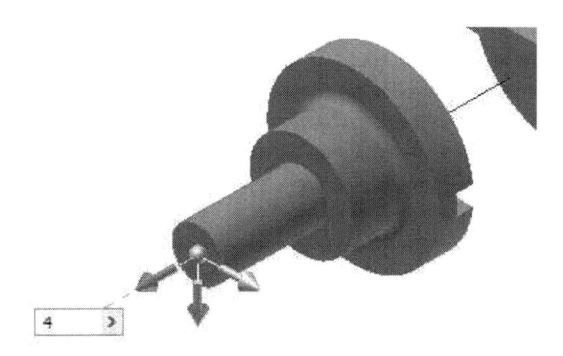

10. Click the **Apply** on the Mini Toolbar.

11. Zoom into the flange and click on the key, as shown. Make sure that the Z axis points backwards.

Assembly Basics

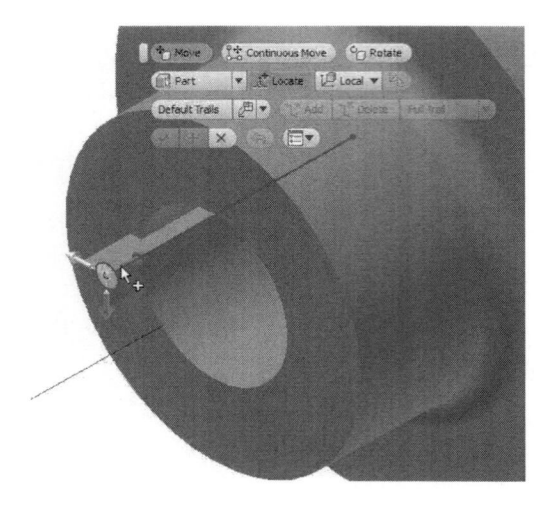

12. Type 3.15 in the box attached to the manipulator and press Enter.

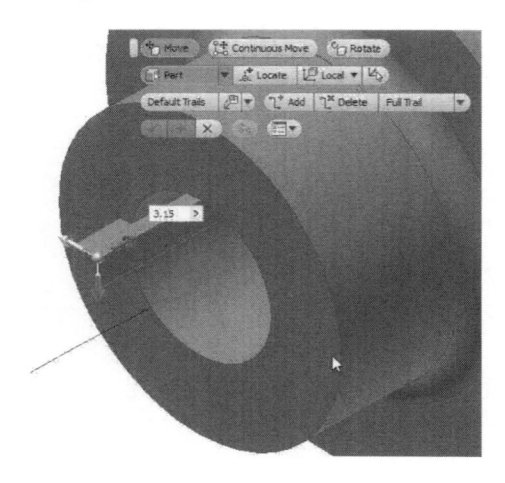

13. Click the **Apply** on the Mini Toolbar.

15. Likewise, explode the other flange subassembly and its parts in the opposite direction. The explosion distances are same.

Animating the Explosion

1. To animate the explosion, click the **Animate** button on the **Presentation** tab.

2. On the **Animation** dialog, type-in **10** in the **Interval** box and **1** in the **Repetitions** box.

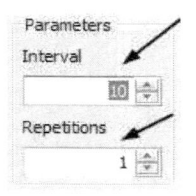

3. Click **Apply**.

4. Click the **Record** button and save the animation file as **Oldham_Explosion.wmv** in the project folder.

5. Leave the default values and click **OK** on the **WMV Export Properties** dialog.

6. Make sure that the **Minimize dialog during recording** option is selected

7. Click the **Auto Reverse** button; the explosion is animated.

8. Click **Cancel**.

9. Click **Save** on the **Quick Access Toolbar**; the **Save As** dialog appears.

10. Type-in **Oldham_coupling** in the **File name** box.

11. Go to the project folder.

12. Click **Save** to save the file.

13. Click **OK**.

14. Click **Application Menu > Close**.

39

Assembly Basics

Creating Drawings

Chapter 4: Creating Drawings

In this chapter, you will generate 2D drawings of the parts and assemblies.

In this chapter, you will:

- Insert standard views of a part model
- Create centerlines and centermarks
- Retrieve model dimensions
- Add additional dimensions and annotations
- Create Custom Sheet Formats and Templates
- Insert exploded view of the assembly
- Insert a bill of materials of the assembly
- Apply balloons to the assembly

TUTORIAL 1
In this tutorial, you will create the drawing of Flange.ipt file created in the second chapter.

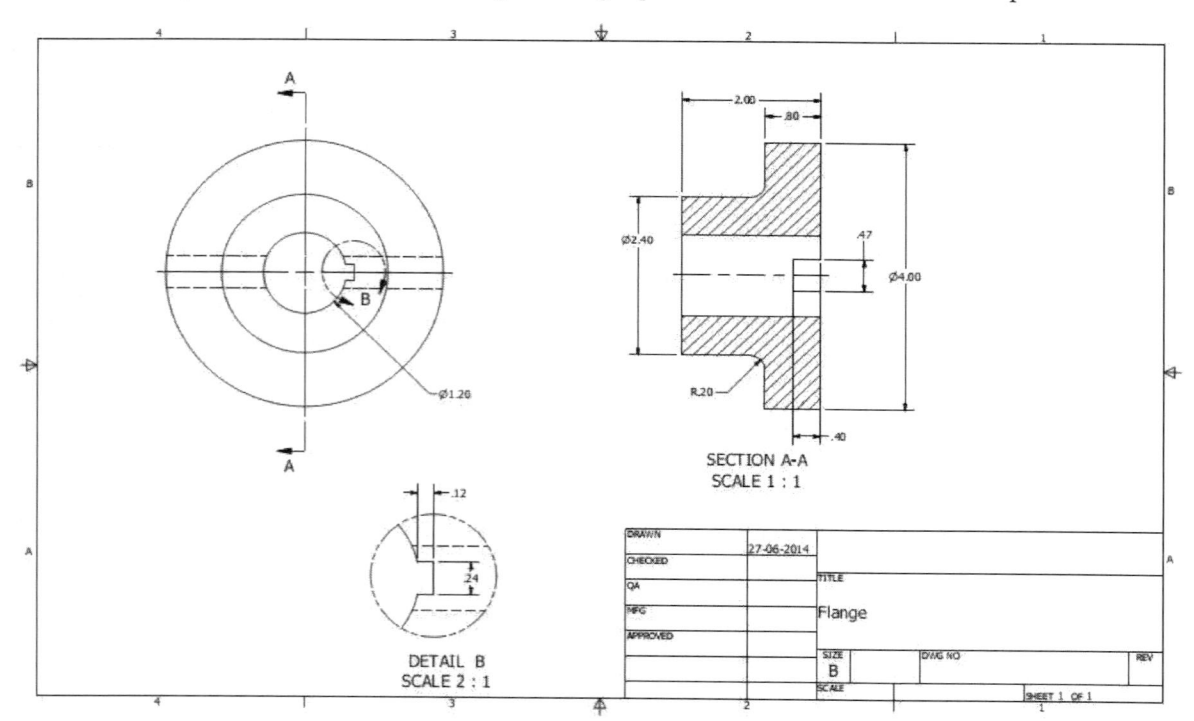

Starting a New Drawing File
1. To start a new drawing, click **Drawing** icon on the welcome screen.

Creating Drawings

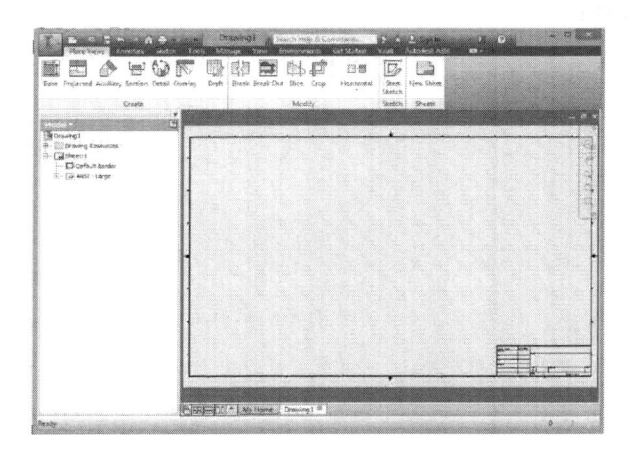

Editing the Drawing Sheet
1. To edit the drawing sheet, right-click on **Sheet:1** in the **Browser window** and select **Edit Sheet** from the shortcut menu.

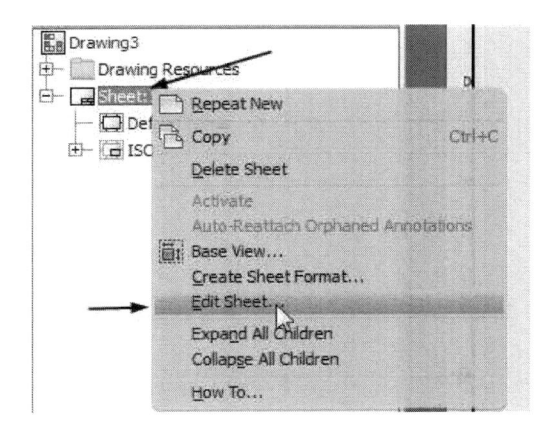

2. On the **Edit Sheet** dialog, set **Size** to **B**.

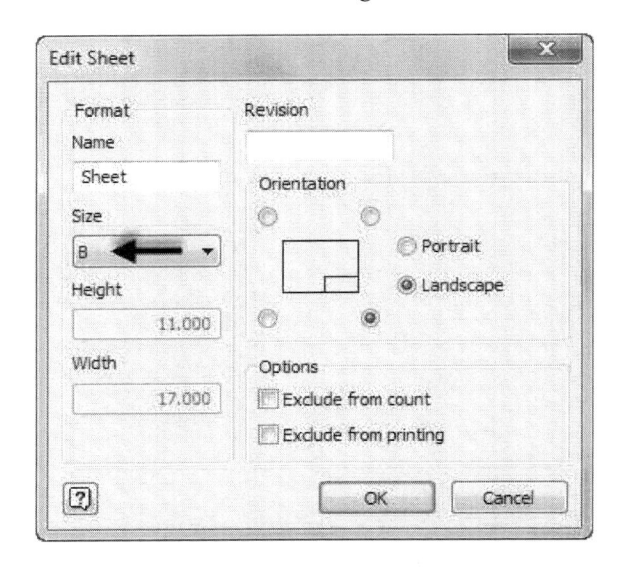

3. Click **OK**.

The drawing views in this tutorial are created in the Third Angle Projection. If you want to change the type of projection, then following the steps given next:

4. Click **Manage > Styles and Standards > Style Editor** on the ribbon.

5. On **Style and Standard Editor** dialog, specify the settings shown in figure.

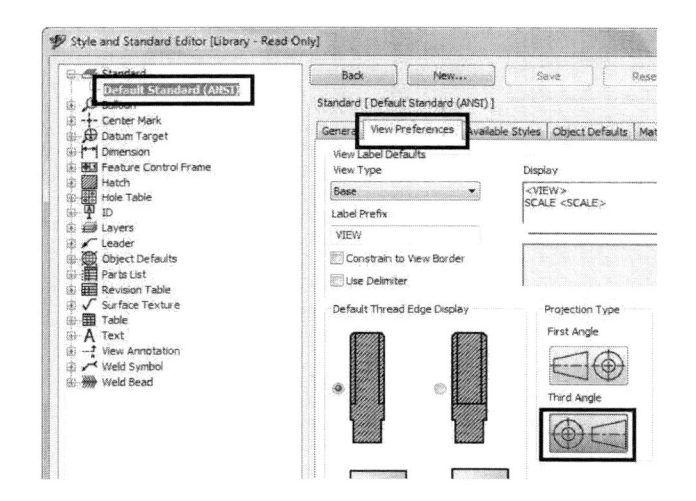

6. Click **Done**.

Generating the Base View
1. To generate the base view, click **Place views > Create > Base** on the ribbon.

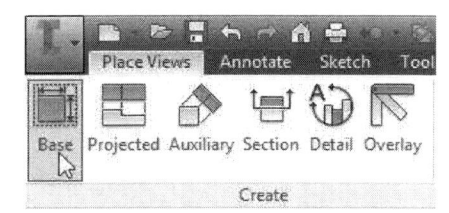

2. On the **Drawing View** dialog, click **Open existing file**.

42

Creating Drawings

3. On the **Open** dialog, browse to the project folder.
4. Set the Files of type to Inventor Files (*.ipt, *.iam, *.ipn), and then double-click on **Flange.ipt**.
5. Set the **Style** to **Hidden Line**.
6. Set **Scale** to **1:1**.
7. Place the view, as shown in figure. The **Projected View** tool gets active.
8. Right-click and select **OK**.

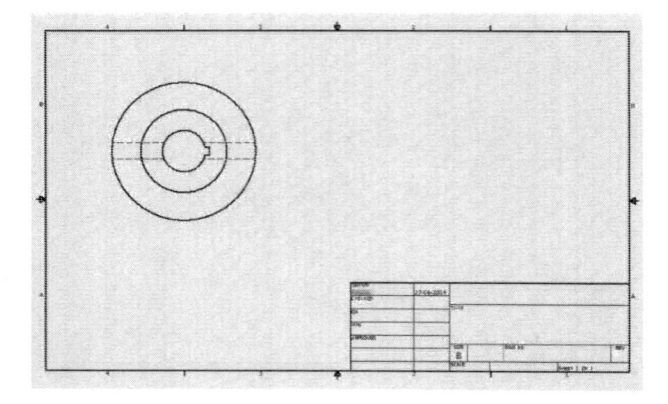

Generating the Section View

1. To create the section view, click **Place Views > Create > Section** on the ribbon.

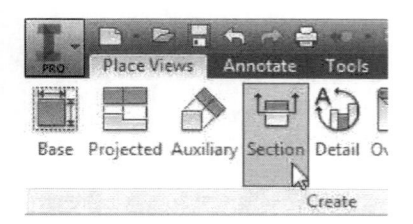

2. Select the base view.
3. Place the cursor on the top quadrant point of the circular edge, as shown.
4. Move the pointer upward and notice the dotted line.

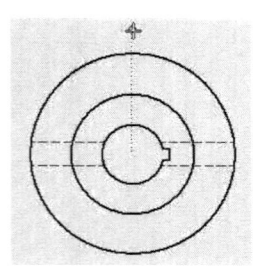

5. Click on the dotted line and draw a vertical line passing through the center point of the view.

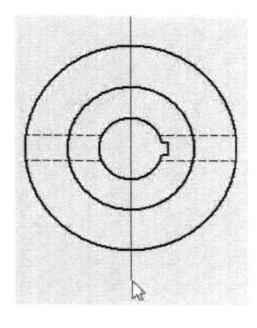

6. Right-click and select **Continue**.

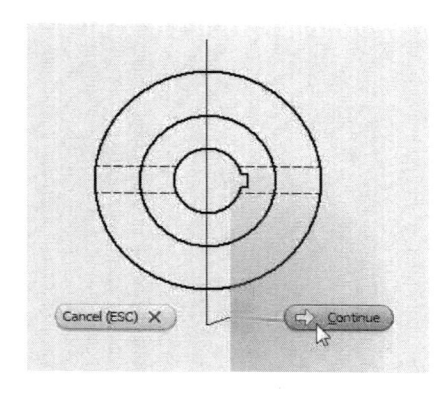

7. Move the cursor toward right and click to place the section view.

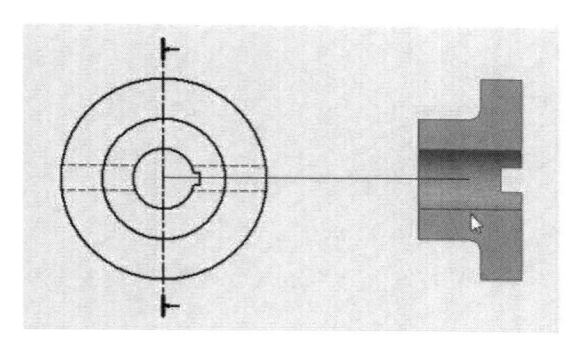

43

Creating Drawings

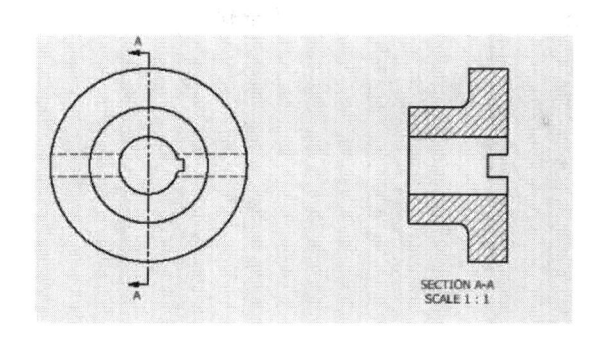

Creating the Detailed View
Now, you have to create the detailed view of the keyway, which is displayed, in the front view.

1. To create the detailed view, click **Place Views > Create > Detail** on the ribbon.

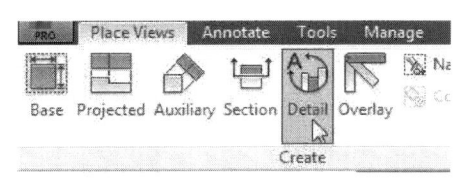

2. Select the base view.

3. On the **Detail View** dialog, specify the settings, as shown next.

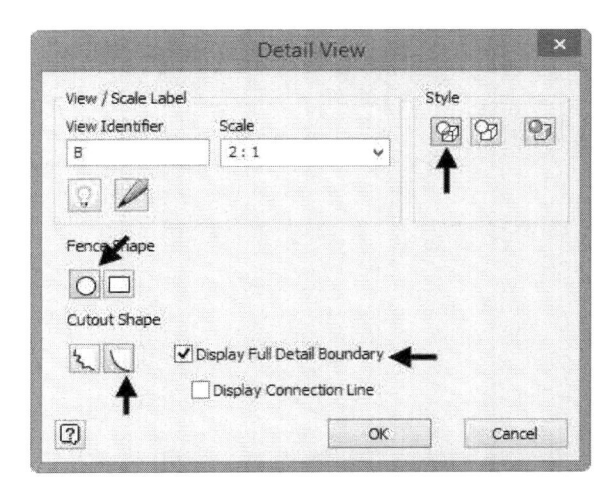

4. Specify the center point and boundary point of the detail view, as shown in figure.

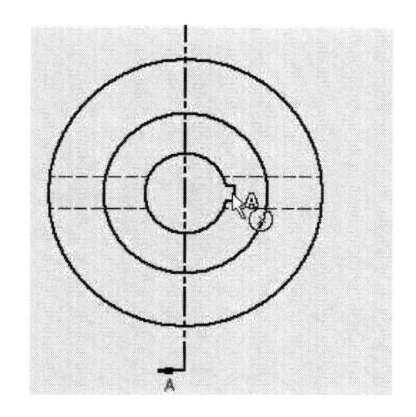

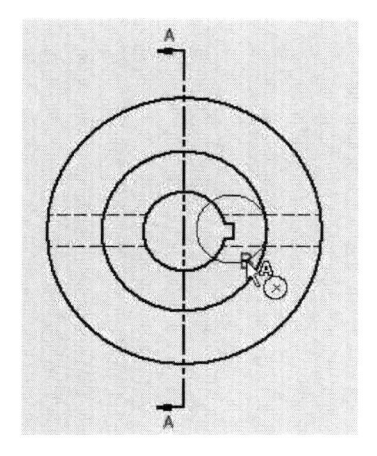

5. Place the detail view below the base view.

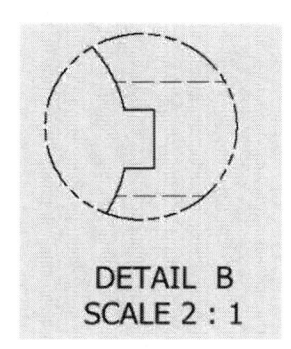

Creating Centermarks and Centerlines
1. To create a center mark, click **Annotate > Symbols > Center Mark** on the ribbon.

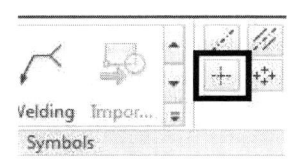

2. Click on the outer circle of the base view.

44

Creating Drawings

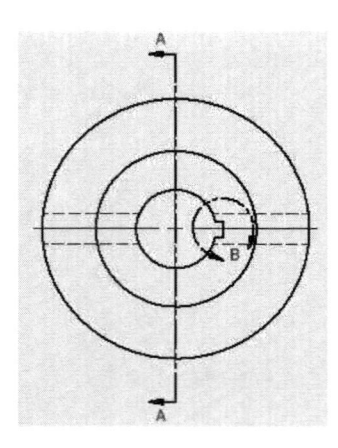

3. To create a centerline, click **Annotate > Symbols > Centerline Bisector** on the ribbon.

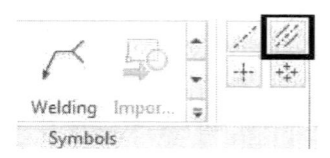

4. Click on the inner horizontal edges of the section view.

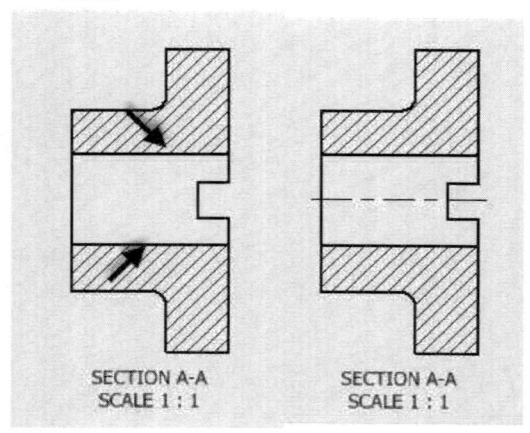

Retrieving Dimensions

Now, you will retrieve the dimensions that were applied to the model while creating it.

1. To retrieve dimensions, click **Annotate > Dimension > Retrieve** on the ribbon.

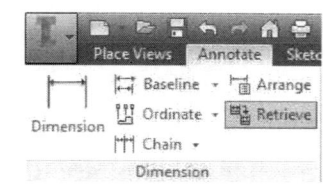

The **Retrieve Dimension** dialog appears.

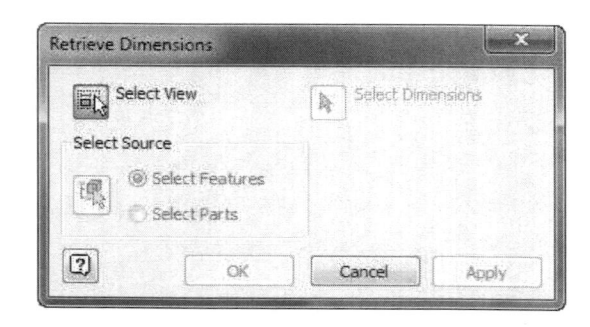

2. Select the section view from the drawing sheet.

3. Click the **Select Dimensions** button on the dialog.

Now, you must select the dimensions to retrieve.

4. Drag a window on the section view to select all the dimensions.

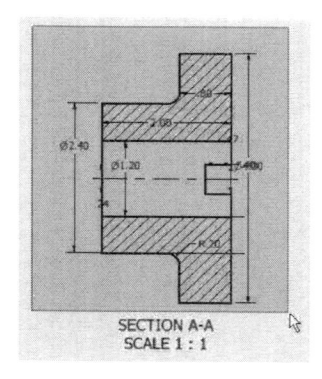

5. Click **Select Features** under the **Select Source** group.

6. Click **OK** to retrieve feature dimensions.

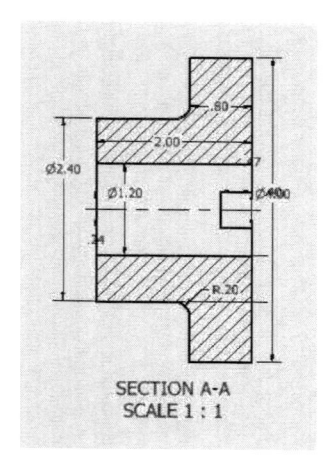

45

Creating Drawings

7. Click **Annotate > Dimension > Arrange** on the ribbon.

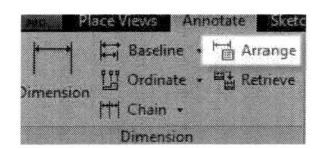

8. Drag a selection box and select all the dimensions of the section view.

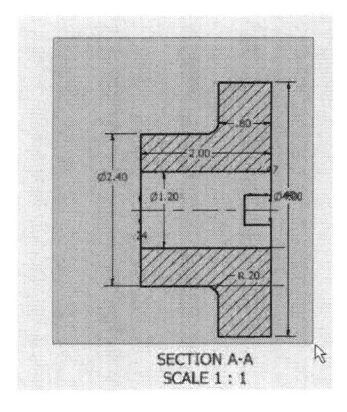

9. Click the right-mouse button and select **OK**.

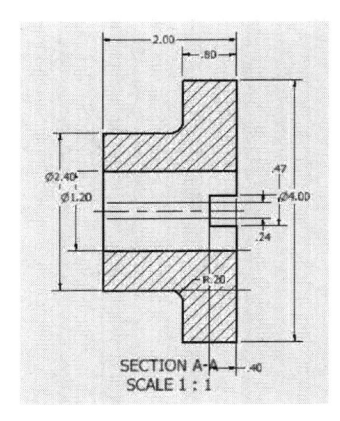

10. Select the unwanted dimensions and press Delete.

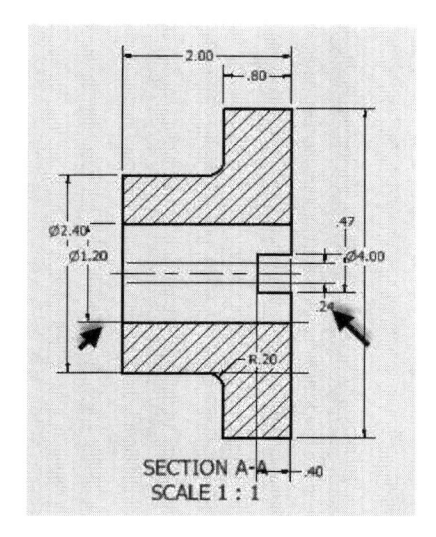

11. Click and drag the dimensions to arrange them properly.

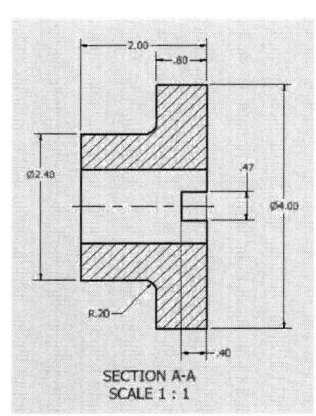

12. Delete the unwanted dimension and arrange the required dimensions, as shown in figure.

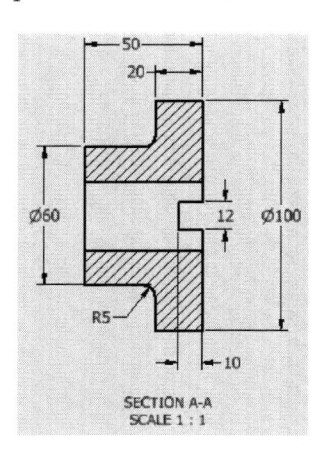

Adding additional dimensions

1. To add dimensions, click **Annotate > Dimension > Dimension** on the ribbon.

Creating Drawings

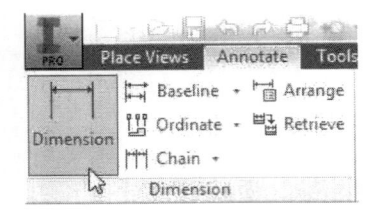

2. Select the center hole on the base view.

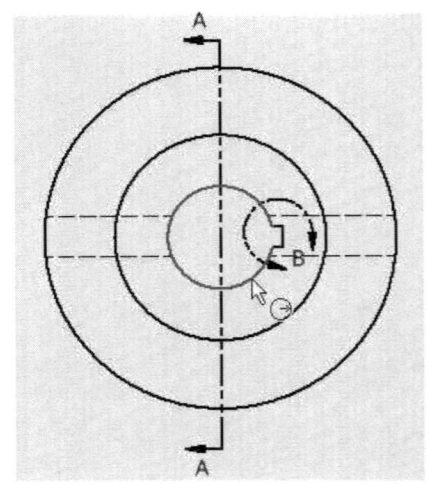

3. Right-click and select **Dimension Type > Diameter**.

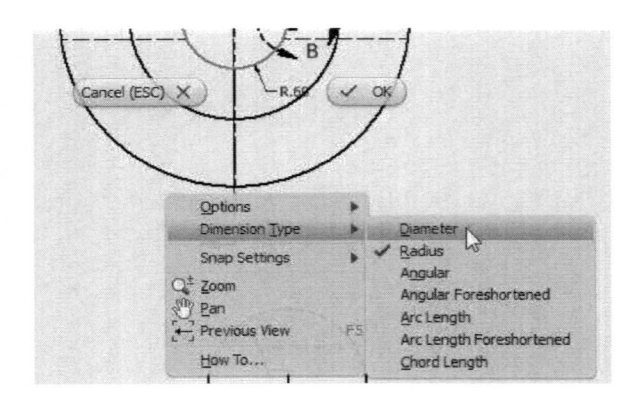

4. Place the dimension, as shown in figure. The **Edit Dimension** dialog appears.

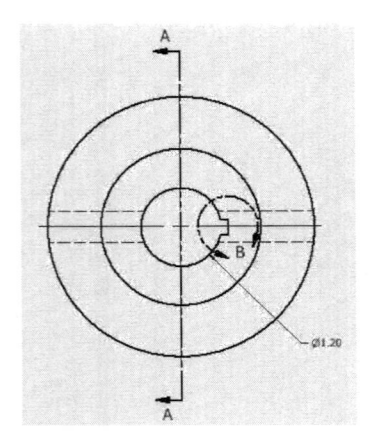

5. Click **OK**.

6. Create the dimensions on the detail view, as shown in figure.

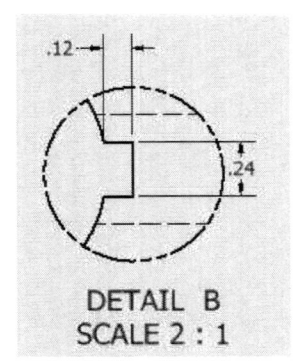

Populating the Title Block

1. To populate the title block, click **Application Menu > iProperties**.

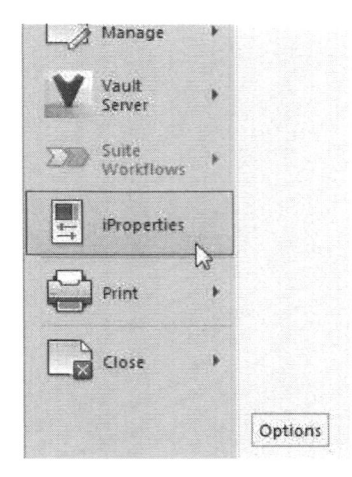

2. On the **Flange iProperties** dialog, click the tabs one-by-one and type-in data in respective fields.

Creating Drawings

3. Click **Apply** and **Close**.

Saving the Drawing

1. Click **Save** on the **Quick Access Toolbar**; the **Save As** dialog appears.

2. Type-in **Flange** in the **File Name** box.

3. Go to the project folder.

4. Click **Save** to save the file.

5. Click **Application Menu > Close**.

TUTORIAL 2

In this tutorial, you will create a custom template, and then use it to create a new drawing.

Creating New Sheet Format

1. On the ribbon, click **Get Started > Launch > New**.

2. On the **Create New File** dialog, click the **Standard.idw** icon.

3. Click **Create** to start a new drawing file.

4. To edit the drawing sheet, right-click on **Sheet:1** in the **Browser window** and select **Edit Sheet** from the shortcut menu.

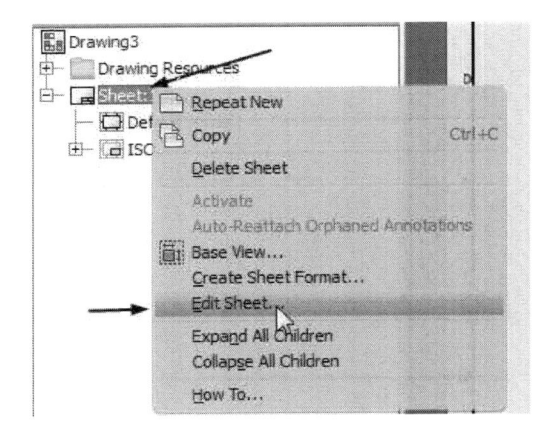

5. On the **Edit Sheet** dialog, set **Size** to **B**.

   Under the **Orientation** section, you can change the orientation of the title block as well as the sheet orientation.

6. Click **OK**.

7. In the **Browser window**, expand the **Drawing Resources > Sheet Formats** folder to view different sheet formats available. Now, you will add a new sheet format to this folder.

8. Click the right mouse button on the **Borders** folder and select **Define New Border**.

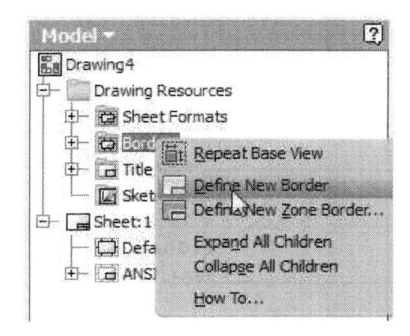

   Now, you can create a new border using the sketch tools available in the **Sketch** tab.

9. Click **Finish Sketch** on the **Sketch** tab of the ribbon.

10. On the **Border** dialog, click **Discard**.

11. In the Browser window, click the right mouse button on the **Borders** folder and select **Define New Zone Border**.

12. On the **Default Drawing Border Parameters** dialog, type-in **4** in the **Vertical Zones** box and click **OK**.

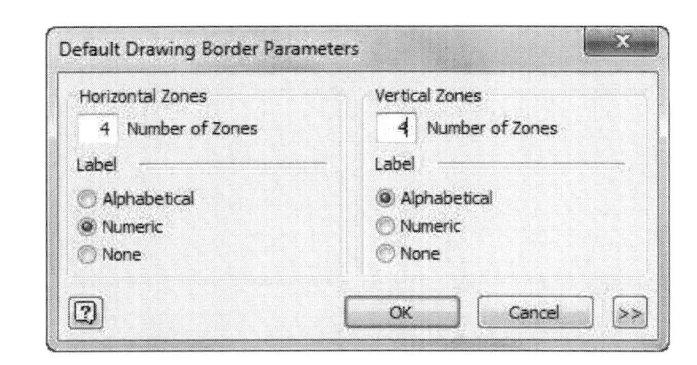

13. Click **Finish Sketch** on the **Sketch** tab of the ribbon.

Creating Drawings

14. On the **Border** dialog, type-in **4-Zone Border** and click **Save**.

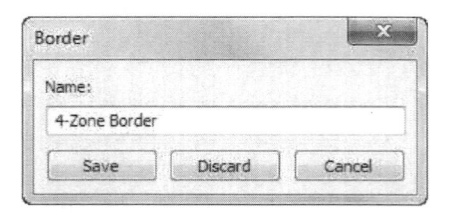

15. Expand the **Title Blocks** folder and click the right mouse button on **ANSI-Large**.

16. Select **Edit** from shortcut menu.

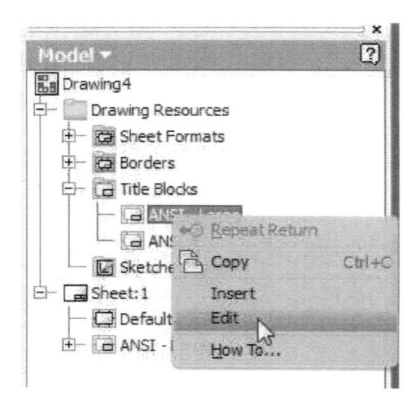

17. On the **Sketch** tab of the ribbon, click **Insert > Image**.

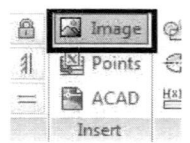

18. Draw a rectangle in the **Company** cell of the title block. This defines the image size and location.

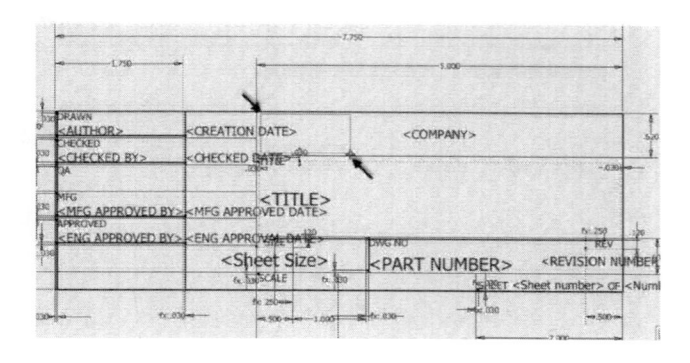

19. Go to the location of your company logo or any other image location. You must ensure that the image is located inside the project folder.

20. Select the image file and click **Open**. This will insert the image into the title block.

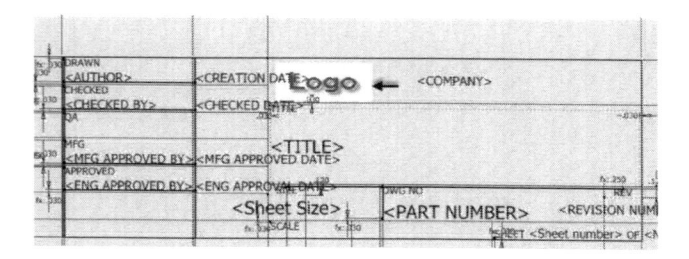

21. Click **Finish Sketch** on the ribbon.

22. Click **Save As** on the **Save Edits** dialog.

23. Type-in **ANSI-Logo** in the **Title Block** dialog.

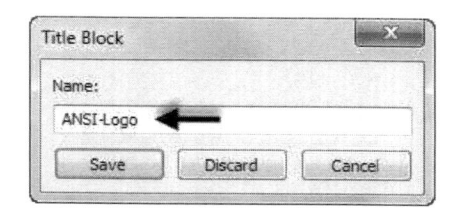

24. Click **Save**.

25. In the Browser window, expand **Sheet:1** and click the right mouse button on **Default Border**.

26. Select **Delete** from the shortcut menu.

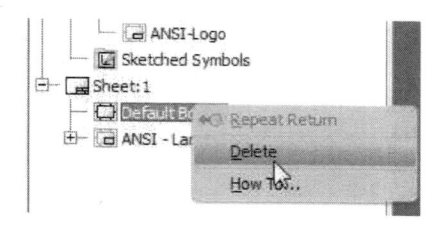

27. Expand the **Borders** folder and click the right mouse button on **4-Zone Border**.

28. Select **Insert** from the shortcut menu.

49

Creating Drawings

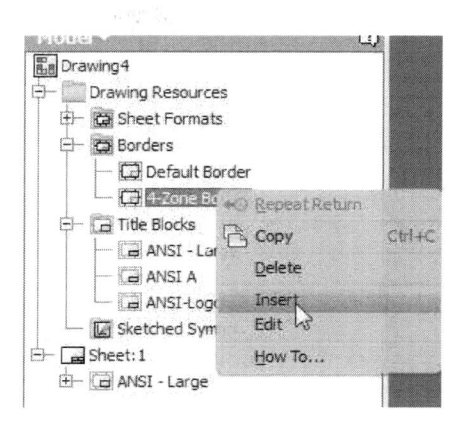

29. Click **OK** on the **Edit Drawing Border Parameters** dialog.

30. Expand **Sheet:1** and click the right mouse button on **ANSI-Large**.

31. Select **Delete** from the shortcut menu.

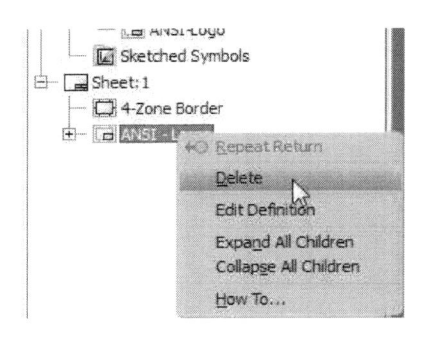

32. Expand the **Title Blocks** folder and click the right mouse button on **ANSI-Logo**.

33. Select **Insert** from the shortcut menu to insert the title block.

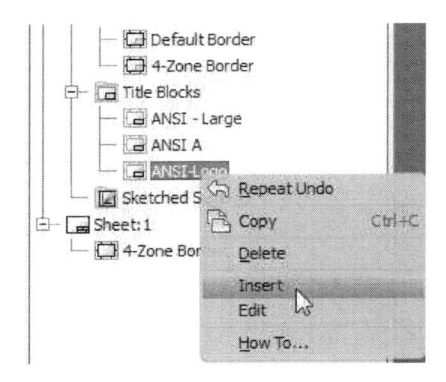

34. Click the right mouse button on **Sheet:1** and select **Create Sheet Format**.

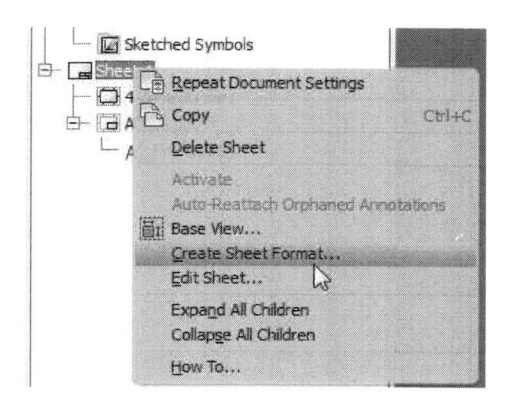

35. Type-in **Custom Sheet** in the **Create Sheet Format** dialog, and then click **OK**.

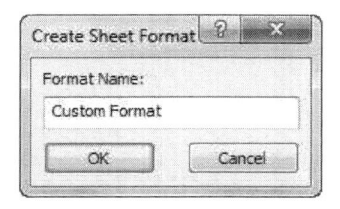

You will notice that the new sheet format is listed in the **Sheet Formats** folder.

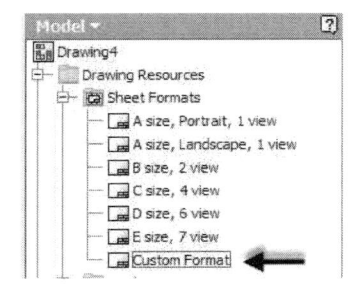

Creating a Custom Template

1. On the ribbon, click **Tools > Options > Document Settings**.

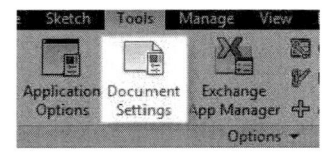

On **Document Settings** dialog, you can define the standard, sheet color, drawing view settings, and sketch settings.

50

Creating Drawings

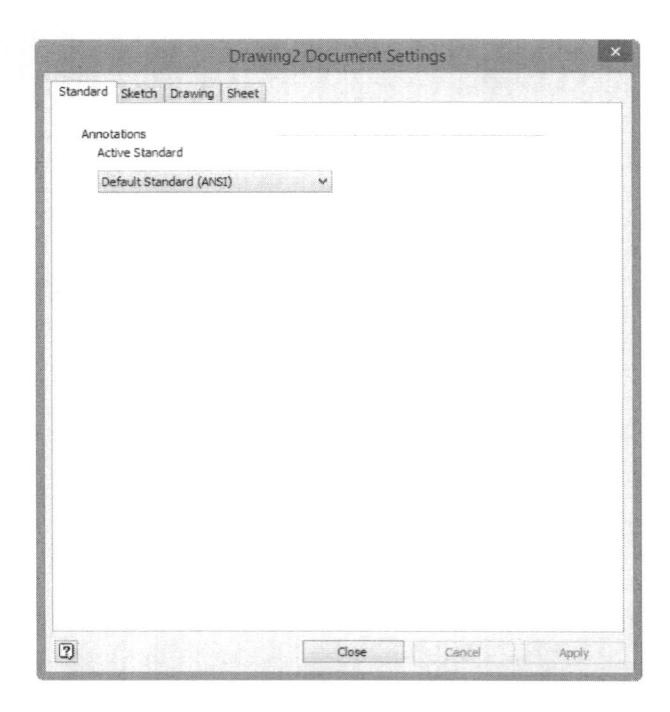

2. Leave the default settings on this dialog and click **Close**.

3. In the Browser window, expand the **Sheet Formats** folder and double-click on **Custom Format**.

4. Click the right mouse button on **Sheet: 2** and select **Delete Sheet** from the shortcut menu.

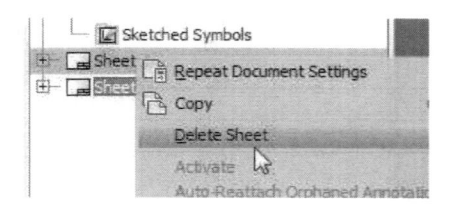

5. Click **OK**.

6. On the ribbon, click **Manage > Styles and Standards > Styles Editor**.

7. On the **Style and Standard Editor** dialog, select **Dimension > Default (ANSI)**.

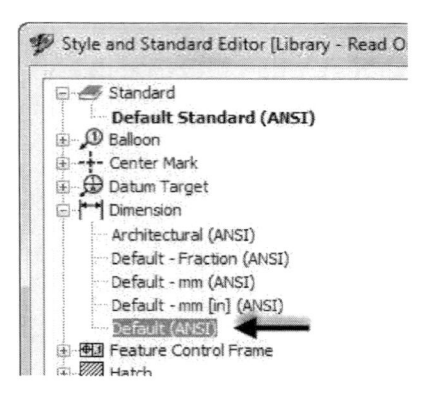

8. Click the **New** button located at the top of the dialog.

9. Type-in **Custom Standard** in the **New Local Style** dialog, and then click **OK**.

10. Click the **Units** tab and set **Precision** to **3.123**.

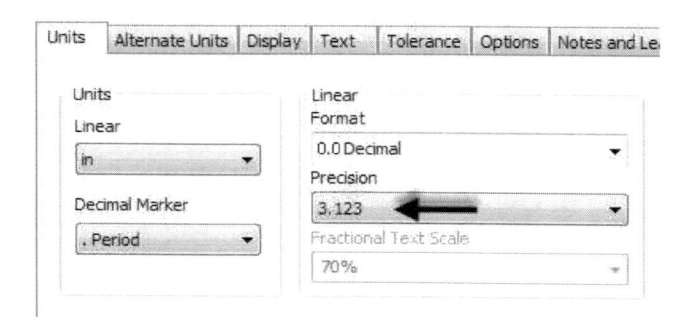

11. Click **Done**, and then **Yes**.

12. On the **Application Menu**, click **Save As > Save Copy As Template**. This will take you to the templates folder on your drive.

13. Type-in **Custom Template** in the **File name** box.

14. Click **Save**.

15. Close the drawing file without saving it.

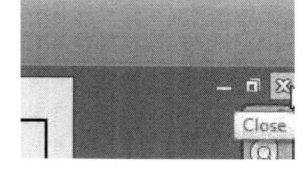

51

Creating Drawings

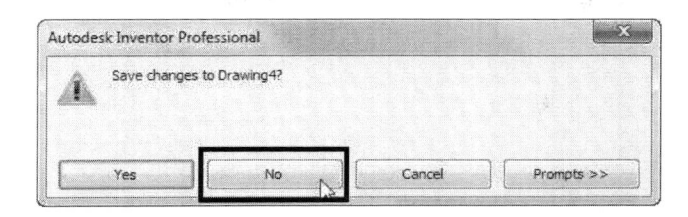

Starting a Drawing using the Custom template

1. On the ribbon, click **Get Started > Launch > New**.

2. On the **Create New File** dialog, click the **Custom Standard.idw** icon.

3. Click **Create** and **OK** to start a new drawing file.

Generating the Drawing Views

1. To generate views, click **Place views > Create > Base** on the ribbon.

2. On the **Drawing View** dialog, click **Open existing file**.

3. Go to the project folder and double-click on **Disc.ipt**.

4. Select **Front** from the ViewCube displayed on the sheet.

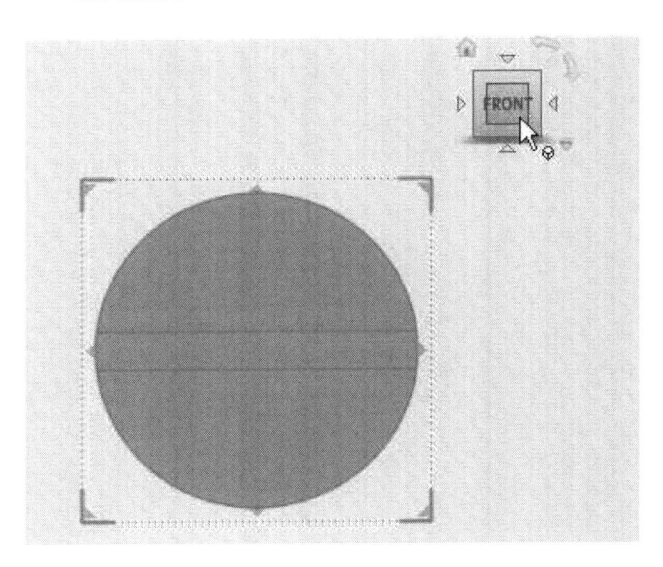

5. Set **Scale** to **1:1**.

6. Place the view at top-center of the drawing sheet; the **Projected View** tool is activated.

7. Move the cursor downwards and click to place the projected view.

8. Right-click and select **OK**.

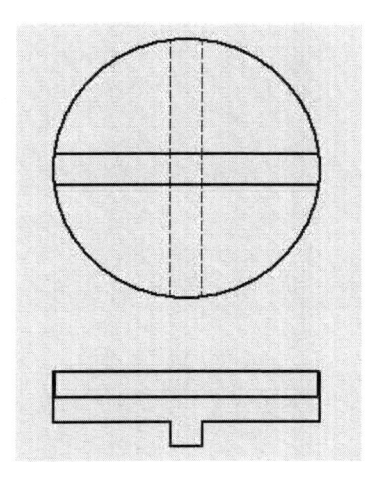

Adding Dimensions

1. On the ribbon, click **Annotate > Dimension > Dimension**.

2. On the ribbon, click **Annotate > Format > Select Style > Custom Standard**.

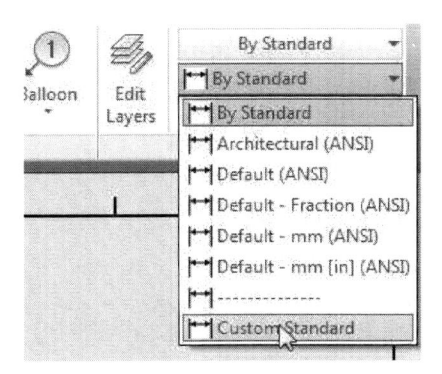

3. Select the circular edge on the base view.

4. Right-click and select **Dimension Type > Diameter**.

5. Place the dimension.

Creating Drawings

6. Click **OK**.

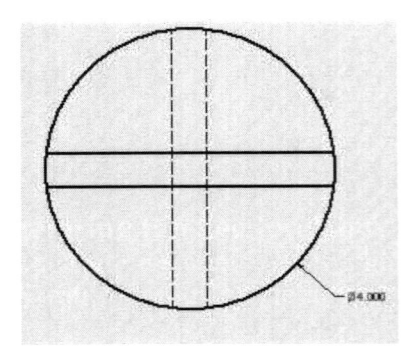

7. Select the horizontal edges on the base view.

8. Move the pointer toward right and click to place the dimension.

9. Click **OK** on the **Edit Dimension** dialog.

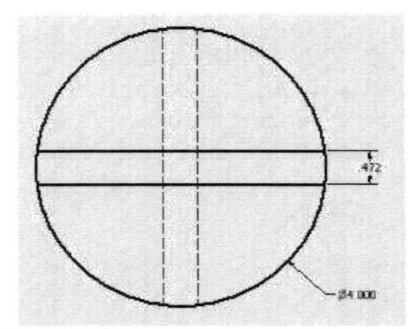

10. Add other dimensions to drawing.

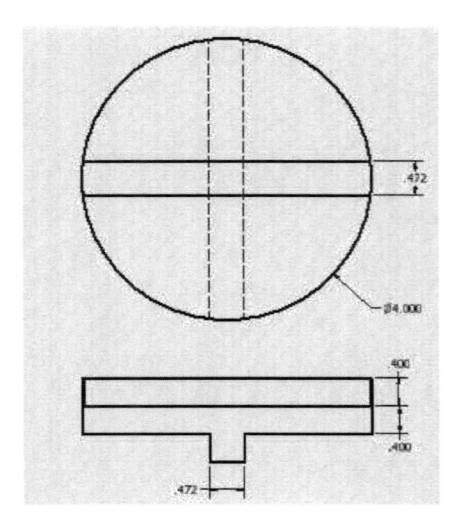

11. Right-click and select **OK** to deactivate the **Dimension** tool.

12. Save and close the drawing file.

TUTORIAL 3
In this tutorial, you will create the drawing of Oldham coupling assembly created in the previous chapter.

Creating a New Drawing File
1. On the ribbon, click **Get Started > Launch > New**.

2. On the **Create New File** dialog, click the **Custom Standard.idw** icon.

3. Click **Create** and **OK** to start a new drawing file.

Generating Base View
1. To generate the base view, click **Place views > Create > Base** on the ribbon; the **Drawing View** dialog appears.

2. Click **Open existing file** on this dialog; the **Open** dialog appears.

3. Go to the project folder and double-click on **Oldham_Coupling.iam**.

4. Click the **Home** icon located above the ViewCube.

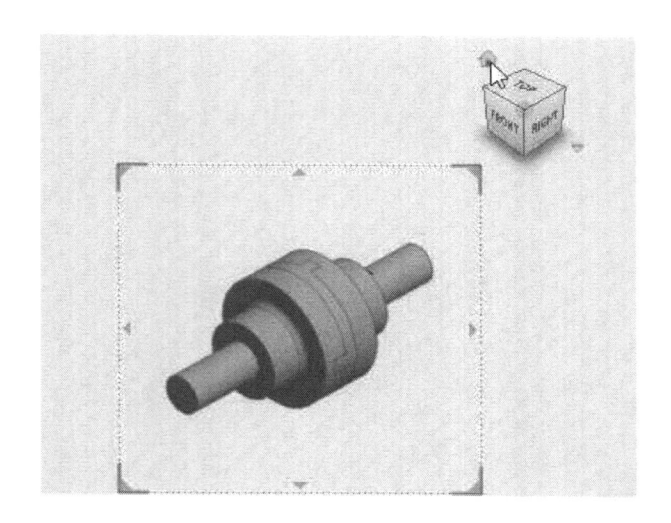

5. Set **Scale** to **1/2**.

53

Creating Drawings

6. Place the view at top left corner; the **Projected View** tool is activated.

7. Right-click and select **OK**.

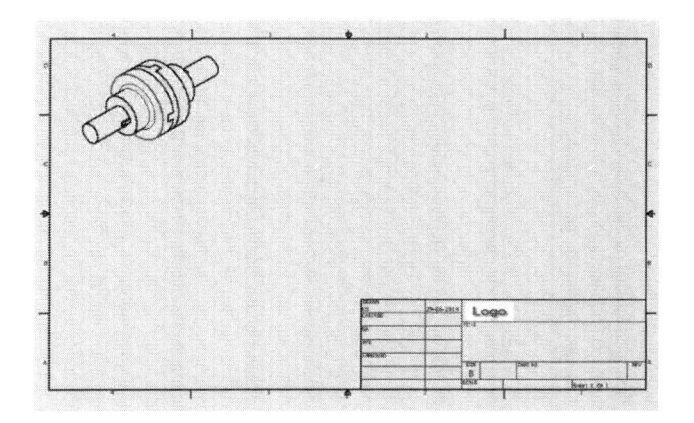

Generating the Exploded View

1. To generate the base view, click **Place views > Create > Base** on the ribbon; the **Drawing View** dialog appears.

2. Click **Open existing file** on this dialog; the **Open** dialog appears.

3. Go to the project folder and double-click on **Oldham_Coupling.ipn**.

4. Click the **Home** icon located above the ViewCube.

5. Set **Scale** to **1/2**.

6. Click in the center of the drawing sheet.

7. Right-click and select **OK**.

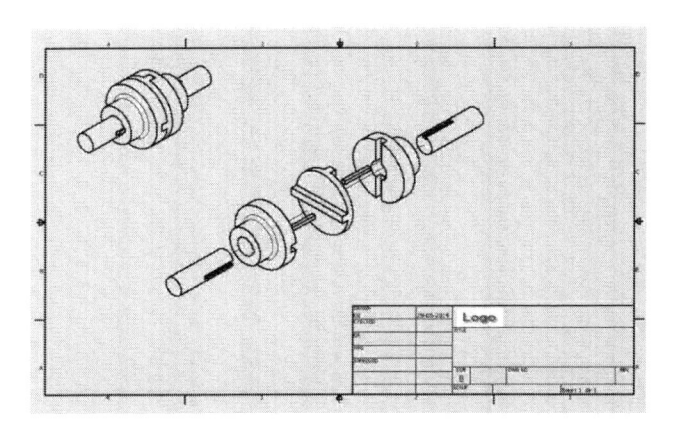

Configuring the Parts list settings

1. Click **Manage > Styles and Standards > Style Editor** on the ribbon; the **Style and Standard Editor** dialog appears.

2. Expand the **Parts List** node and select **Parts List (ANSI)**.

3. Click the **Column Chooser** button under the **Default Columns Settings** group; the **Parts List Column Chooser** dialog appears.

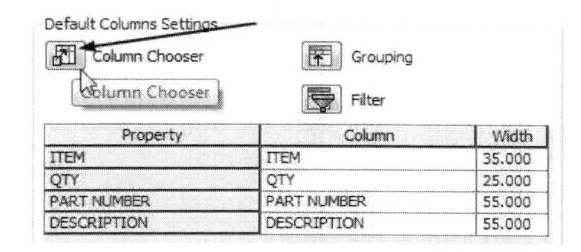

4. On this dialog, select **DESCRIPTION** from the **Selected Properties** list and click the **Remove** button.

5. Select **PART NUMBER** from the **Selected Properties** list and click **Move Up**.

6. Click **OK**.

7. Click **Save** and then **Done**.

Creating the Parts list

1. To create a parts list, click **Annotate > Table > Parts List** on the ribbon; the **Parts List** dialog appears.

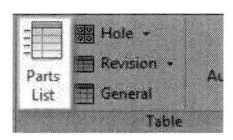

2. Select the exploded view.

3. Select **Parts Only** from the **BOM View** drop-down under the **BOM Settings and Properties** group.

Creating Drawings

4. Click **OK** twice.

5. Place the part list above the title block.

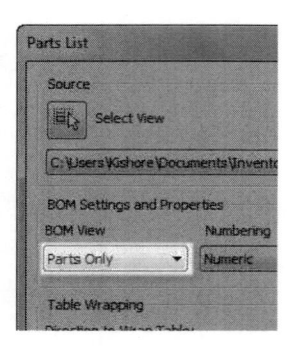

PARTS LIST		
ITEM	PART NUMBER	QTY
1	Disc	1
2	Flange	2
3	Shaft	2
4	Key	2

Creating Balloons

1. To create balloons, click **Annotate > Table > Balloon > Auto Balloon** on the ribbon; the **Auto-Balloon** dialog appears.

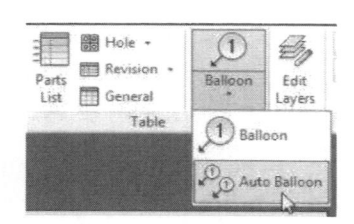

2. Select the exploded view.

3. Select all the parts in the exploded view.

4. Select **Horizontal** from the **Placement** group.

5. Click the **Select Placement** button in the **Placement** group.

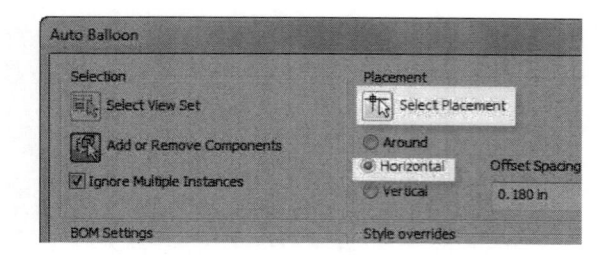

6. Click above the exploded view.

7. Click **OK** to place the balloons.

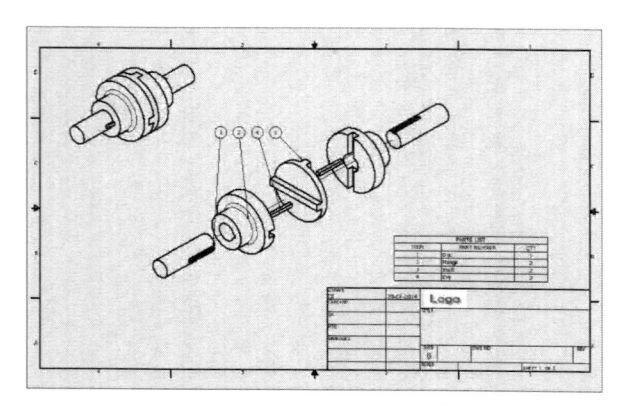

Saving the Drawing

1. Click **Save** on the **Quick Access Toolbar**; the **Save As** dialog appears.

2. Type-in **Oldham_Coupling** in the **File Name** box.

3. Go to the project folder.

4. Click **Save** to save the file.

5. Click **OK**.

6. Click **Application Menu > Close**.

Creating Drawings

Additional Modeling Tools

Chapter 5: Additional Modeling Tools

In this chapter, you create models using additional modeling tools. You will learn to:

- Create slots
- Create circular patterns
- Create holes
- Create chamfers
- Create shells
- Create rib features
- Create coils
- Create a loft feature
- Create an emboss feature
- Create a thread
- Create a sweep feature
- Create a grill feature
- Create a replace faces
- Create a face fillet
- Create a variable fillet
- Create a boss feature
- Create a lip feature

TUTORIAL 1
In this tutorial, you create the model shown in figure:

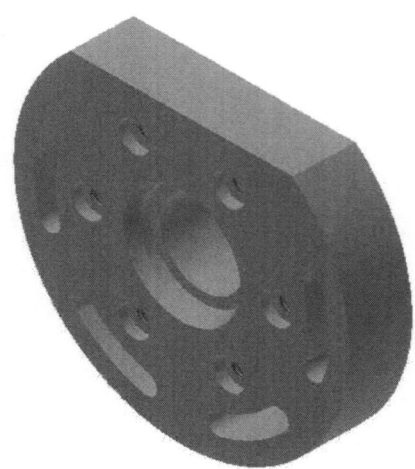

Creating the First Feature
1. Create a new project with the name **Autodesk Inventor 2016 Learn by doing**.

2. Open a new Inventor part file using the **Standard.ipt** template.

3. Click the **Start 2D sketch** button and select the XY Plane.

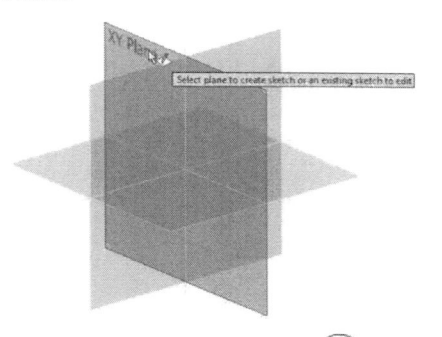

4. Click the **Circle Center Point** button and draw a circle.

5. Click the **Line** button and draw a horizontal line on the top portion of the circle.

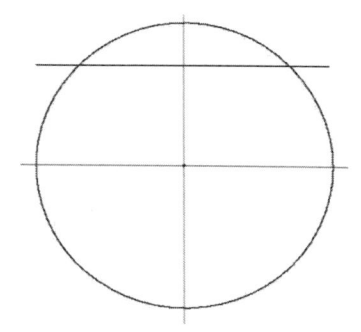

6. Click the **Trim** button on the **Modify** panel and trim the unwanted portions of the sketch, as shown below.

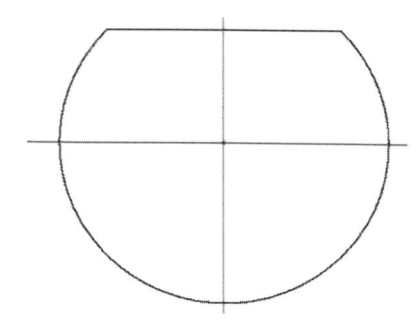

7. Apply dimensions to the sketch (Radius=0.63, vertical length=1.102). To apply the vertical

57

Additional Modeling Tools

length dimension, activate the **Dimension** tool and select the horizontal line. Move the pointer downward and place the cursor on the bottom quadrant point of the arc. Click when the symbol appears.

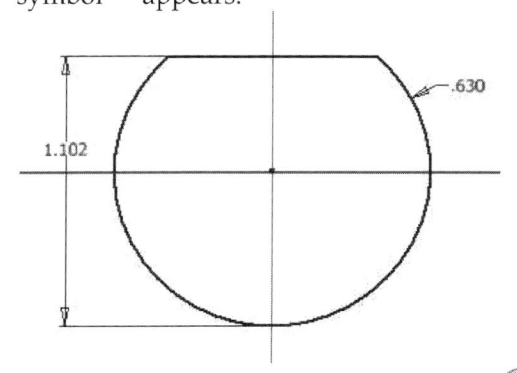

8. Click **Rectangle > Slot Center Point Arc** on the **Create** panel.

9. Select the origin as the center point.

10. Select the start point of the slot arc.

11. Select the end point of the slot arc.

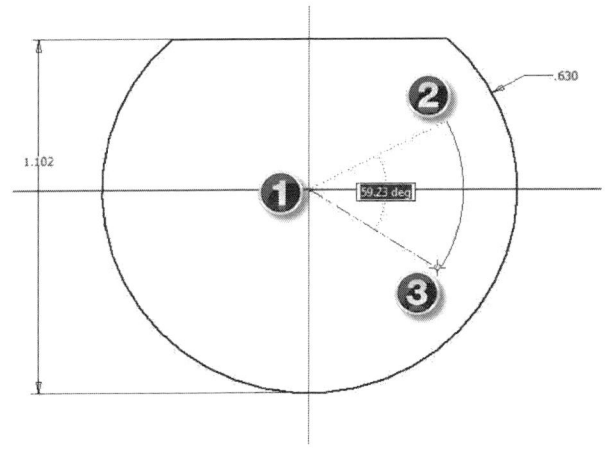

12. Move the cursor outward from the arc and click.

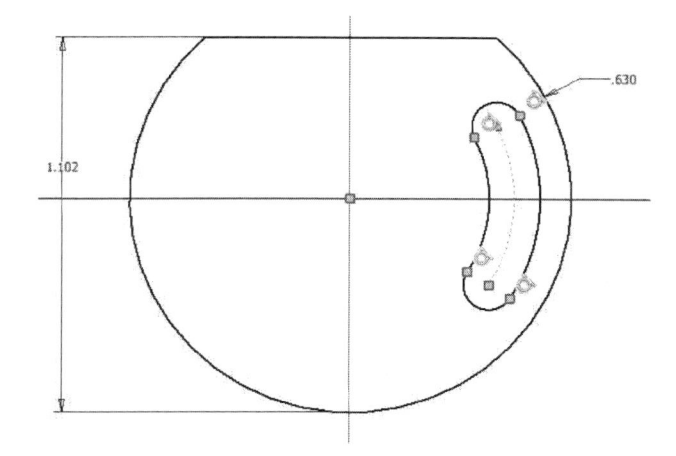

13. Click the **Dimension** button on the **Constrain** panel.

14. Select the start point of the slot arc.

15. Select the center point of the slot arc.

16. Select the end point of the slot arc.

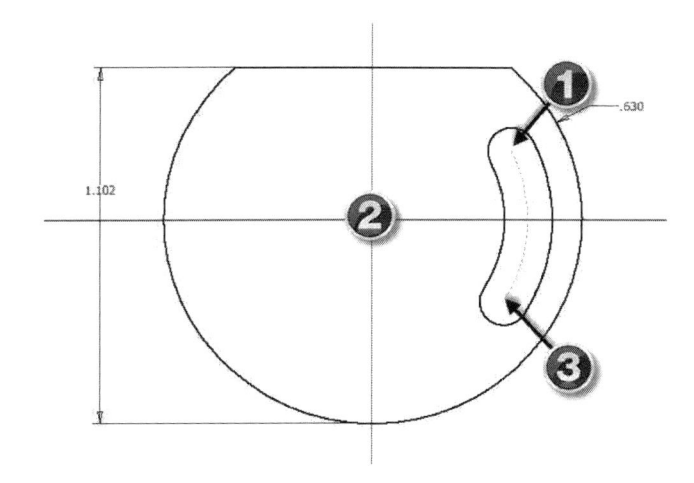

17. Place the angular dimension of the slot; the **Edit Dimension** box appears.

18. Enter **30** in the **Edit Dimension** box and click the green check.

58

Additional Modeling Tools

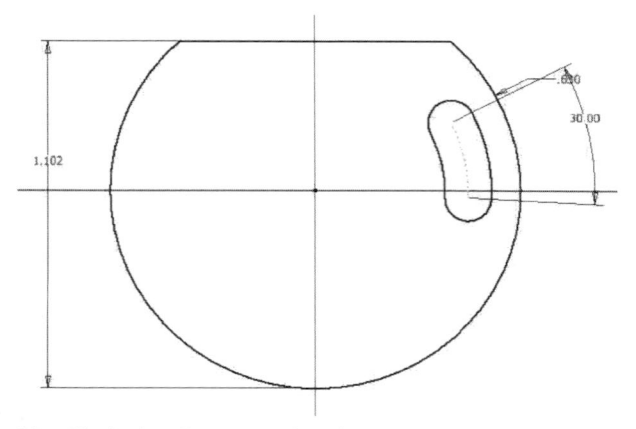

19. Click the **Construction** button on the **Format** panel.

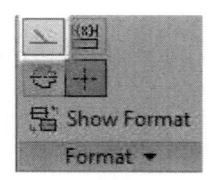

20. Click the **Line** button on the **Create** panel.

21. Draw a horizontal line passing through the origin.

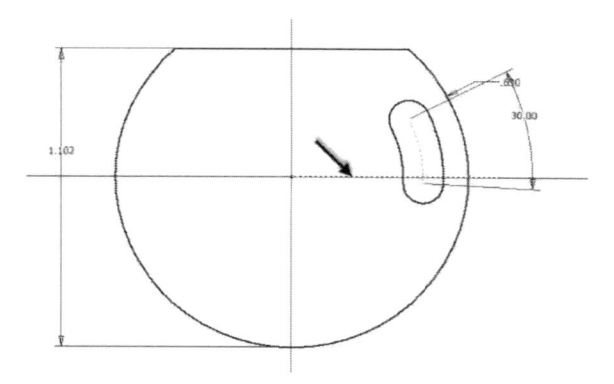

22. Click the **Symmetric** button on the **Constrain** panel.

23. Select the end caps of the slot.

24. Select the construction line; the slot is made symmetric about the construction line.

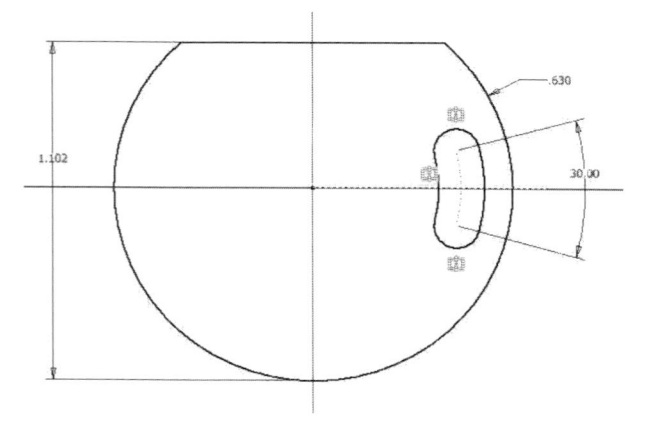

25. Apply other dimensions to the slot.

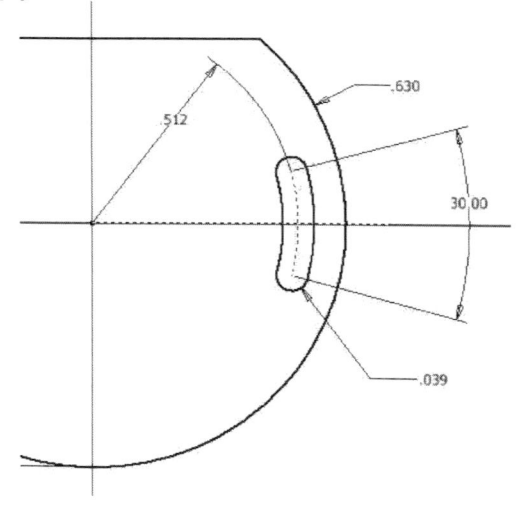

26. Click the **Circular Pattern** button on the **Pattern** panel; the **Circular Pattern** dialog appears.

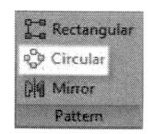

27. Select all the elements of the slot.

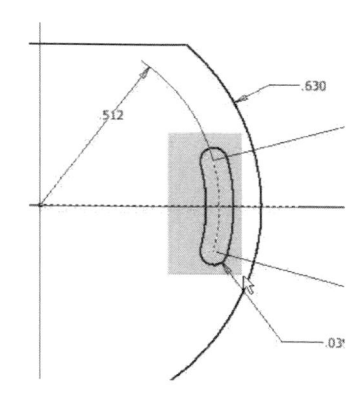

59

Additional Modeling Tools

28. Click the cursor button located on the right-side on the dialog.

29. Select the origin point of the sketch.

30. Enter **4** in the **Count** box and **180** in the **Angle** box.

31. Click the **Flip** button.

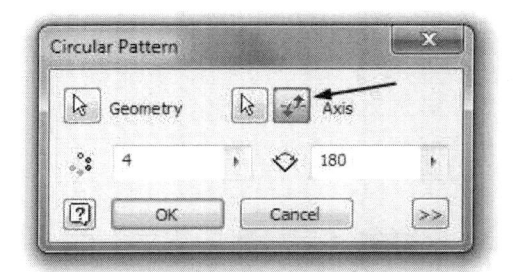

The preview of the circular pattern appears.

32. Click **OK** to create the circular pattern.

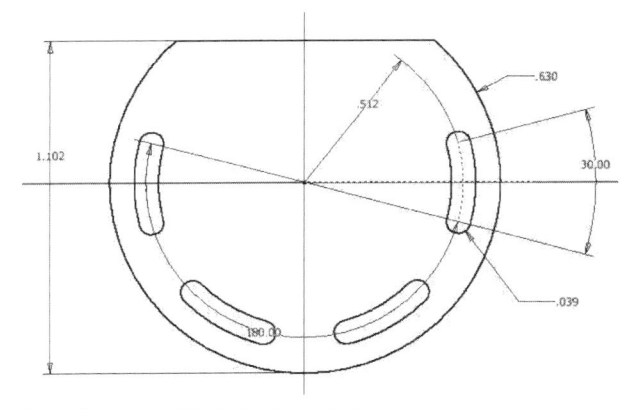

33. Click the **Finish Sketch** button.

34. Extrude the sketch up to 0.236 distance.

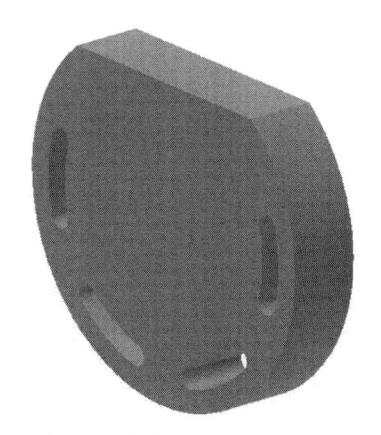

Adding the Second feature
1. Create a sketch on the back face of the model.

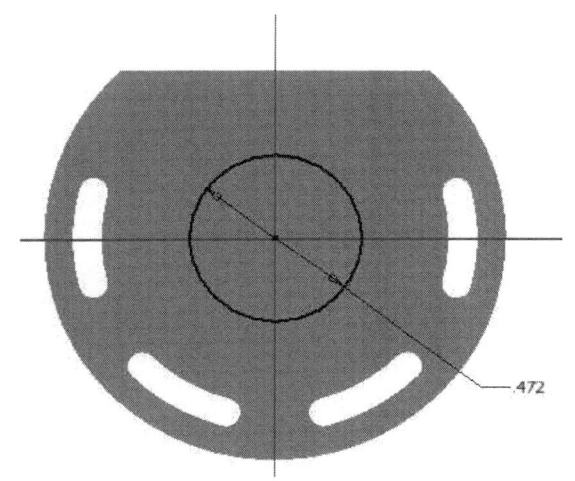

2. Extrude the sketch up to 0.078 distance.

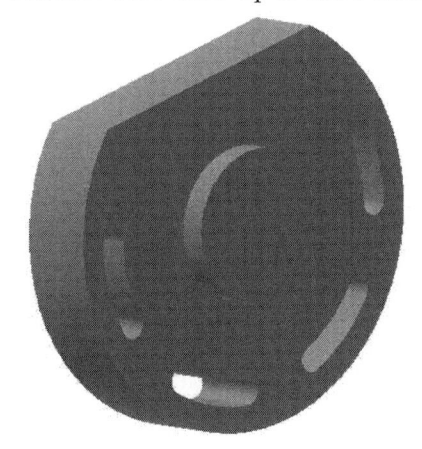

Creating a Counterbore Hole
In this section, you will create a counterbore hole concentric to the cylindrical face.

1. Click the **Hole** button on the **Modify** panel; the **Hole** dialog appears.

Additional Modeling Tools

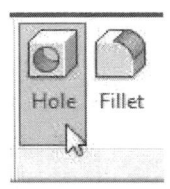

2. Set the parameters in the **Hole** dialog, as shown in figure.

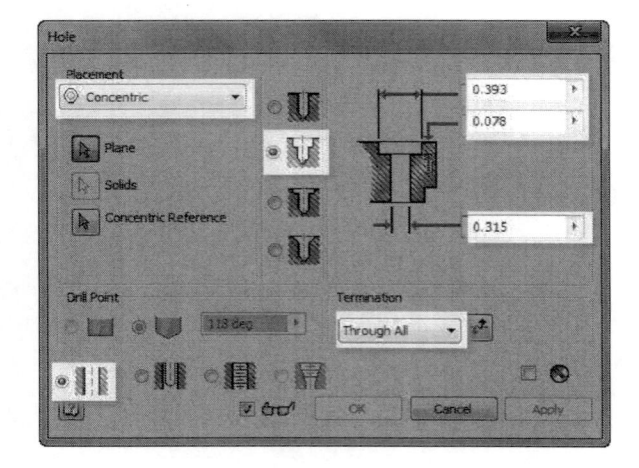

3. Click on the front face of the model; the preview of the hole appears.

Now, you need to specify the concentric reference.

4. Select the cylindrical face of the model; the hole is made concentric to the model.

5. Click **OK**; the counterbore hole is created.

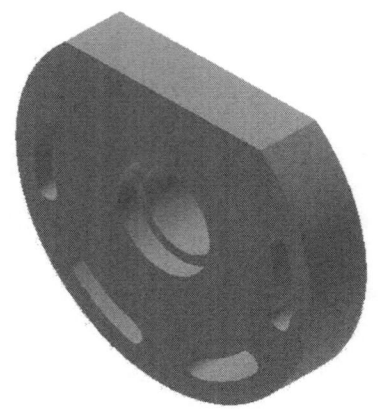

Creating a Threaded hole

In this section, you will create a hole using a sketch point.

1. Click the **Start 2D Sketch** button and front face of the model.

2. Click the **Point** button on the **Create** panel.

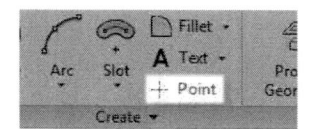

3. Place the point on the front face of the model.

4. Click the **Horizontal** button on the **Constrain** panel.

5. Select the point and sketch origin; the point becomes horizontal to the origin.

6. Create a horizontal dimension of 0.354 between point and origin.

Additional Modeling Tools

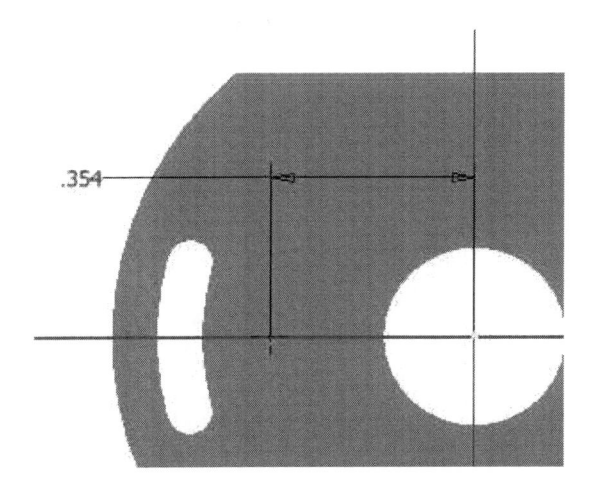

7. Click **Finish Sketch**.

8. Click the **Hole** button on the **Modify** panel; the **Hole** dialog appears.

9. On the **Hole** dialog, set **Placement** to **From Sketch**.

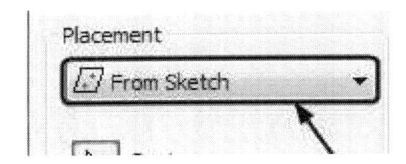

10. Select the **Counterbore** option.

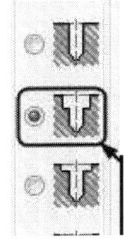

11. Set the **Counterbore Diameter** to 0.118.

12. Set the **Counterbore Depth** to 0.039.

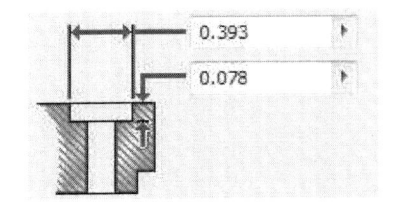

13. Select the **Tapped Hole** option.

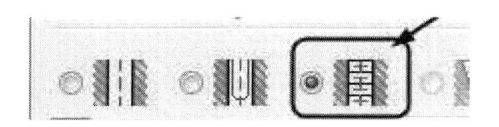

14. Set the **Thread Type** to **ANSI Unified Screw Threads**.

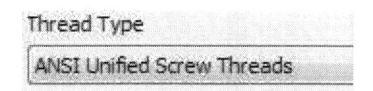

15. Set the **Size** to **0.073**.

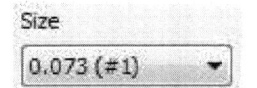

16. Set the **Designation** to **1-64 UNC**.

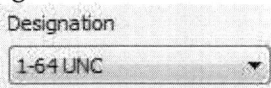

17. Select the **Full Depth** option.

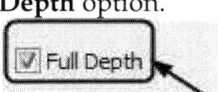

18. Set the **Direction** to **Right Hand**.

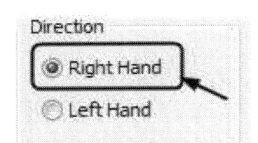

19. Click **OK** to create the hole.

Creating a Circular Pattern

1. Click the **Circular Pattern** button on the **Pattern** panel; the **Circular Pattern** dialog appears.

62

Additional Modeling Tools

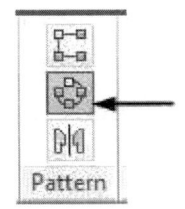

2. Select the threaded hole created in the previous section.

3. Click the **Rotation Axis** button on the dialog.

4. Select the outer cylindrical face of the model.

5. Enter **6** in the **Occurrence** box and **360** in the **Angle** box.

6. Click **OK** to create the circular pattern.

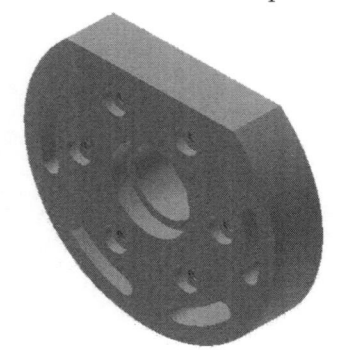

Creating Chamfers

1. Click the **Chamfer** button on the **Modify** panel.

2. Click the **Distance and Angle** button on the dialog.

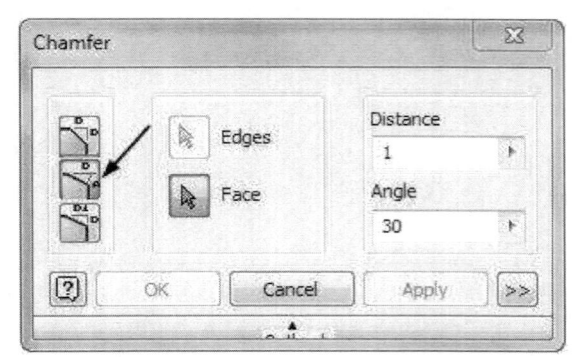

3. Select the cylindrical face of the counterbore hole at the center.

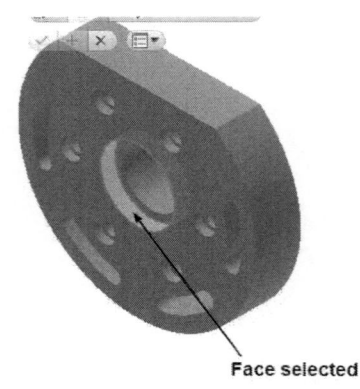

4. Select the circular edge of the counterbore hole.

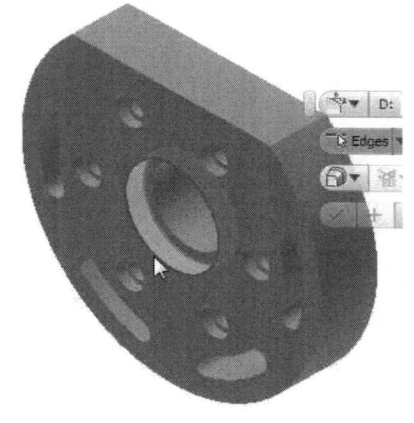

5. Enter 0.039 in the **Distance** box and 30 in the **Angle** box.

6. Click **OK** to create the chamfer.

7. Save the model and close it.

TUTORIAL 2

In this tutorial, you will create the model shown in figure.

Additional Modeling Tools

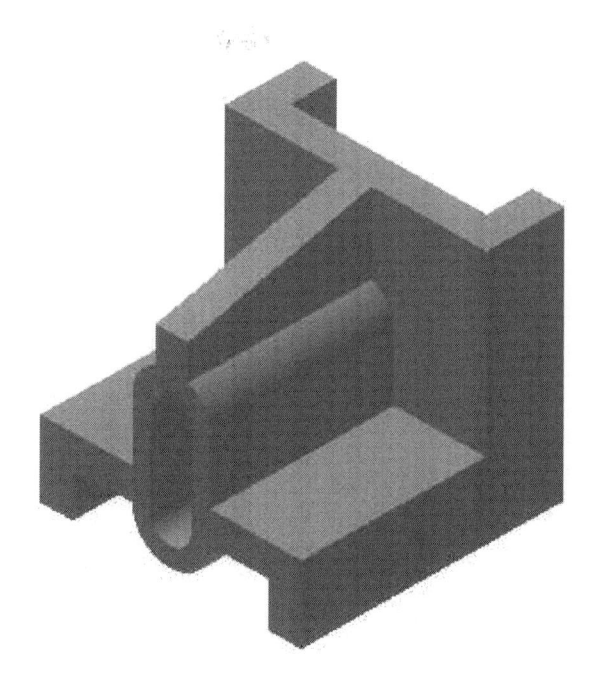

Creating the first feature

1. Open a new Inventor part file using the **Standard.ipt** template.

2. On the ribbon, click **3D Model > Sketch > Start 2D Sketch**.

3. Select the YZ plane.

4. Draw an L-shaped sketch using the **Line** tool and dimension it.

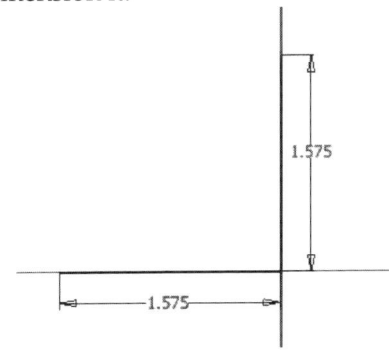

5. Click the **Offset** button on the **Modify** panel.

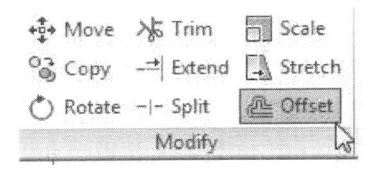

6. Select the sketch and specify the offset position.

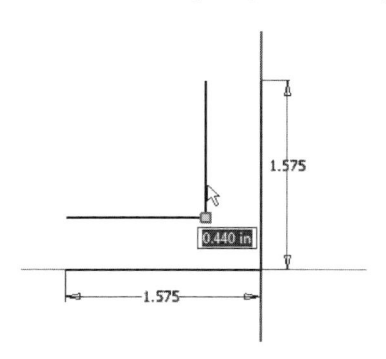

7. Click the **Line** button and draw lines closing the offset sketch.

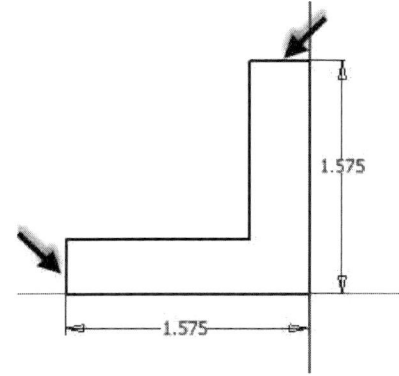

8. Add the offset dimension to the sketch.

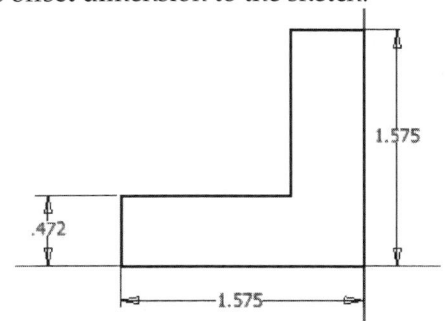

9. Click **Finish Sketch**.

10. Click **3D Model > Create > Extrude** on the ribbon.

11. Select the **Symmetric** option from the Mini toolbar.

64

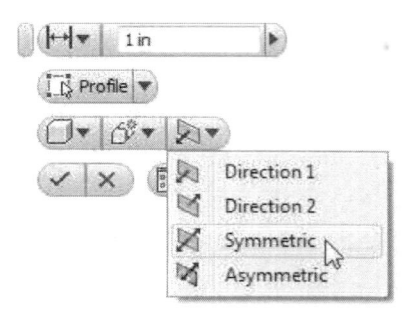

Additional Modeling Tools

12. Set the **Distance** to 1.575.

13. Click **OK** to create the first feature.

Creating the Shell feature

You can create a shell feature by removing a face of the model and applying thickness to other faces.

1. Click **3D Model > Modify > Shell** on the ribbon; the **Shell** dialog appears.

2. Set **Thickness** to 0.197.

Now, you need to select the faces to remove.

3. Select the top face and the back face of the model.

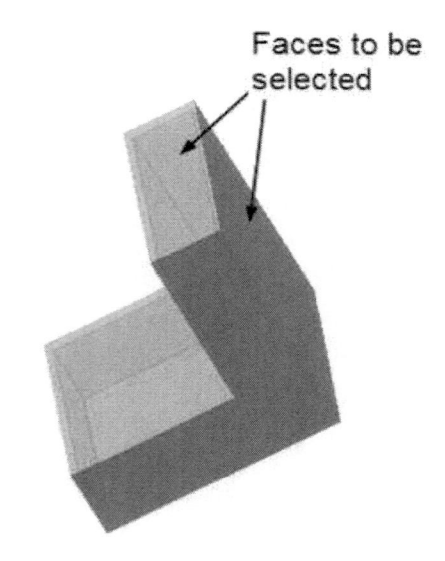

4. Select the front face and the bottom face of the model.

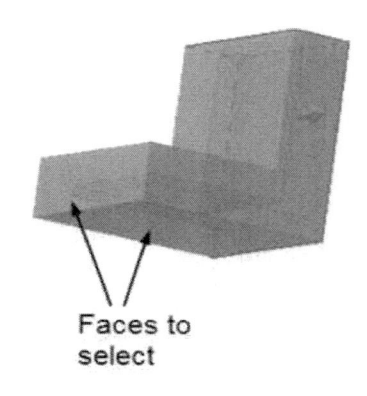

5. Click **OK** to shell the model.

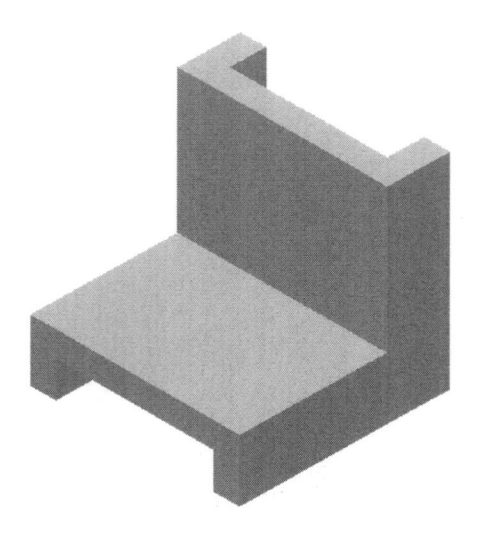

65

Additional Modeling Tools

Creating the Third feature

1. Click **3D Model > Sketch > Start 2D Sketch** on the ribbon.

2. Select the front face of the model.

3. Click **Sketch > Create > Slot Center to Center** on the ribbon.

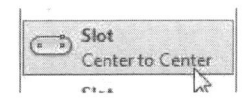

4. Draw a slot by selecting the first, second, and third points.

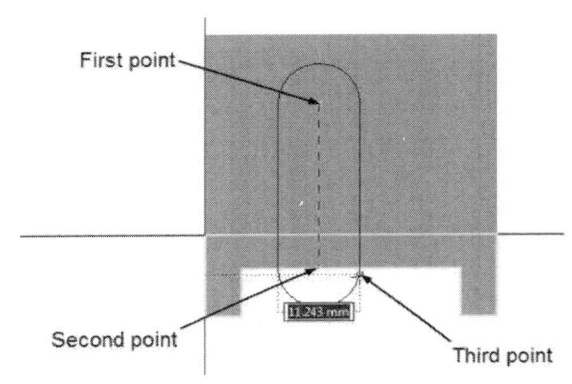

5. Apply dimensions to the slot.

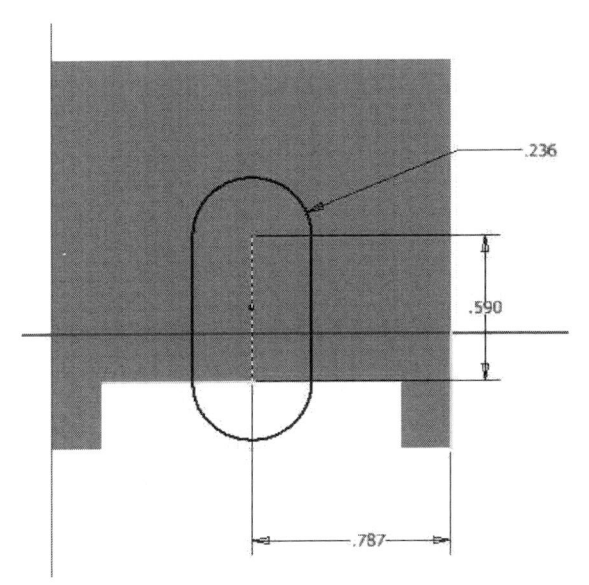

6. Click **Finish Sketch**.

7. Click **3D Model > Create > Extrude** on the ribbon.

8. Select the sketch.

9. Select the **To** option from the **Extents** drop-down.

10. Select the back face of the model.

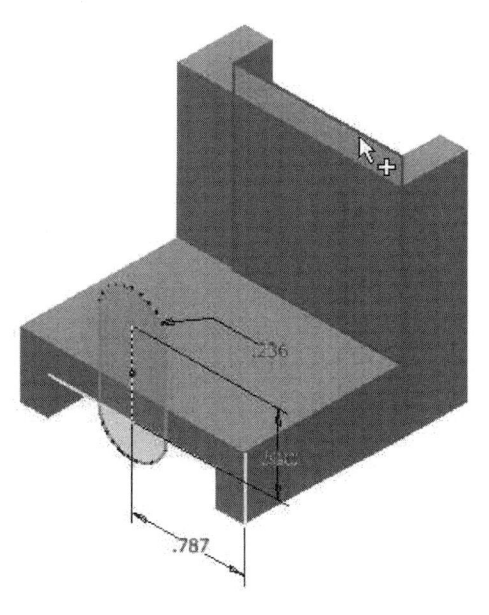

11. Click the **Join** button on the dialog.

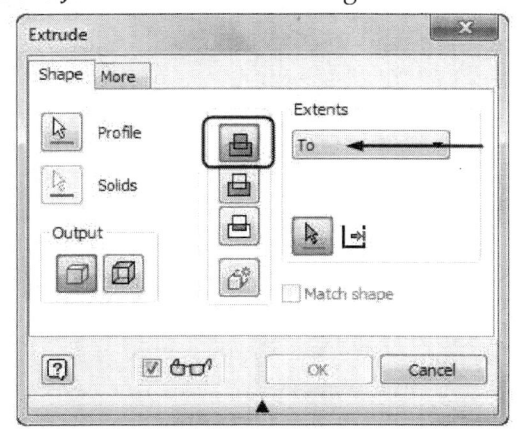

12. Click **OK** to create the feature.

66

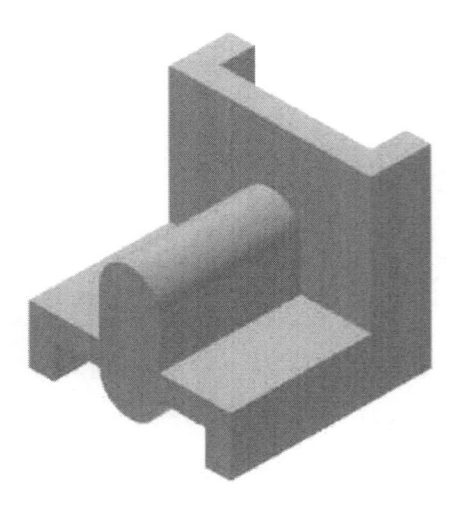

Additional Modeling Tools

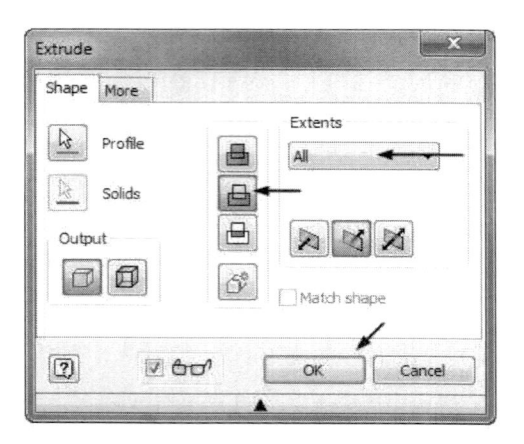

7. Click **OK** to create the cut feature.

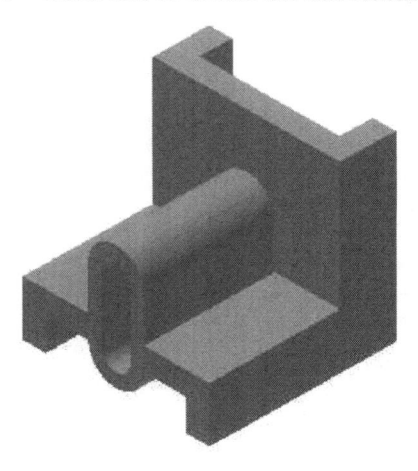

Creating a Cut Feature
1. Create the sketch on the front face of the model, as shown below.

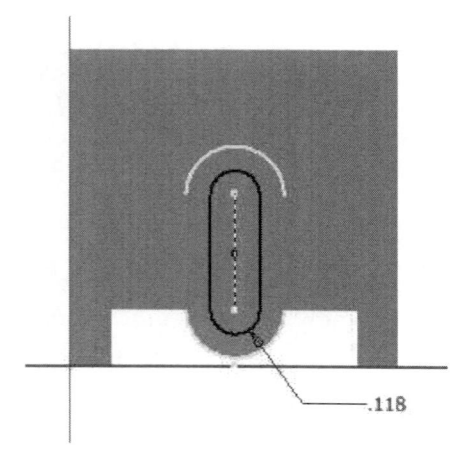

2. Finish the sketch.

3. Click **3D Model > Create > Extrude** on the ribbon.

4. Select the sketch.

5. Select the **All** option from the **Extents** drop-down.

6. Click the **Cut** button on the dialog.

Creating the Rib Feature
In this section, you will create a rib feature at the middle of the model. To do this, you must create a mid plane.

1. To create a mid plane, click **3D Model > Work Features > Plane > Midplane between Two Parallel Planes** on the ribbon.

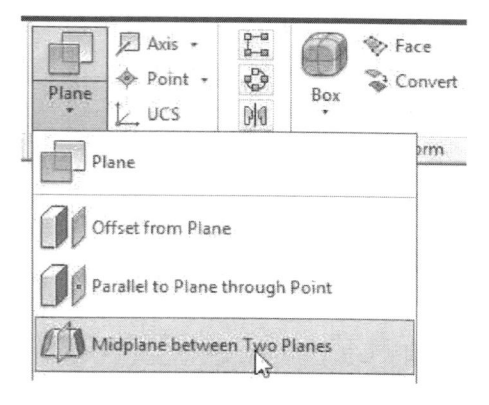

2. Select the right face of the model.

67

Additional Modeling Tools

3. Select the left face of the model; the midplane is created.

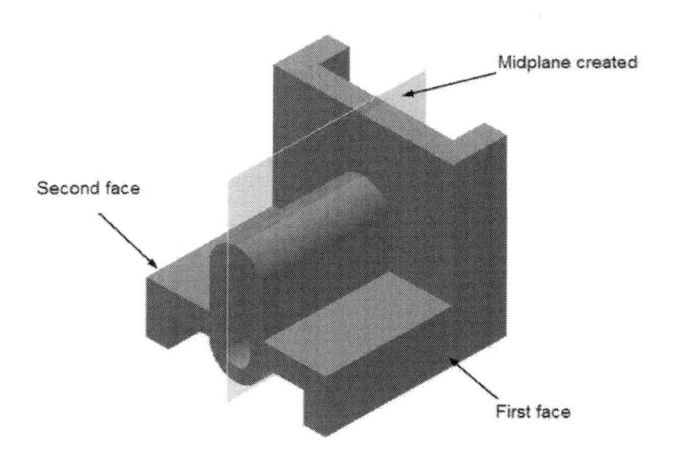

4. Click **3D Model > Sketch > Start 2D Sketch** on the ribbon.

5. Select the mid plane.

6. Click the **Slice Graphics** button at the bottom of the window.

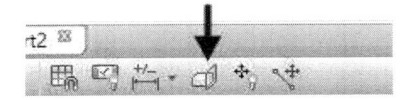

7. Click **Sketch > Create > Project Geometry > Project Cut Edges** on the ribbon; the edges cut by the sketch plane are projected.

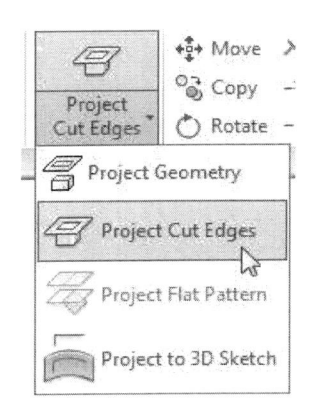

8. Draw the sketch, as shown below.

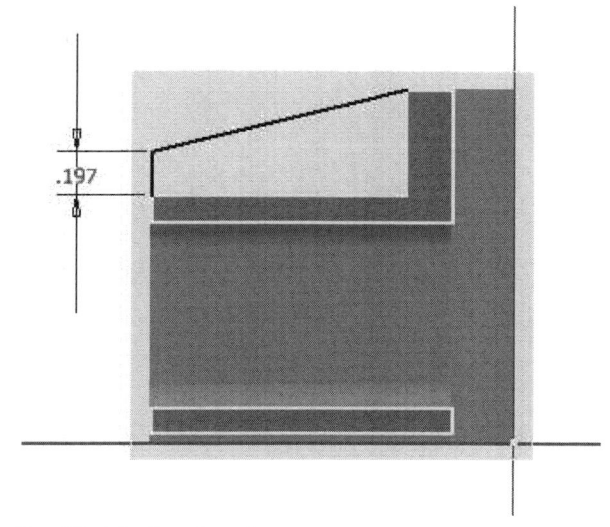

9. Finish the sketch.

10. Click **3D Model > Create > Rib** on the ribbon; the **Rib** dialog appears.

11. Select the sketch.

12. Click the **Parallel to Sketch** button on the dialog.

13. Click the **Direction 1** button.

14. Set **Thickness** to 0.197.

15. Click the **To Next** button.

16. Click the **Symmetric** button below the **Thickness** box.

17. Click **OK** to create the rib feature.

68

Additional Modeling Tools

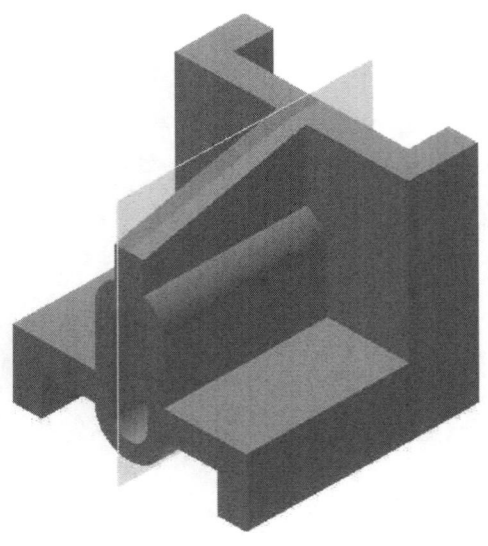

18. To hide the midplane, select it and right-click.

19. Click **Visibility** on the Marking Menu; the plane will be hidden.

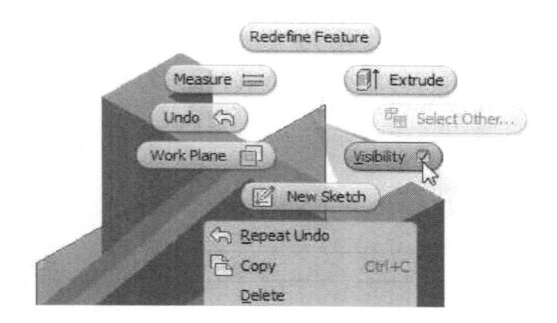

20. Save the Model and close it.

TUTORIAL 3
In this tutorial, you will create a helical spring using the **Coil** tool.

Creating the Coil
1. Open a new Inventor file using the **Standard.ipt** template.

2. Create a sketch on the XY plane.

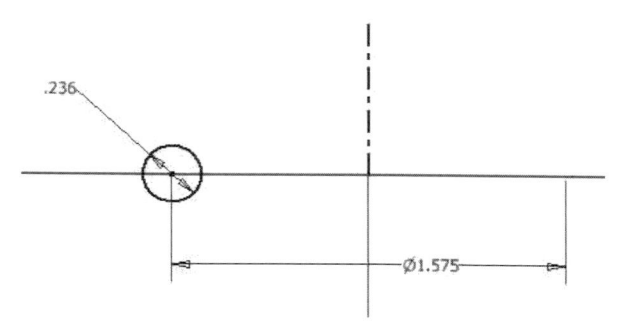

3. Finish the sketch.

4. To create a coil, click **3D Model > Create > Coil** on the ribbon; the **Coil** dialog appears.

In addition, the profile is automatically selected. Now, you need to select the axis of the coil.

5. Select the centerline as the axis.

Additional Modeling Tools

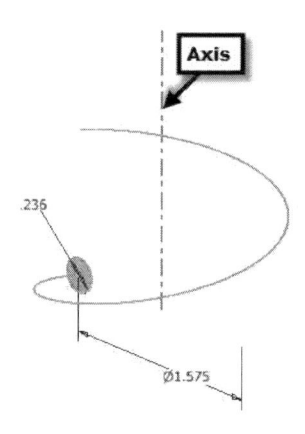

6. Click the **Coil Size** tab on the dialog.

7. In the **Coil Size** tab, specify the settings as given next.

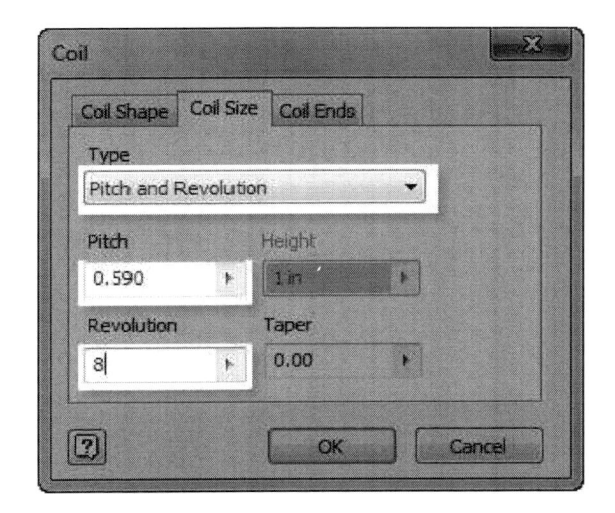

8. Click the **Coil Ends** tab on the dialog.

9. Specify the settings in the **Coil Ends** tab, as given next.

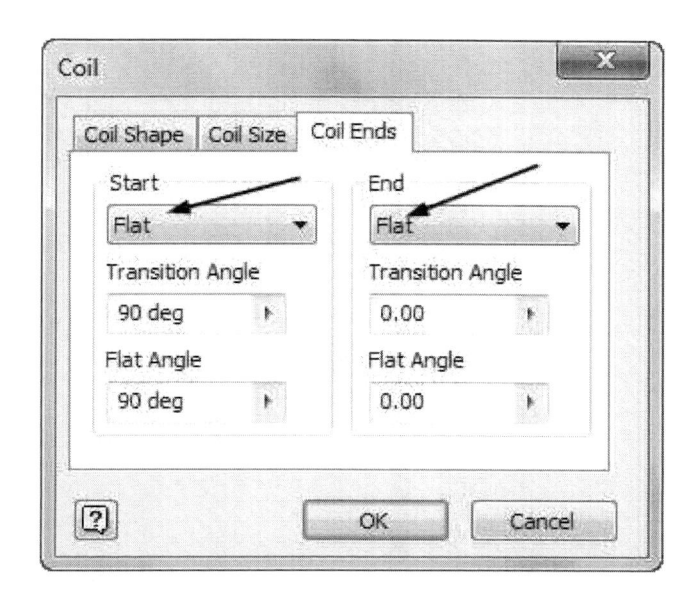

10. Click **OK** to create the coil.

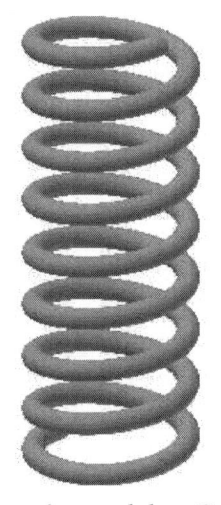

11. Save the model as **Coil.ipt** and close the file.

TUTORIAL 4

In this tutorial, you create a shampoo bottle using the **Loft**, **Extrude**, and **Coil** tools.

Additional Modeling Tools

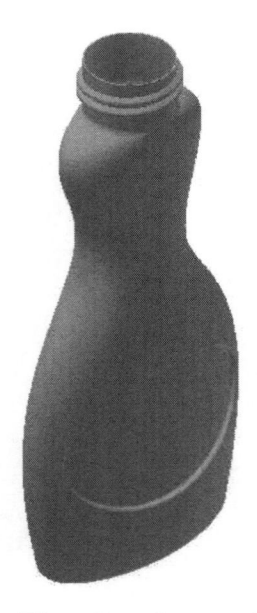

Creating First Section and Rails
To create a swept feature, you need to create sections and guide curves.

1. Open a new Part file.

2. Click **3D Model > Sketch > Start 2D Sketch** on the ribbon.

3. Select the XZ plane.

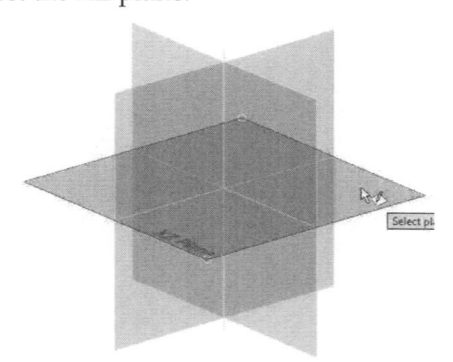

4. Click **Sketch > Create > Circle > Ellipse** on the ribbon.

5. Draw the ellipse by selecting the points.

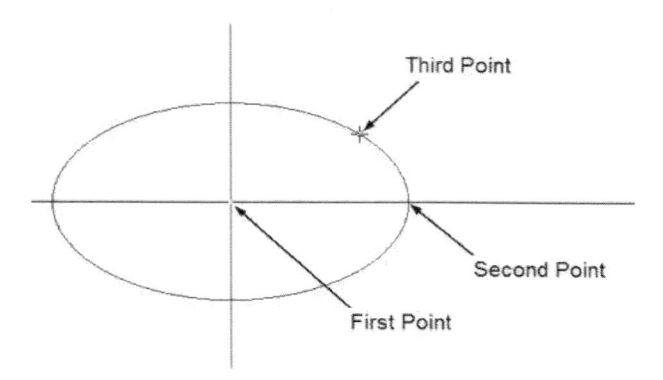

6. Add dimensions to the sketch.

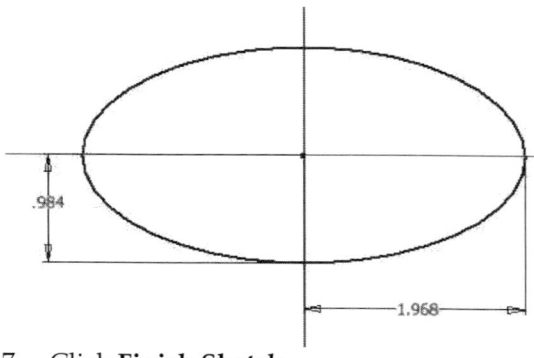

7. Click **Finish Sketch**.

8. Click **3D Model > Sketch > Start 2D Sketch** on the ribbon.

9. Select the YZ plane.

10. Click **Sketch > Create > Line > Spline Interpolation** on the ribbon.

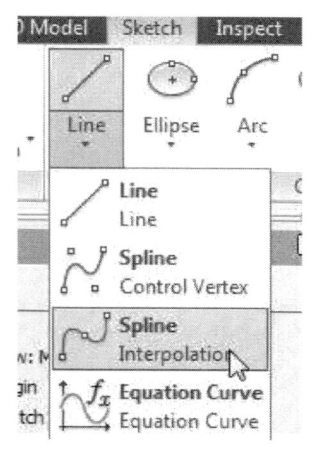

11. Select seven points to define the spline.

12. Click the right mouse button and select **Create**.

Additional Modeling Tools

The spline will be similar to the one shown in figure.

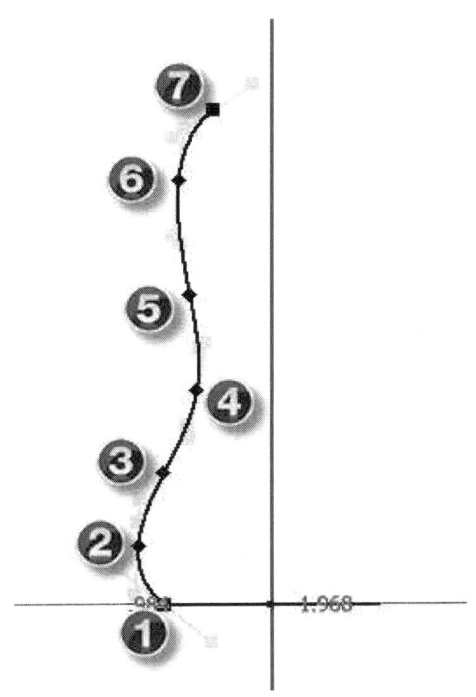

13. Draw a vertical construction line passing through the origin.

14. Apply dimension to the spline, as shown in figure.

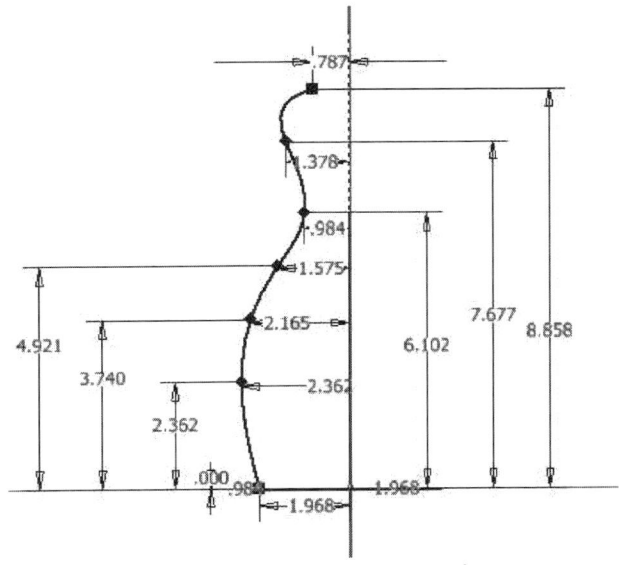

15. Click **Sketch > Pattern > Mirror** on the ribbon; the **Mirror** dialog appears.

16. Select the spline.

17. Click **Mirror line** on the **Mirror** dialog, and then select the construction line.

18. Click **Apply**, and then click **Done**.

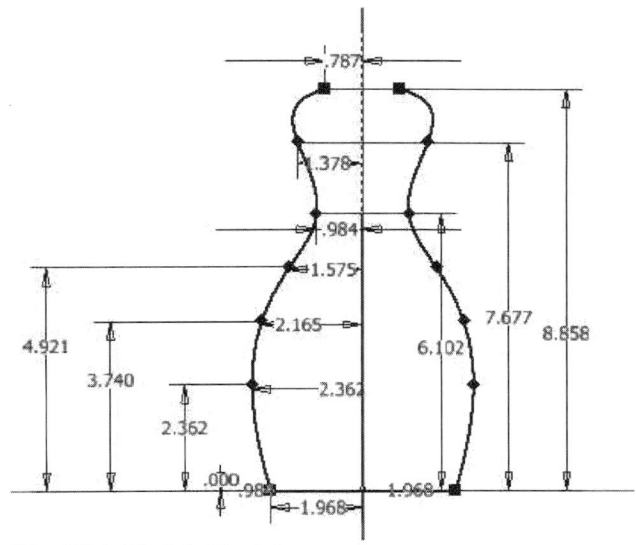

19. Click **Finish Sketch**.

Creating the second section

1. Click **3D Model > Work Features > Plane > Offset from Plane** on the ribbon.

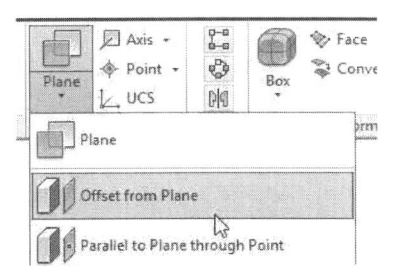

2. Select the XZ plane from the Browser window.

3. Enter **8.858** in the **Distance** box.

4. Click **OK**.

5. Start a sketch on the newly created datum plane.

6. Create a circle of 1.575 diameter.

Additional Modeling Tools

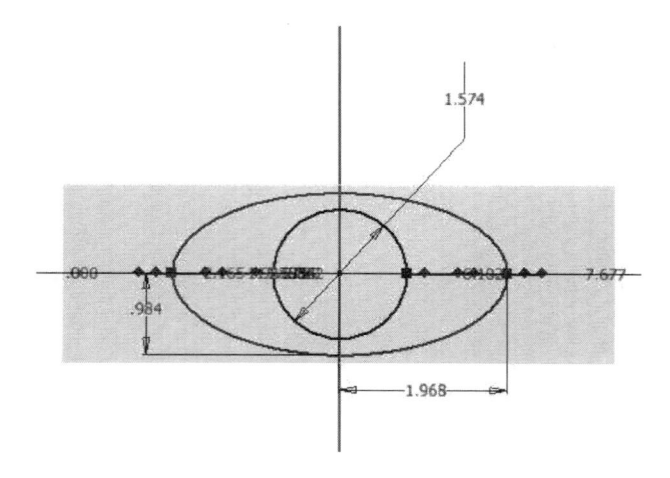

7. Click **Finish Sketch**.

Creating the Loft feature

1. To create a loft feature, click **3D Model > Create > Loft** on the ribbon; the **Loft** dialog appears.

2. Select the **Rails** option on the dialog.

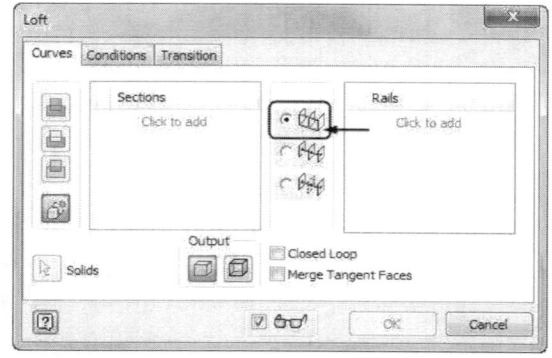

3. Click **Click to add** in the **Sections** group and select the circle.

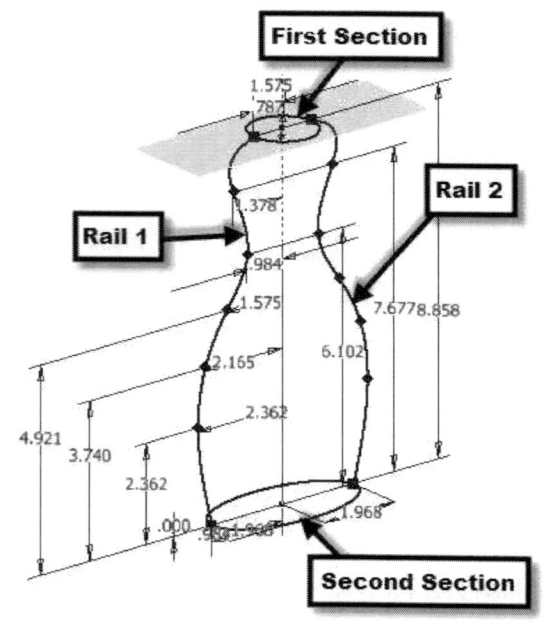

4. Select the ellipse.

5. Click **Click to add** in the **Rails** group.

6. Select the first rail.

7. Select the second rail.

8. Click **OK** to create the loft feature.

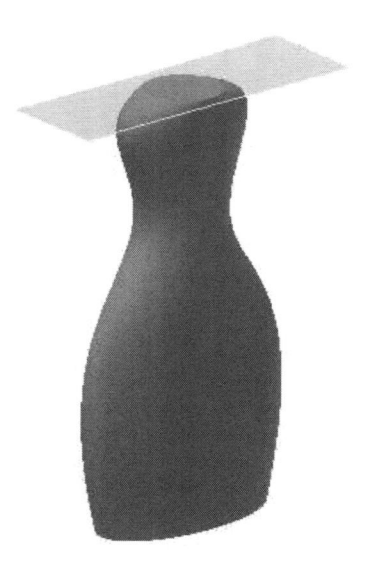

Creating the Extruded feature

1. Create a circle on the top of the sweep feature.

2. Click the **Extrude** button on the **Create** panel.

73

Additional Modeling Tools

3. Extrude the circle upto 1 in.

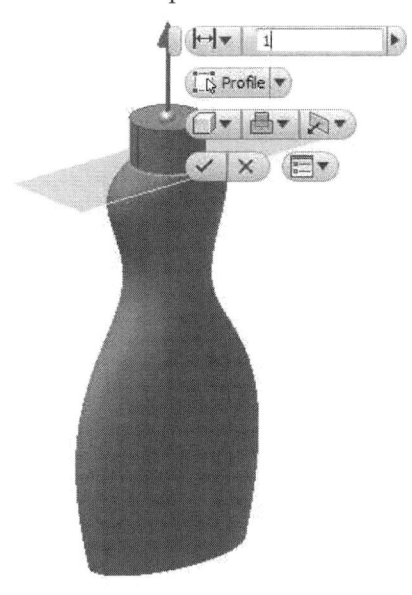

Creating the Emboss feature
1. Click **3D Model > Work Features > Plane > Offset from Plane** on the ribbon.

2. Select the YZ plane from the Browser window.

3. Enter **2** in the **Distance** box.

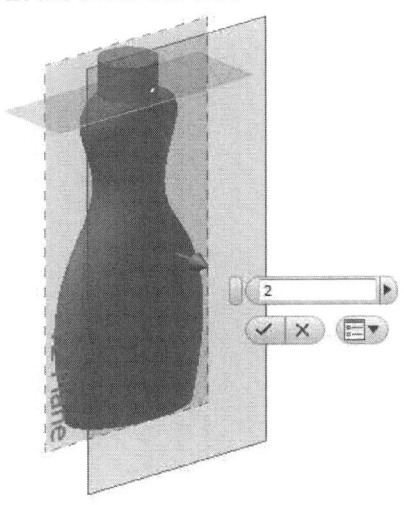

4. Create a sketch on the plane, as shown in figure.

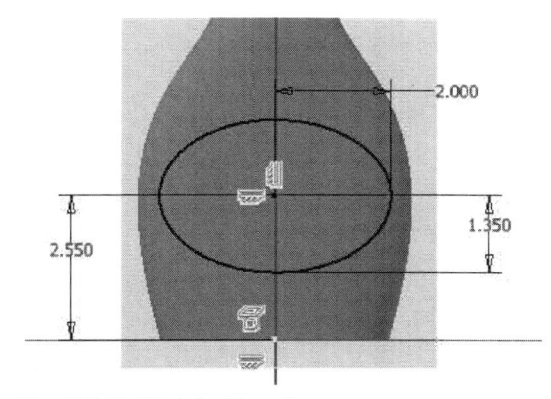

5. Click **Finish Sketch**.

6. Click **3D Model > Create > Emboss** on the ribbon; the **Emboss** dialog appears.

7. Click the **Engrave from Face** button on the dialog.

8. Set the **Depth** to 0.125.

9. Click **OK** to create the embossed feature.

Mirroring the Emboss feature
1. Click **3D Model > Pattern > Mirror** on the ribbon.

2. Select the emboss feature from the model geometry.

3. On the **Mirror** dialog, click the **Mirror Plane** button, and then select the YZ Plane from the Browser window.

4. Click **OK** to mirror the emboss feature.

Additional Modeling Tools

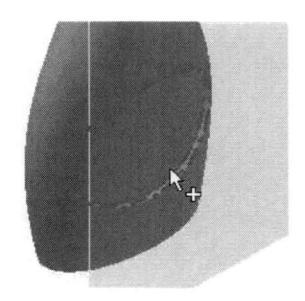

Creating Fillets
1. Click **3D Model > Modify > Fillet** on the ribbon; the **Fillet** dialog appears.

2. Click on the bottom and top edges of the swept feature.

3. Set **Radius** to 0.2.

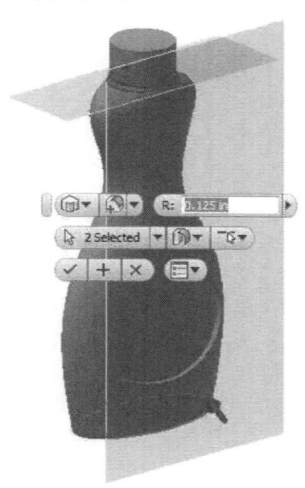

4. Click **Click to add** on the dialog.

5. Set **Radius** to 0.04.

6. Select the edges of the emboss features, and click **OK**.

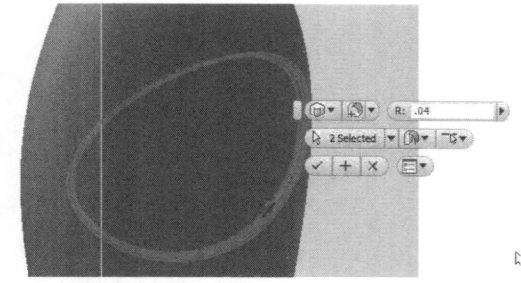

Shelling the Model
1. Click **3D Model > Modify > Shell** on the ribbon; the **Shell** dialog appears.

2. Set **Thickness** to 0.03.

3. Select the top face of the cylindrical feature.

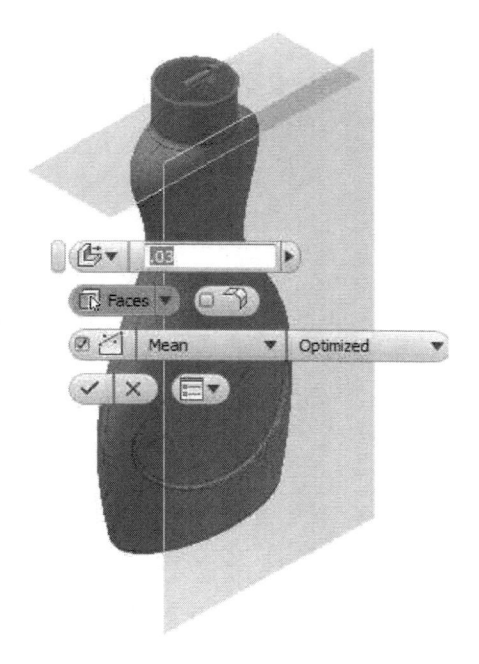

4. Click **OK** to create the shell.

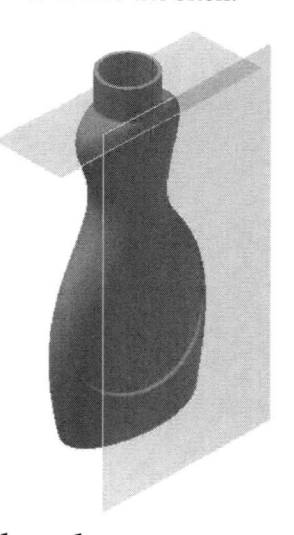

Adding Threads
1. Start a sketch on the YZ Plane.

2. Draw the thread profile.

Additional Modeling Tools

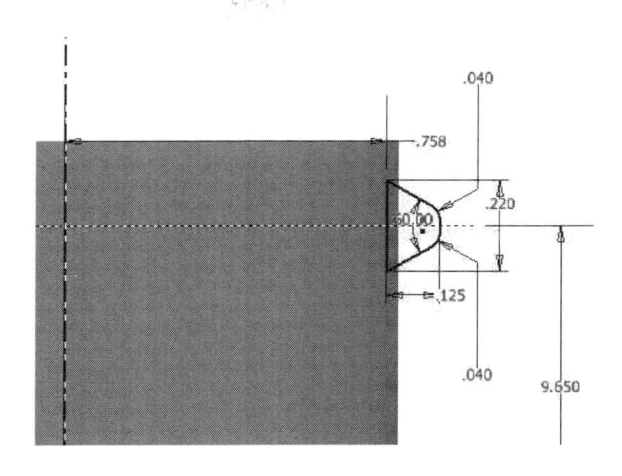

3. Draw the thread axis.

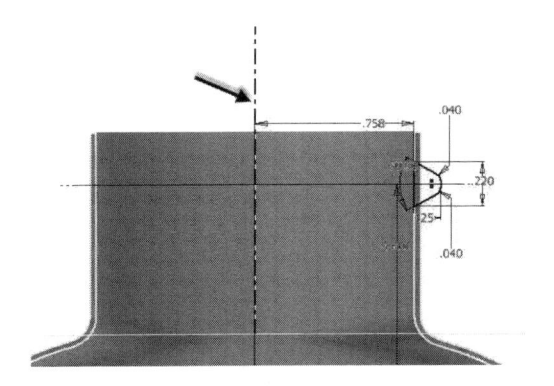

4. Click **Finish Sketch**.

5. On the ribbon, click **3D Model > Create > Coil**.

6. Select the axis of the coil.

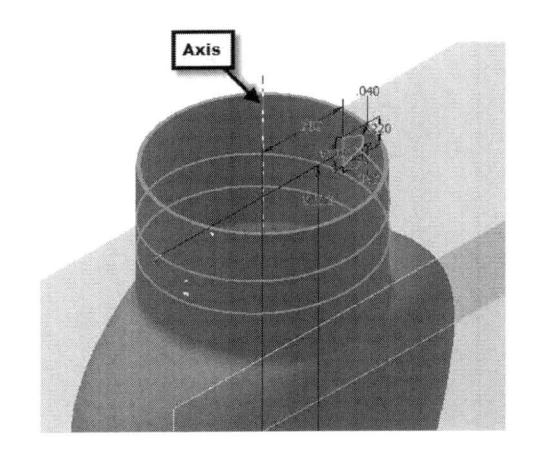

7. On the dialog, click the **Coil Size** tab and select **Type > Pitch and Revolution**.

8. Type-in **0.275** and **2** in the **Pitch** and **Revolution** boxes, respectively.

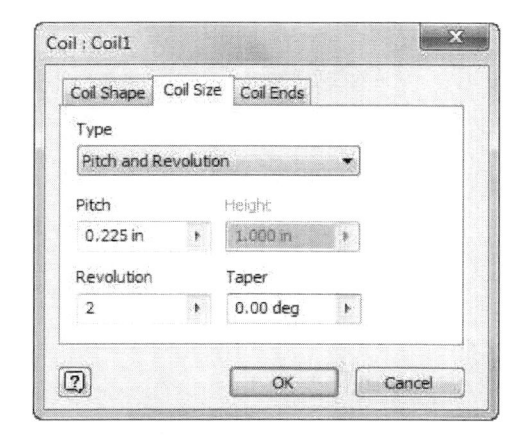

9. Click **OK**.

10. Start a sketch on the YZ Plane.

11. On the ribbon, click Sketch > Create > Project Geometry.

12. Select the edges of the end face of the thread.

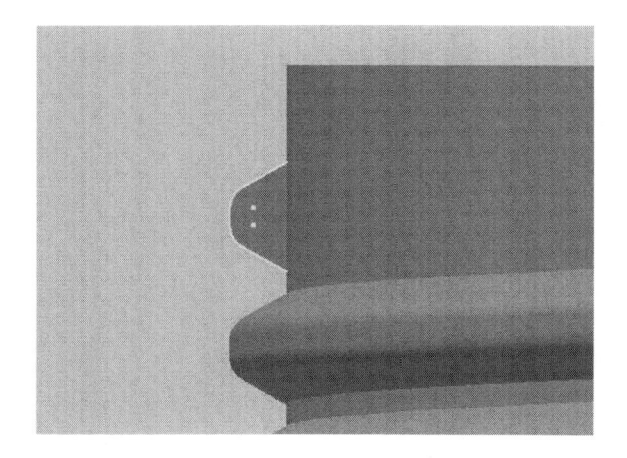

Additional Modeling Tools

13. Draw a straight line connecting the end points of the projected elements.

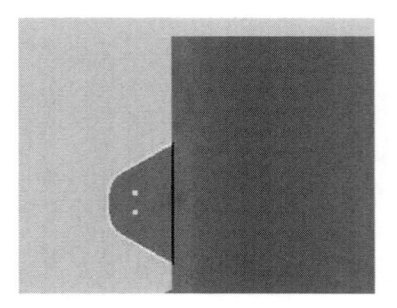

14. Click **Finish Sketch**.

15. Activate the **Revolve** tool and click on the vertical line of the sketch.

16. On the dialog, select **Extents > Angle**, and then type-in **100** in the **Angle1** box.

17. Click the **Direction 2** button.

18. Click **OK**.

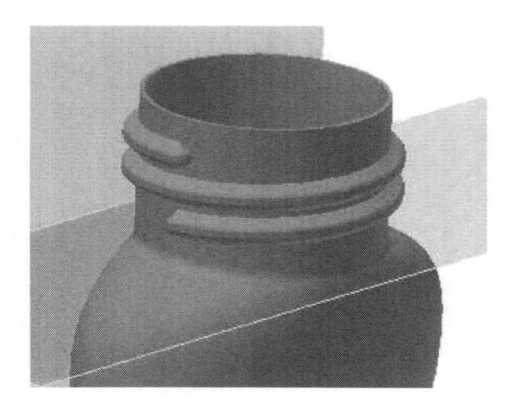

19. Likewise, blend the other end of the thread.

20. Save the model.

TUTORIAL 5
In this tutorial, you create a chair.

Creating a 3D Sketch
1. Start a new part file using the **Standard.ipt** template.

2. Click the **Home** icon located above the ViewCube. This changes the view orientation to Home.

3. On the ribbon, click **3D Model > Sketch > Start 2D Sketch > Start 3D Sketch**.

77

Additional Modeling Tools

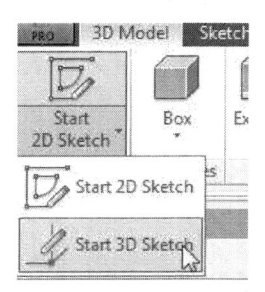

4. On the **3D Sketch** tab of the ribbon, click **Draw > Line**.

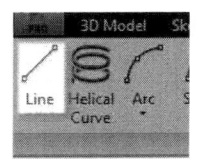

5. Expand the **Draw** panel on the ribbon and activate the **Precise Input** option.

6. On the **Precise Input** toolbar, click the **Reset to Origin** button.

7. Select the **Relative** option from the drop-down available on the **Precise Input** toolbar.

8. On the **Precise Input** toolbar, type-in 0, 0, 0 in the X, Y, and Z boxes, respectively. Press Enter to specify the first point.

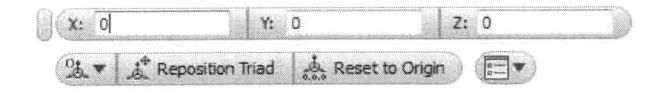

9. Type-in 12 in the **X** box and press Tab on your keyboard.

10. Likewise, type-in 0 in the **Y** and **Z** boxes. Press Enter to specify the second point.

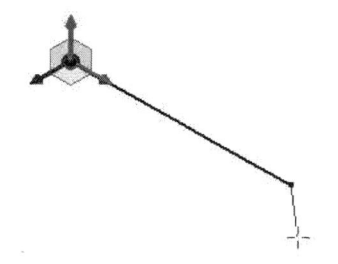

11. Type-in 0, 0, and 20 in the X, Y, and Z boxes, respectively. Press Enter.

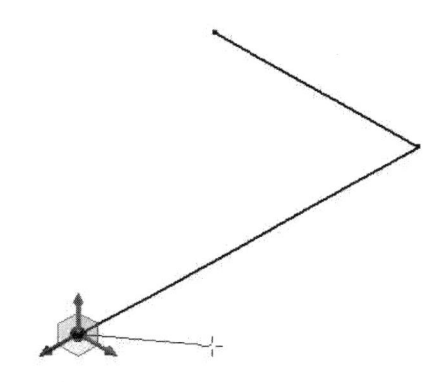

12. Type-in 0,18, 0 in the X, Y, and Z boxes, respectively. Press Enter.

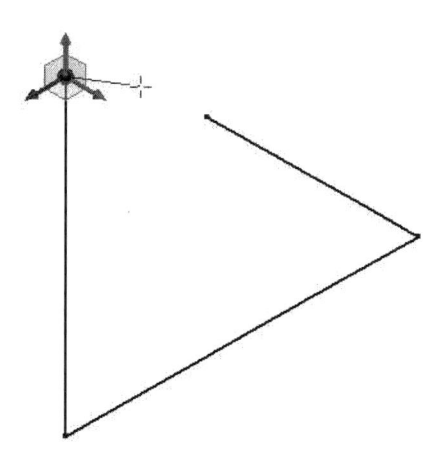

13. Type-in 0, 0 and -22 in the X, Y and Z boxes, respectively. Press Enter.

78

Additional Modeling Tools

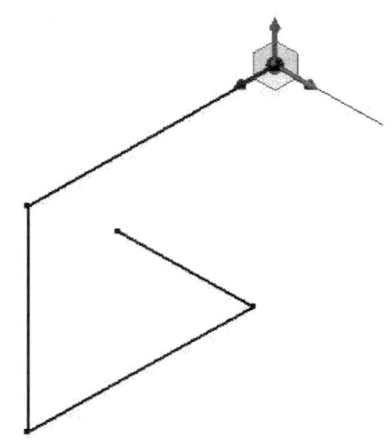

14. Type-in 0, 18, and 0 in the X, Y, and Z boxes, respectively. Press Enter.

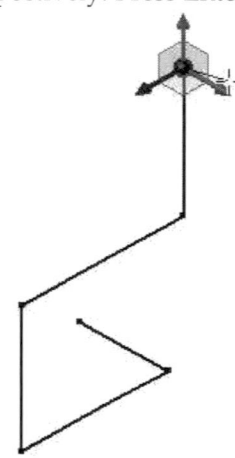

15. Type-in -12, 0, and 0 in the X, Y, and Z boxes, respectively. Press Enter.

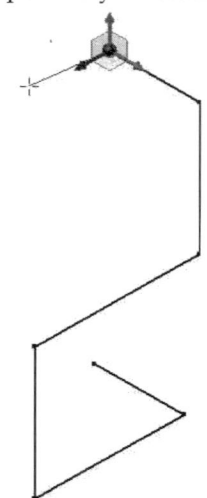

16. Click the right mouse button and select **OK**.

17. On the **3D Sketch** tab of the ribbon, click **Pattern > Mirror**.

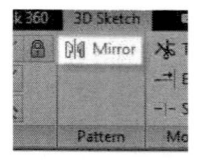

18. Drag a selection box and select all the sketch elements.

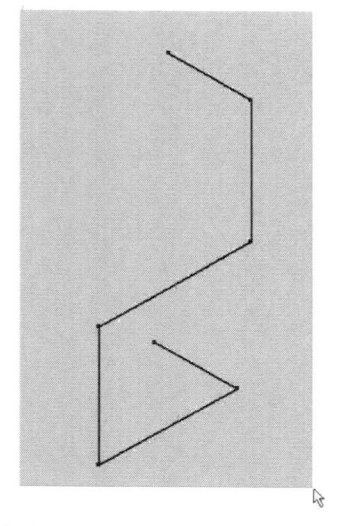

19. Click the **Mirror Plane** button on the dialog, and then select YZ Plane from the Browser window.

20. Click **Apply** and **Done** on the dialog.

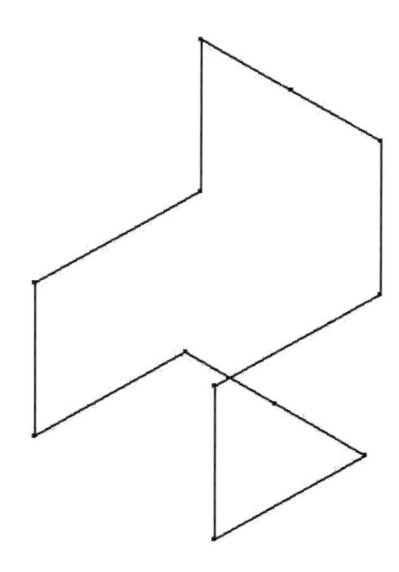

21. On the ribbon, click **3D Sketch > Draw > Bend**.

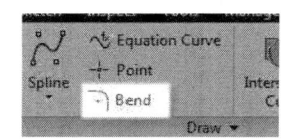

Additional Modeling Tools

22. Type-in 3 in the **Bend** dialog and select the intersecting lines, as shown in figure.

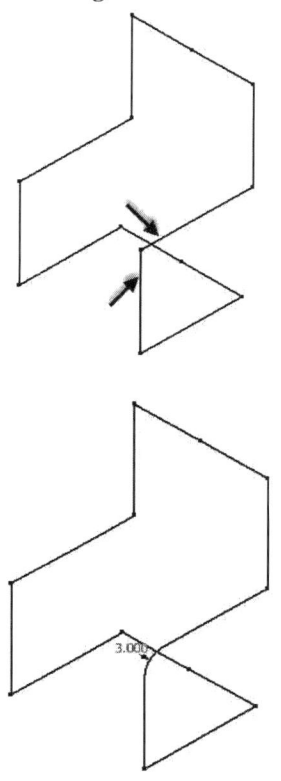

23. Likewise, bend the other corners of the 3D sketch.

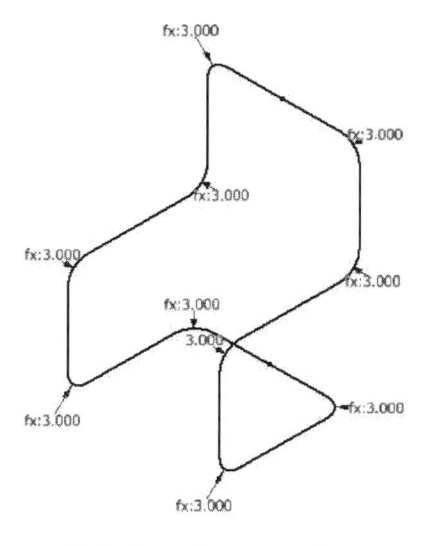

24. Click the right mouse button and select **OK**.

25. On the ribbon, click **3D Sketch > Constrain > Fix**.

26. Select the origin point of the sketch.

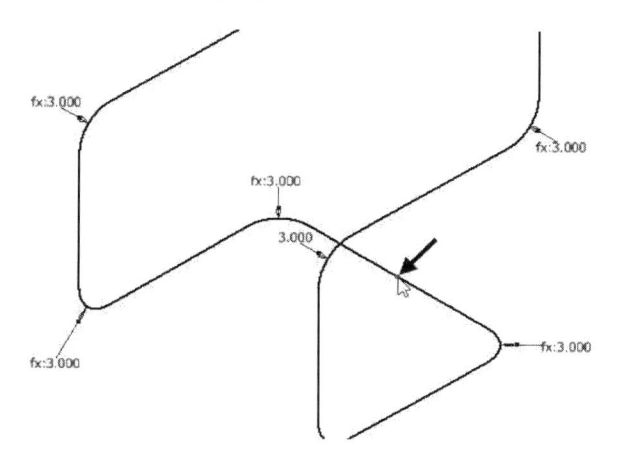

27. Add dimensions to fully define the sketch.

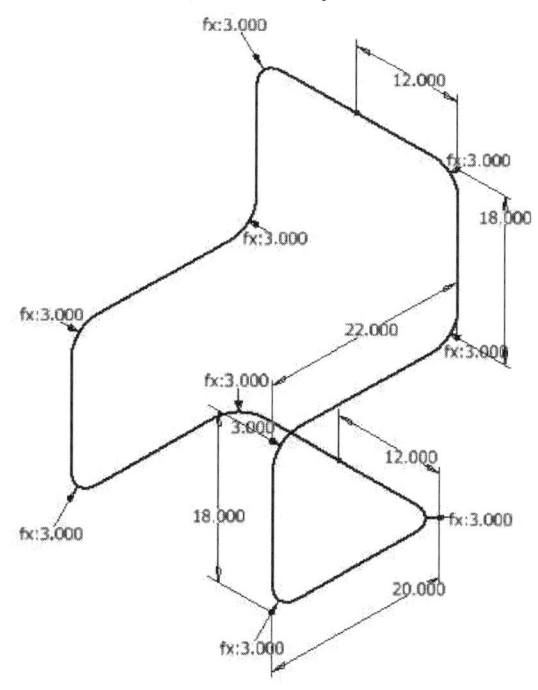

28. Click **Finish Sketch** on the ribbon.

29. On ribbon, click **3D Model > Work Features > Plane > Normal to Axis through Point**.

Additional Modeling Tools

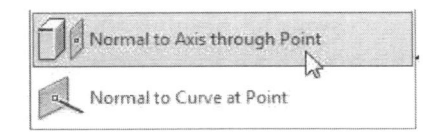

30. Click on the horizontal line of the sketch and its end point.

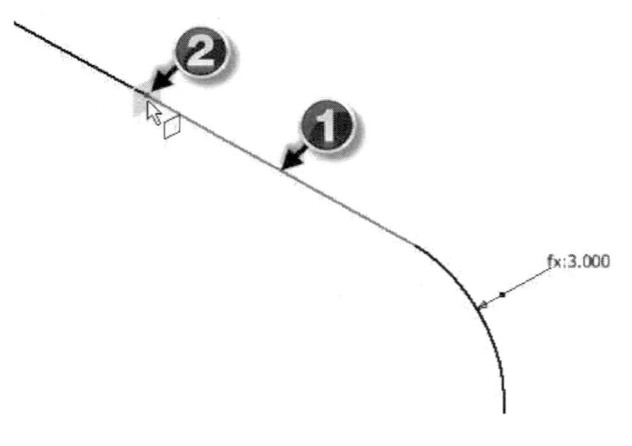

31. Start a 2D sketch on the new plane and create two concentric circles.

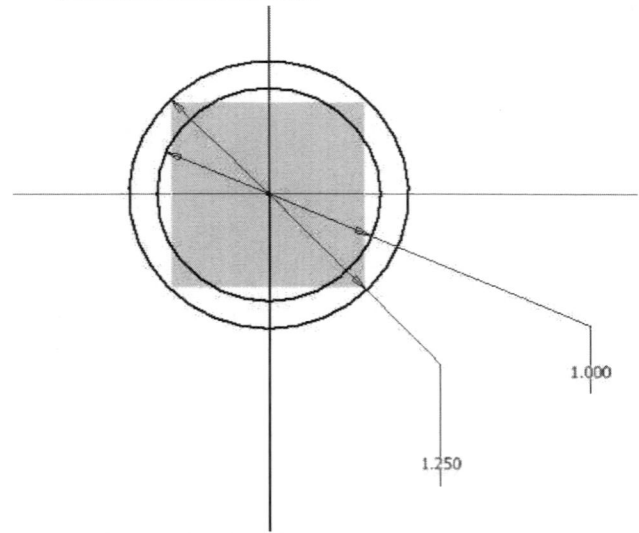

32. Click **Finish Sketch**.

Creating the Sweep feature

1. On the ribbon, click **3D Model > Create > Sweep**.

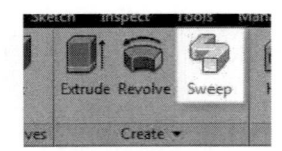

2. Zoom into the circular sketch and click in the outer loop.

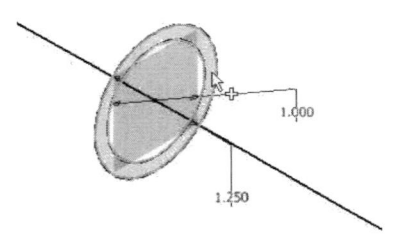

3. Click on the 3D sketch to define the sweep path.

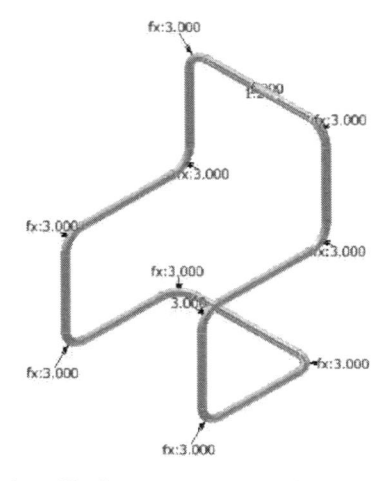

4. Click **OK** to sweep the profile.

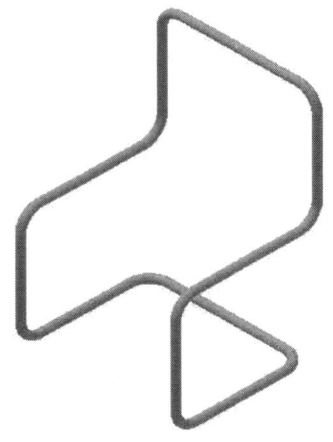

5. Start a sketch on the YZ Plane.

6. Draw two concentric circles and dimension them.

81

Additional Modeling Tools

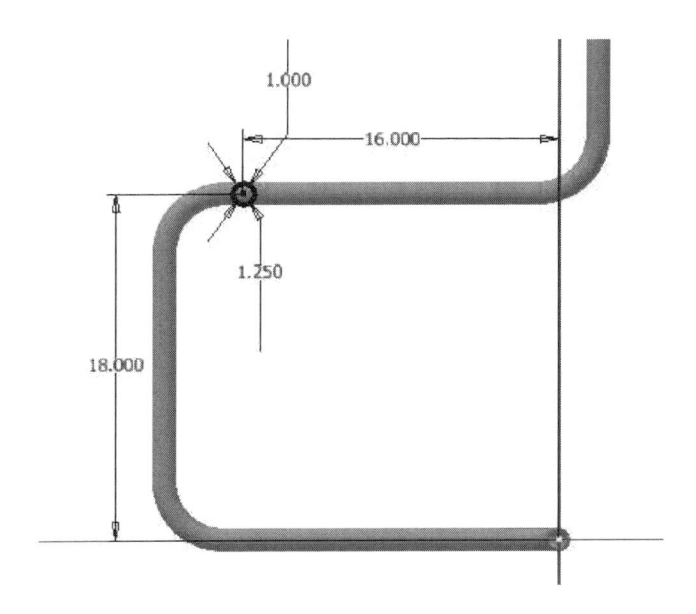

7. Click **Finish Sketch**.

8. Activate the **Extrude** tool and click in the outer loop of the sketch.

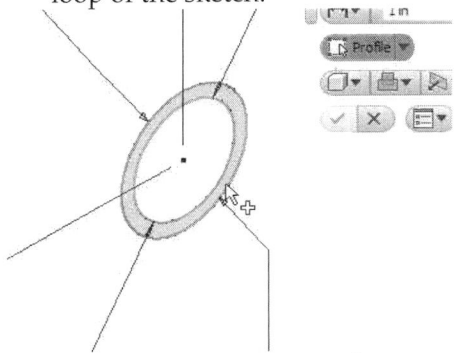

9. On the **Extrude** dialog, select **Extents > Between**.

10. Click on the tubes on both sides of the sketch.

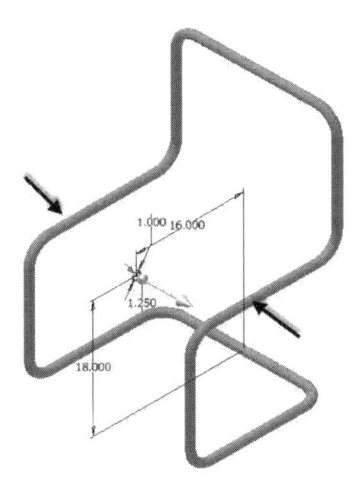

11. On the **Extrude** dialog, uncheck the **Check to terminate feature on the extended face** options.

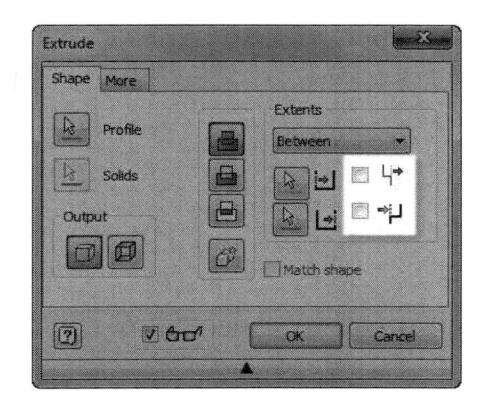

12. Click **OK** to extrude the sketch.

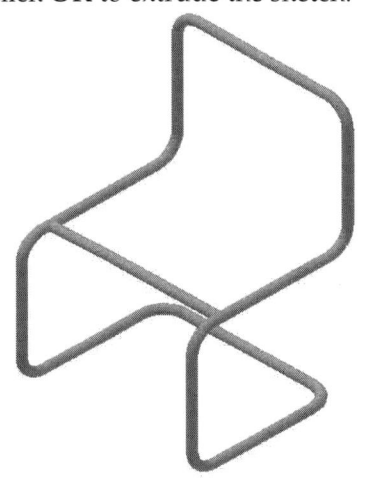

Creating the Along Curve pattern

1. On the Browser window, click the right mouse button on the **3D Sketch** and select **Visibility**.

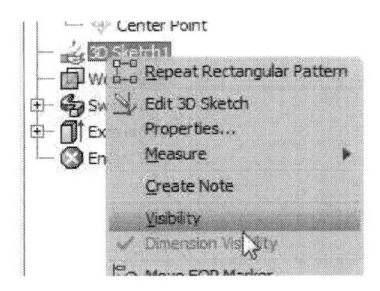

2. On the ribbon, click **3D Model > Pattern > Rectangular Pattern**.

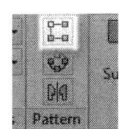

Additional Modeling Tools

3. Click on the extrude feature.

4. On the **Rectangular Pattern** dialog, click the **Direction 1** button, and then click on the **3D sketch**.

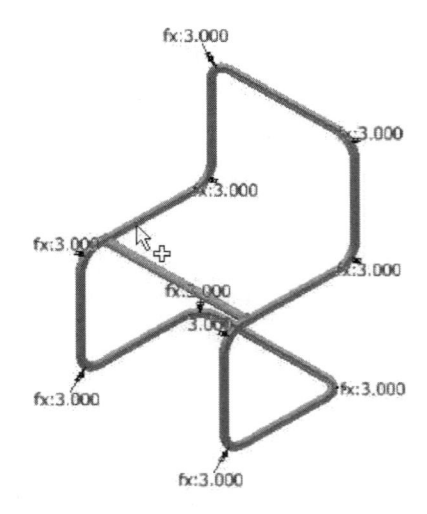

5. Type-in **3** and **23** in the **Column Count** and **Column Spacing** boxes, respectively.

6. Select **Spacing > Distance** from the drop-down menu.

7. Click the double-arrow button located at the bottom of the dialog. This expands the dialog.

8. Set the **Orientation** to **Direction 1**.

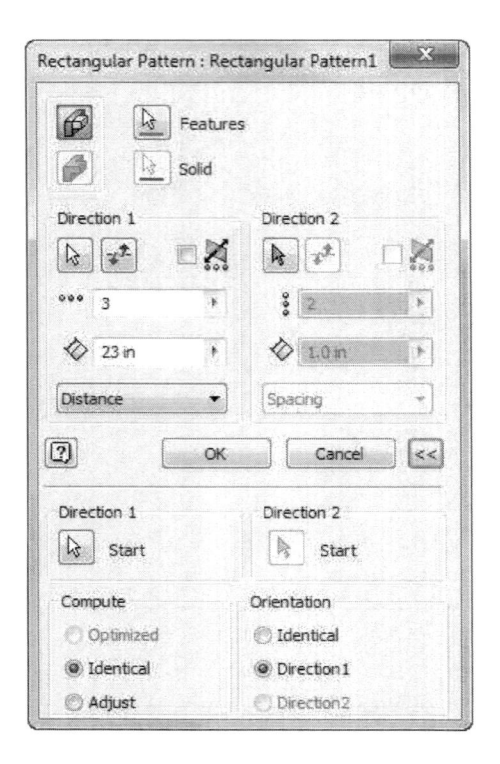

9. Click **OK** to pattern the extruded feature.

10. On the Browser window, click the right mouse button on the 3D sketch and select **Visibility**. This hides the 3D sketch.

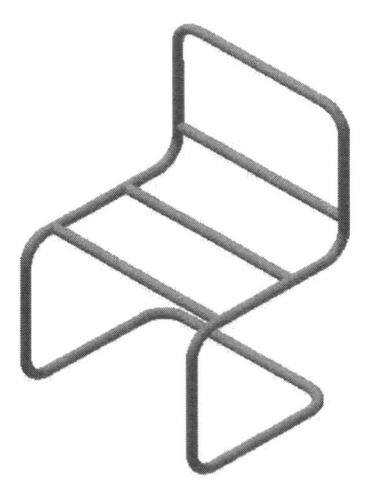

Creating the Freeform feature

1. On the ribbon, click **3D Model > Work Features > Plane**.

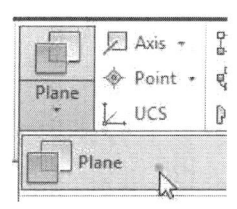

Additional Modeling Tools

2. On the **Browser window**, click the XZ Plane. A plane appears on the XZ Plane.

3. Click on the extruded feature. A plane appears tangent to the extruded feature.

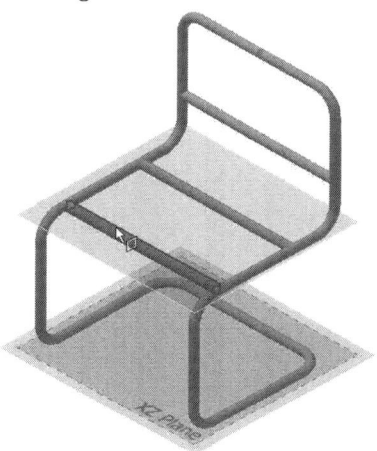

4. Start a sketch on the new plane.

5. Place a point on the sketch plane and add dimensions to position it.

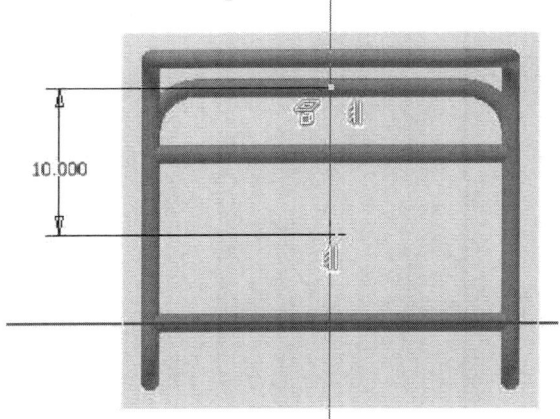

6. Click **Finish Sketch**.

7. On the ribbon, click **3D Model > Freeform > Box**.

8. Select the plane tangent to the extruded feature.

9. Select the sketch point to define the location of the freeform box.

10. Click and drag the side-arrow of the freeform box.

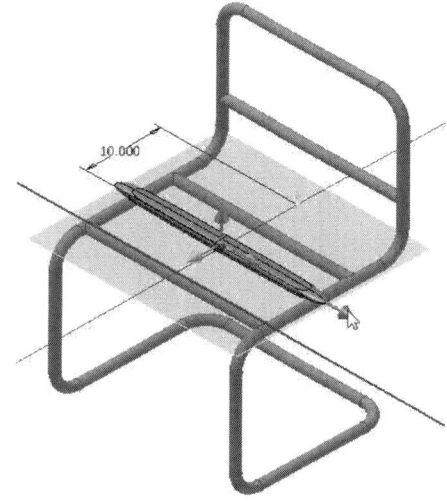

11. Click and drag the front arrow of the freeform box.

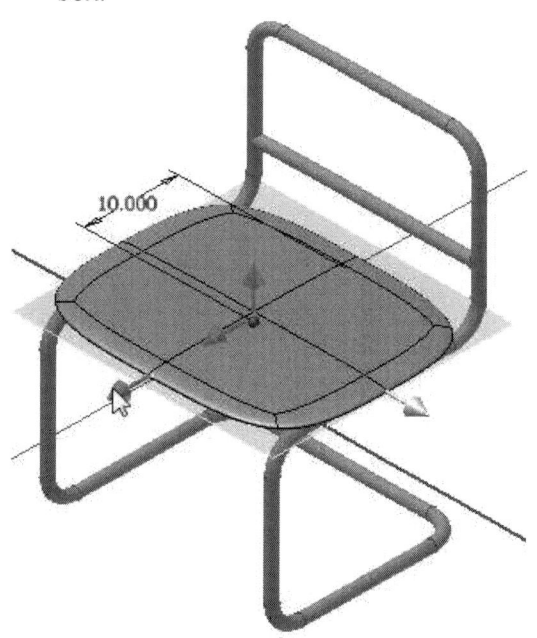

12. Click and drag the top arrow to increase the height of the freeform box.

Additional Modeling Tools

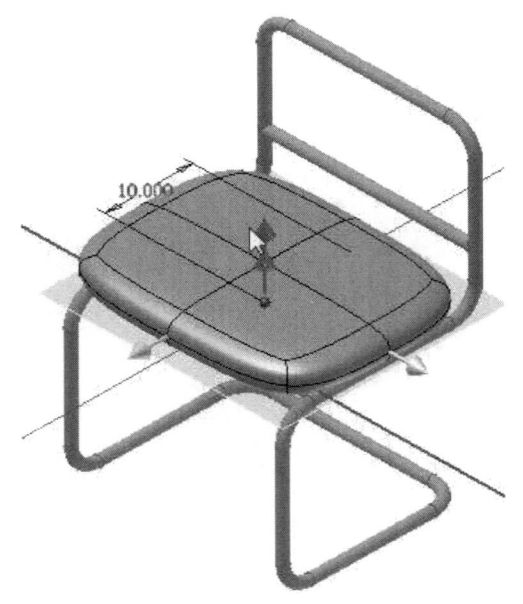

13. On the **Box** dialog, type-in 4, 1, and 2 in the **Faces** boxes, respectively.

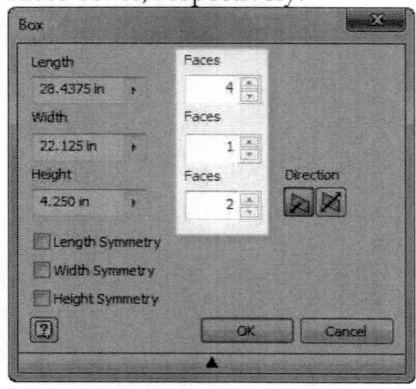

14. Click **OK** to create the freeform shape.

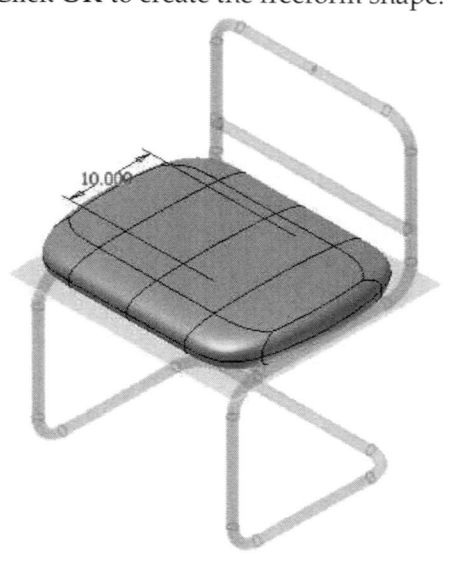

Editing the Freeform Shape

1. On the ribbon, click **Freeform > Edit > Edit Form**.

2. Hold the Ctrl key and click on top faces of the freeform shape.

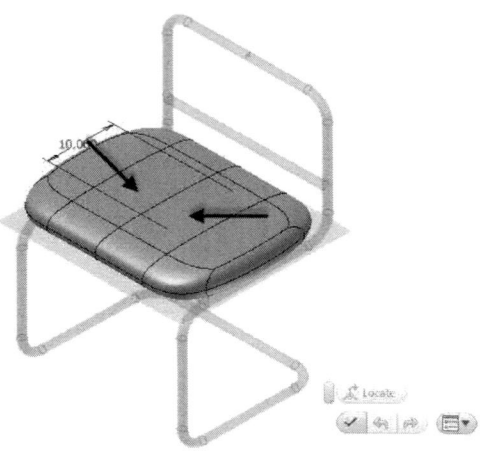

3. Click on the arrow pointing upwards.

4. Drag it downwards.

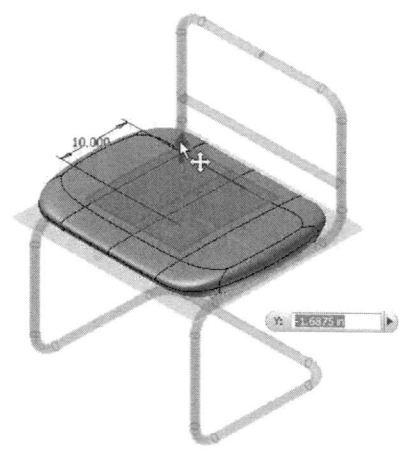

5. Click **OK** on the dialog.

6. On the ribbon, click **Freeform > Edit > Edit Form**.

7. Hold the Ctrl key and click on the two edges at the front.

85

Additional Modeling Tools

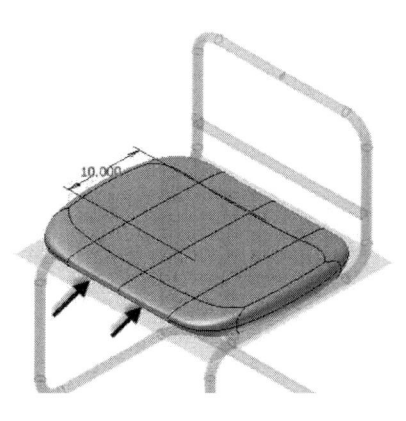

8. Drag the vertical arrow downwards.

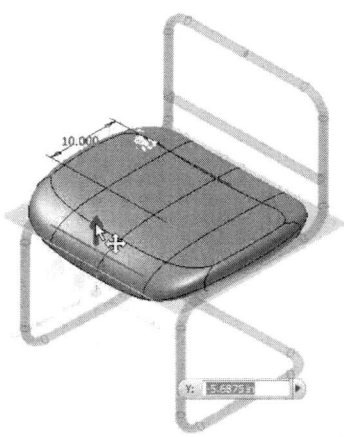

9. Click **OK** on the Edit Form dialog.

10. Click **Finish Freeform** on the ribbon.

Create another Freeform box

1. On the ribbon, click **3D Model > Work Features > Plane**.

2. On the Browser window, click the XY Plane.

3. Click on the vertical portion of the sweep feature to create a plane tangent to it.

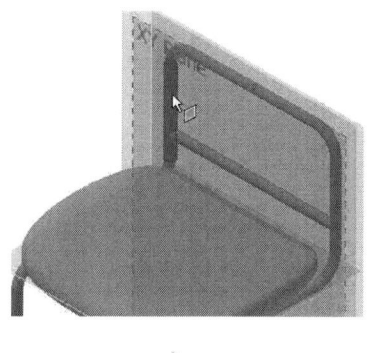

4. Start a sketch on the new plane.

5. Place a point and add dimensions to it.

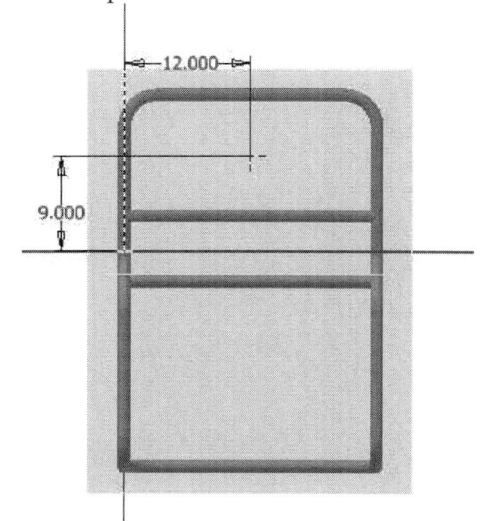

6. Click **Finish Sketch**.

86

Additional Modeling Tools

7. Activate the Freeform **Box** tool.

8. Select the new plane and click on the sketch point.

9. On the **Box** dialog, type-in 27, 16, and 3 in the **Length**, **Width**, and **Height** boxes, respectively.

10. Click **OK**, and then click **Finish Freeform**.

11. Save and close the file.

TUTORIAL 6
In this tutorial, you create a bolt.

Start a new part file
1. Start a new part file using the **Standard.ipt** template.

2. On the ribbon, click **3D Model > Primitives > Primitive drop-down > Cylinder**.

3. Click on the YZ Plane.

4. Click the origin point of the sketch to define the center point of the circle.

5. Move the pointer and type-in 0.75 in the box, and then press Enter.

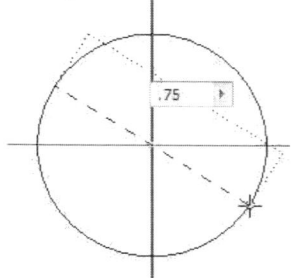

6. Type-in 3 in the **Distance** box and press Enter.

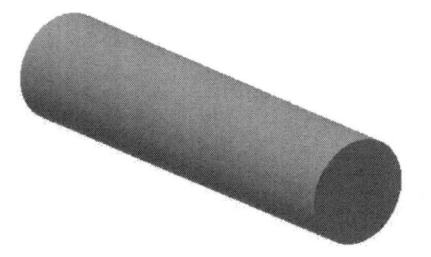

Creating the second feature
1. Start a sketch on the YZ Plane.

2. On the ribbon, click **Sketch > Create > Rectangle** drop-down **> Polygon**.

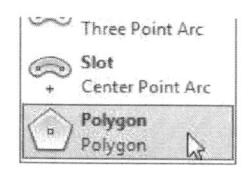

3. Click the sketch origin.

4. Type-in 6 in the **Polygon** dialog

5. Move the pointer vertically upward. You will notice that a dotted trace line appears between the origin point and the pointer.

87

Additional Modeling Tools

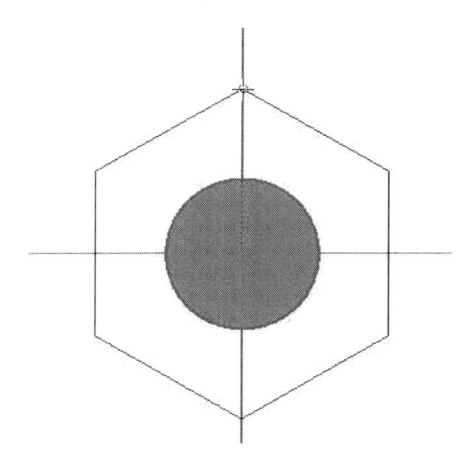

6. Click to create the polygon.

7. Click **Done** on the dialog.

8. On the ribbon, click the **Sketch > Format > Construction**.

9. Activate the **Line** tool and select the vertices of the polygon.

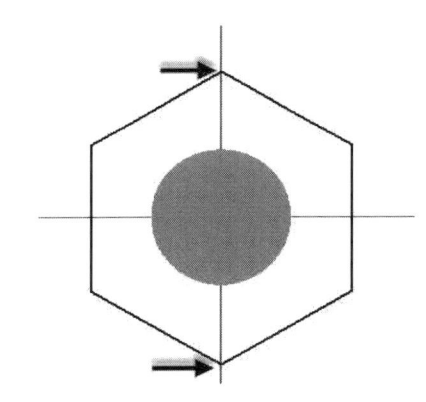

10. Activate the **Dimension** tool and create a dimension, as in figure.

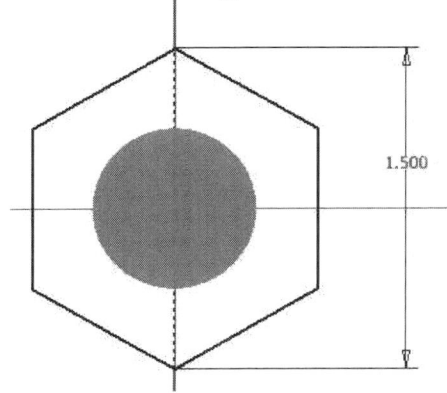

11. Finish the sketch.

12. Activate the **Extrude** tool and select the sketch.

13. On the **Extrude** dialog, type-in 0.5 in the **Distance** box.

14. Use the **Direction 1** or **Direction 2** buttons to make sure that the polygon is extruded toward left.

15. Click **OK**.

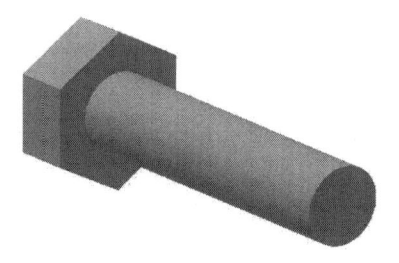

Adding Threads

1. On the ribbon, click **3D Model > Modify > Thread**.

2. Click on the cylindrical face of the model geometry.

3. On the **Thread** dialog, uncheck the **Full Length** option and type-in **1.5** in the **Length** box.

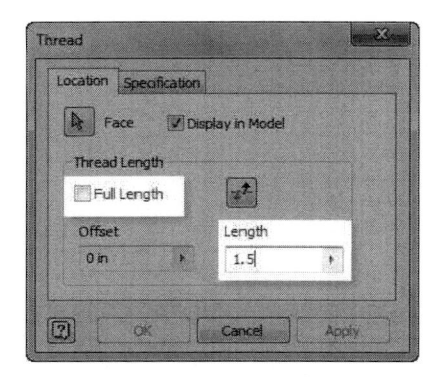

4. Click the **Specification** tab to specify the thread settings.

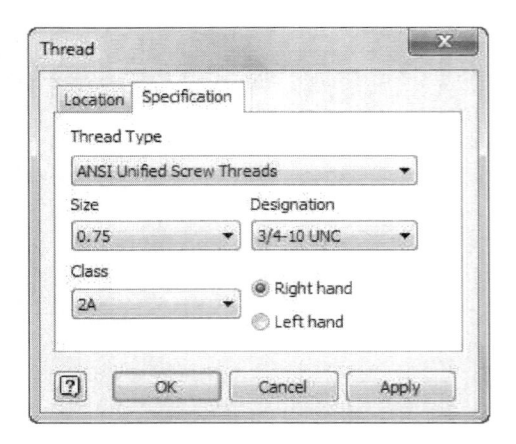

Additional Modeling Tools

5. Click **OK** to add thread.

Creating iParts

iParts allow you to design a part with different variations, sizes, materials and other attributes. Now, you will create different variations of the bolt created in the previous section.

1. On the ribbon, click **3D Model > Manage > Parameters**. This opens the **Parameters** dialog.

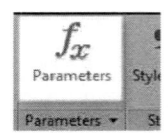

2. On the **Parameters** dialog, type-in **Diameter** in the first cell of the **Model Parameters** table.

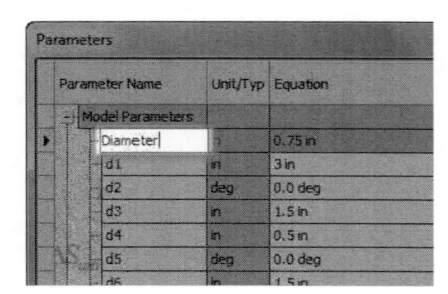

3. Likewise, update the names of other parameters.

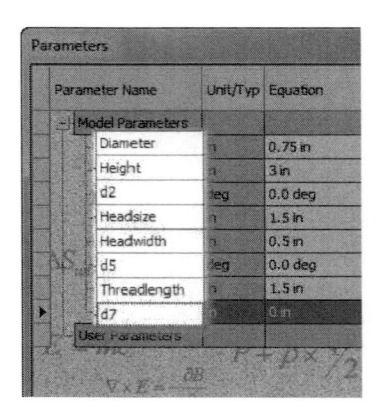

4. Click **Done** on the **Parameters** dialog.

5. Click the right mouse button in the graphics window and select **Dimension Display > Expression**.

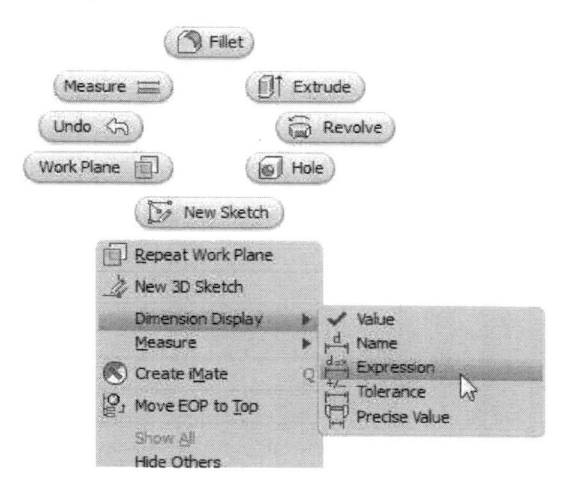

6. On the Browser window, click the right mouse button on the **Extrusion1** and select **Show Dimensions**. You will notice that the dimensions are shown along with the names.

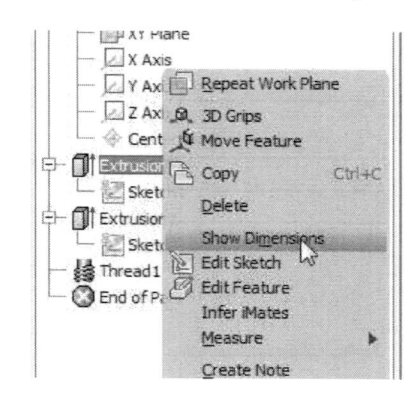

89

Additional Modeling Tools

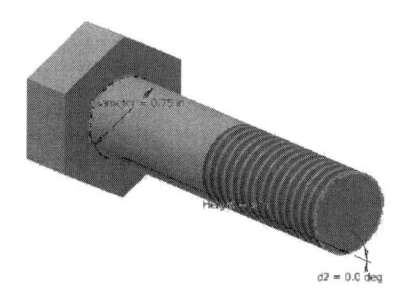

7. On the ribbon, click **Manage > Author > Create iPart**.

This opens the **iPart Author** dialog. In this dialog, you will define the parameters to create other versions of the model geometry.

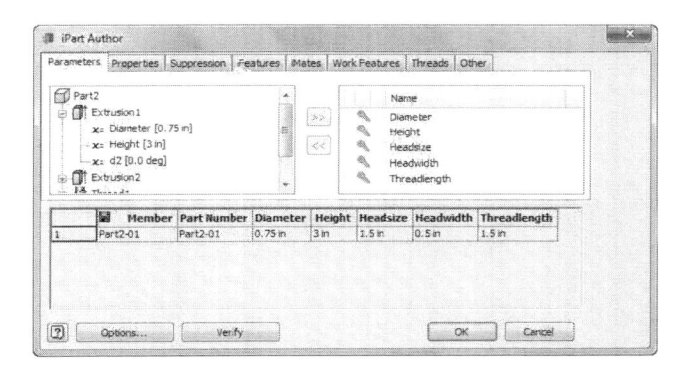

The table at the bottom of this dialog shows the parameters for the iPart factory. You will notice that the renamed parameters are automatically added to the table. If you want to add more parameters to the table, then select them from the section located at the left side. Click the arrow button pointing towards right. Likewise, if you want to remove a parameter from the table, then select it from the right side section and click the arrow pointing toward left.

8. Now, click the right mouse button on the table and select **Insert Row**. Notice that a new row is added to the table.

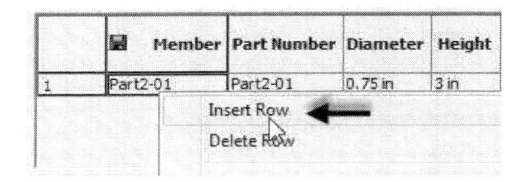

9. Likewise, insert another row.

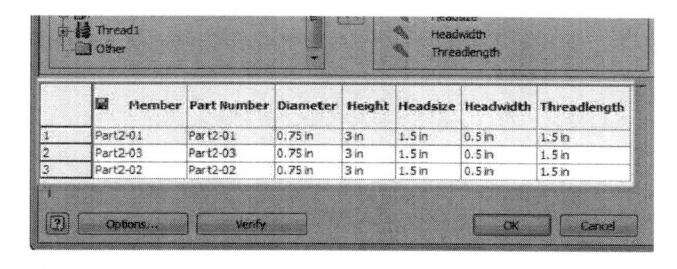

10. In the second row of the table, type-in new values (5, 0.75, and 3) in the Height, Headwidth, and Threadlength boxes. This creates the second version of the bolt.

11. In the third row of the table, type-in new values in (2, 0.75, and 3) the Headsize, Headwidth, and Threadlength boxes. This creates the third version of the bolt.

Now, you have to set the default version of the bolt.

12. Click the right mouse button on the third row of the table and select **Set As Default Row**.

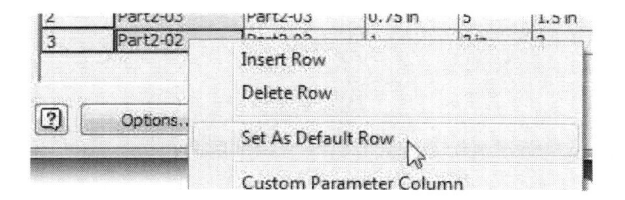

13. Click **OK** to close the dialog. Notice that the default version of the bolt changes.

Additional Modeling Tools

In the Bowser Bar, you will notice that the **Table** item is added.

14. Expand the **Table** item in the Browser Window to view the different variations of the iPart. Notice that the activated version of the iPart is designated by a check mark.

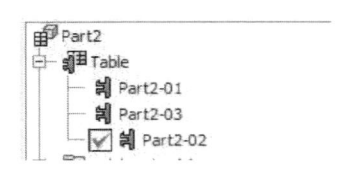

15. Double-click on any other version of the iPart to activate it.

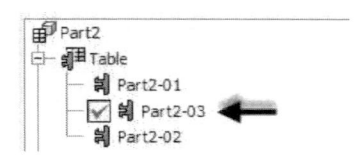

If you want to make changes to any version of the bolt, then click the right mouse button on it and select **Edit table**.

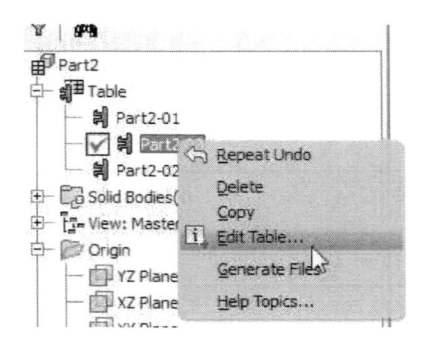

If you want to edit the table using a spreadsheet, then click the right mouse button on **Table** and select **Edit via Spreadsheet**. Click **OK** on the message box.

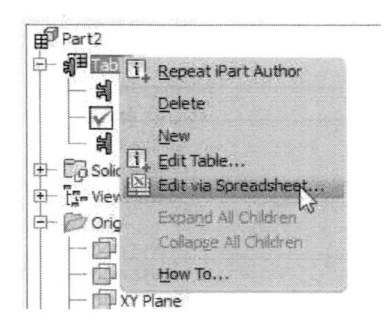

Now, modify the values in the spreadsheet and close it. A message pops up asking you to save the changes. Click **Yes** to save the changes.

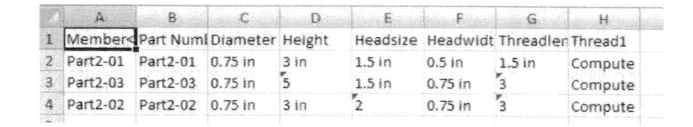

	A	B	C	D	E	F	G	H
1	Members	Part Numl	Diameter	Height	Headsize	Headwidt	Threadlen	Thread1
2	Part2-01	Part2-01	0.75 in	3 in	1.5 in	0.5 in	1.5 in	Compute
3	Part2-03	Part2-03	0.75 in	5	1.5 in	0.75 in	3	Compute
4	Part2-02	Part2-02	0.75 in	3 in	2	0.75 in	3	Compute

If you want to save anyone of the iPart versions as a separate part file, then click the right mouse button on it and select **Generate Files**.

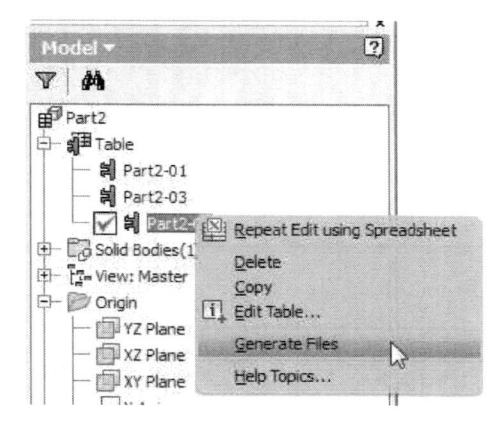

91

Additional Modeling Tools

16. Save and close the file.

TUTORIAL 7

In this tutorial, you create a plastic casing.

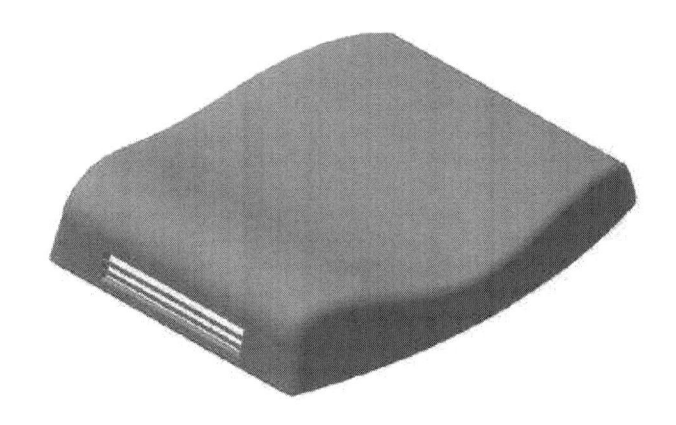

Creating the First Feature

1. Open a new Autodesk Inventor part file using the **Standard.ipt** template.

2. Create a sketch on the XZ Plane, as shown in figure.

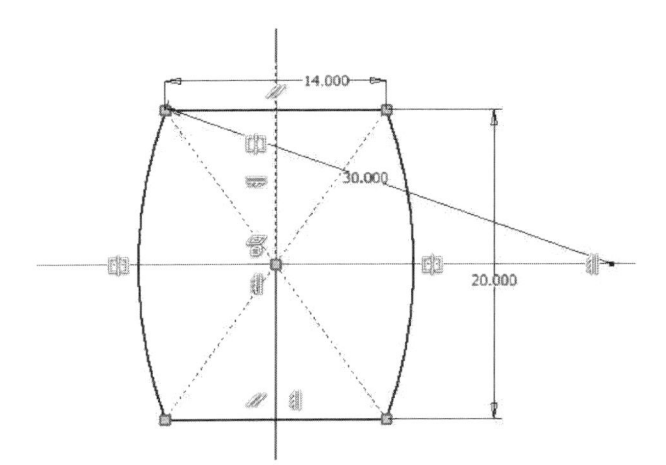

3. Click **Finish Sketch**.

4. Click the **3D Model > Create > Extrude** on the ribbon; the **Extrude** dialog appears.

5. Set the **Distance** to 3.15.

6. Click the **More** tab and set the **Taper** angle to -10.

7. Click the **OK** button.

Creating the Extruded surface

1. Click **3D Model > Sketch > Start 2D Sketch** on the ribbon and select the XY Plane.

2. Click the **Slice Graphics** button at the bottom of the window or press **F7** on the keyboard.

3. Click **Sketch > Create > Line > Spline Interpolation** on the ribbon.

4. Create a spline, as shown in figure.

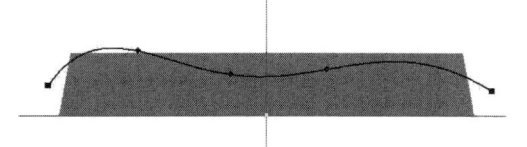

5. Apply dimensions to the spline, as shown below.

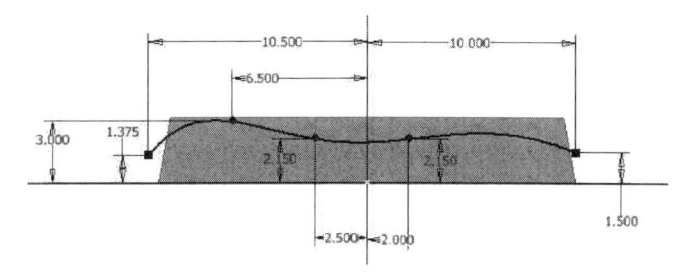

6. Click **Finish Sketch**.

7. Click the **Extrude** button.

8. On the **Extrude** dialog, set the **Output** type to **Surface**.

92

Additional Modeling Tools

9. Set the **Extents** type to **Distance**.

10. Select the **Symmetric** button.

11. Extrude the sketch up to 17 in distance.

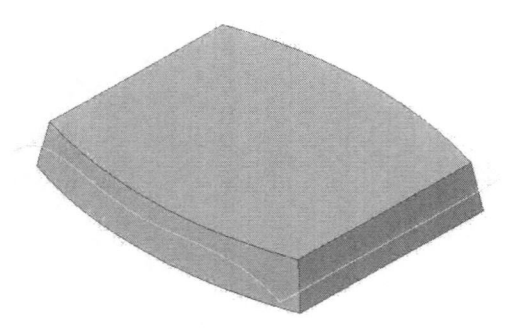

Replacing the top face of the model with the surface

1. On the **Surface** panel of the **3D Model** ribbon, click the **Replace Face** button; the **Replace Face** dialog appears.

Now, you need to select the face to be replaced.

2. Select the top face of the model.

Next, you need to select the replacement face or surface.

3. Click the **New Faces** button on the dialog and select the extruded surface.

You can also use a solid face to replace an existing face.

4. Click **OK** to replace the top face with a surface.

5. Hide the extruded surface.

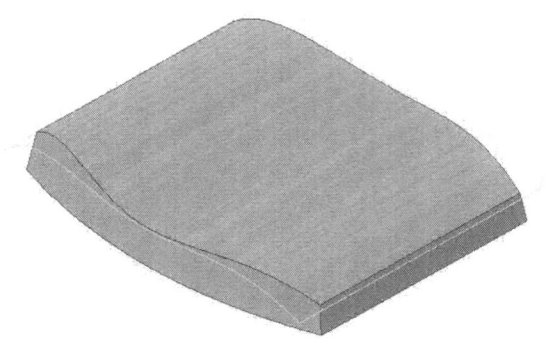

6. Hide the extruded surface by clicking the right mouse button on it and un-checking **Visibility**.

Creating a Face fillet

1. Click the **Fillet** button on the **Modify** panel.

2. Click the **Face Fillet** button on the **Fillet** dialog.

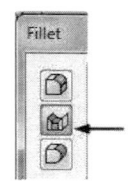

3. Select the top surface as the first face and the inclined front face as the second face.

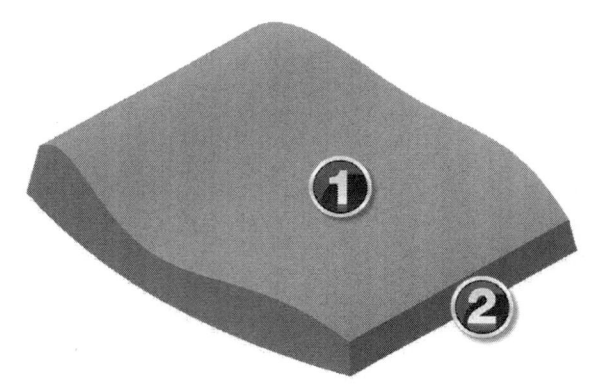

4. Set the **Radius** to 1.5 and click the **OK** button to create the face fillet.

93

Additional Modeling Tools

5. Likewise, apply a face fillet of 1.5 radius between top surface and the back inclined face of the model.

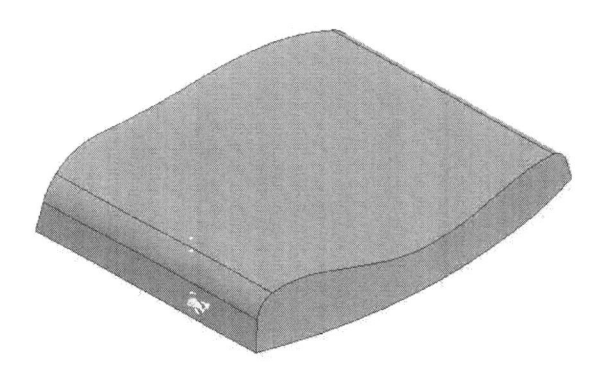

Creating a Variable Radius fillet

1. Click the **Fillet** button on the **Modify** panel.

2. Click the **Variable** tab on the **Fillet** dialog.

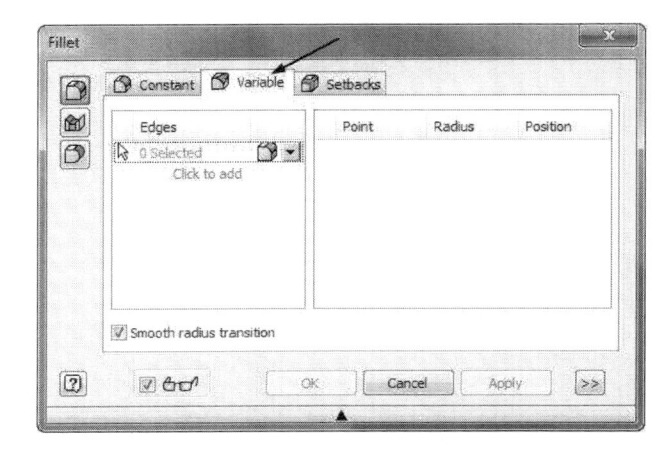

3. Select the curved edge on the model; the preview of the fillet appears.

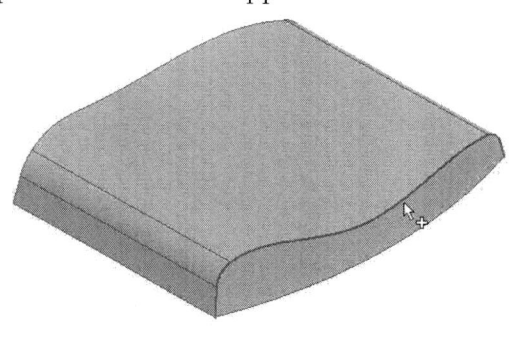

4. Select a point on the fillet, as shown in figure.

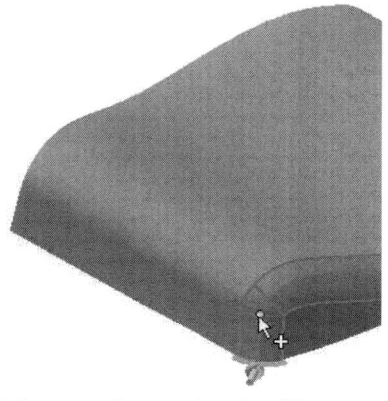

5. Select another point the fillet, as shown in figure.

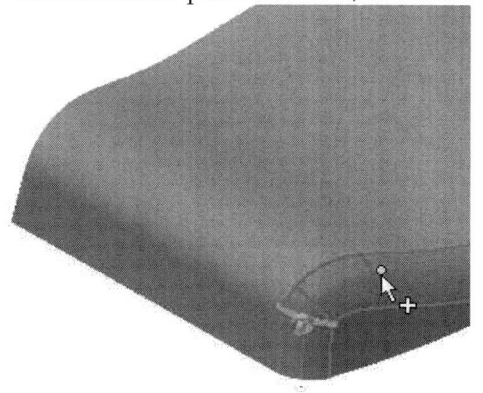

6. Set the radii of the **Start**, **End**, **Point 1** and **Point 2** as shown below.

Point	Radius	Position
Start	.6	0.0
End	.6	1.0
Point 1	1	0.0000
Point 2	.8	0.9103

You can also specify the fillet continuity type. By default, the **Tangent Fillet** type is specified.

Additional Modeling Tools

7. Select **Smooth (G2) Fillet** type.

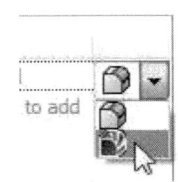

8. Make sure the **Smooth radius transition** option is checked.

9. Click **OK** to create the variable fillet.

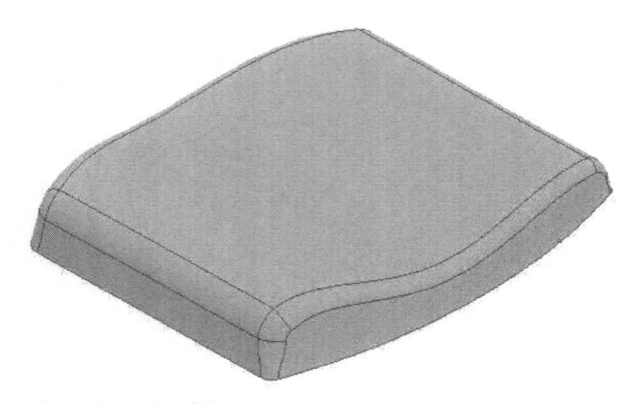

Mirroring the fillet

10. Click the **Mirror** button on the **Pattern** panel; the **Mirror** dialog appears.

11. Select the variable radius fillet from the model.

12. Click the **Mirror Plane** button on the dialog.

13. Select the **XY Plane** from the Browser window.

14. Click **OK** to mirror the fillet.

Shelling the Model

1. Click the **Shell** button on the **Modify** panel; the **Shell** dialog appears.

2. Click the **Inside** button on the dialog and set the **Thickness** to 0.2 in.

3. Rotate the model and select the bottom face.

4. Click **OK**.

Creating the Boss Features

1. Click **3D Model > Sketch > Start 2D Sketch** on the ribbon and select the bottom face of the model.

95

Additional Modeling Tools

2. Draw a rectangle with **Construction** button selected on the **Format** panel.

3. Apply dimensions to the rectangle.

4. Click the **Point** button on the **Create panel**.

5. Place four points at corners of the rectangle.

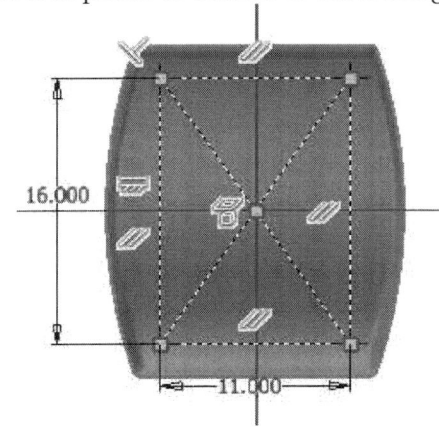

6. Click **Finish Sketch**.

Now, you will create bosses by selecting the points created in the sketch.

7. On the ribbon, click the **Show Panels** button located at the right side, and then select Plastic Part from the menu.

8. Click the **Boss** button on the **Plastic Part** panel; the **Boss** dialog appears.

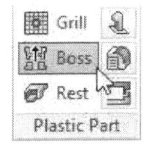

9. Click the **Thread** button on the dialog.

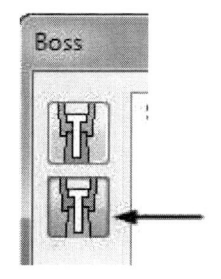

10. Select the **From Sketch** option from the **Placement** group.

11. Select the points located on the corners of the rectangle; the bosses are placed at the selected points.

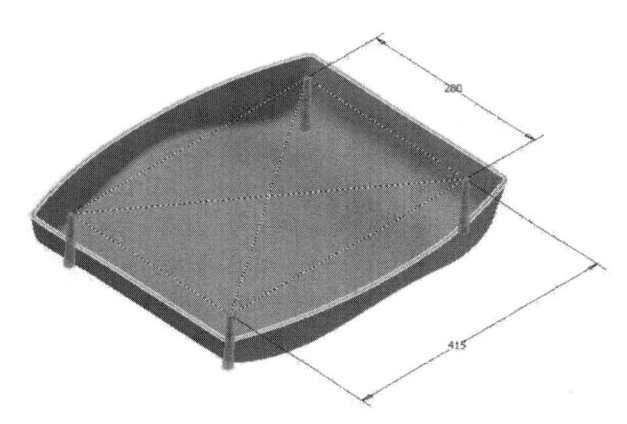

12. Click the **Thread** tab and specify the parameters, as shown below.

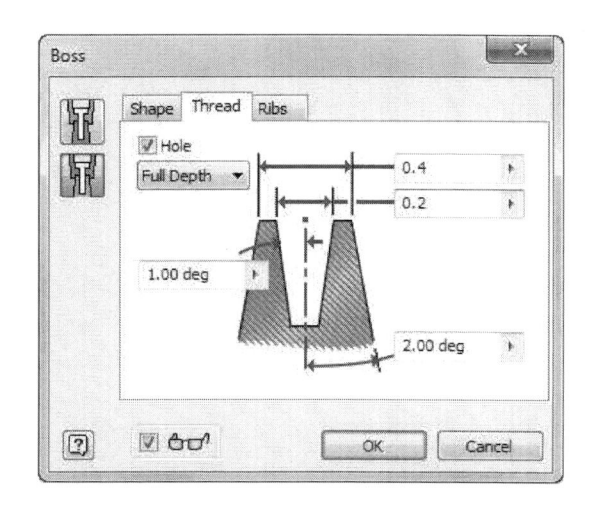

Additional Modeling Tools

13. Click the **Ribs** tab and check the **Stiffening Ribs** option.

14. Set the rib parameters, as shown next.

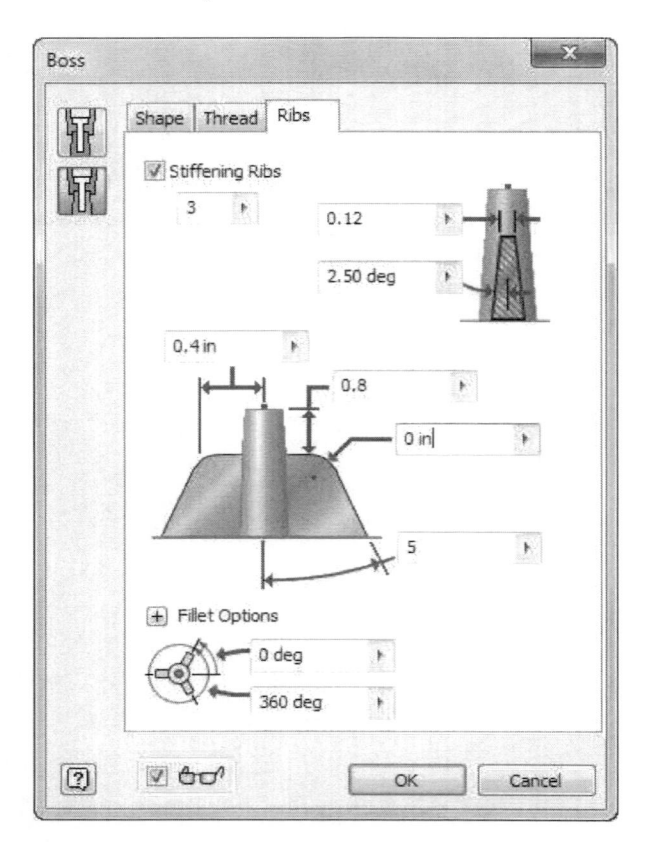

15. Expand the **Fillet options**.

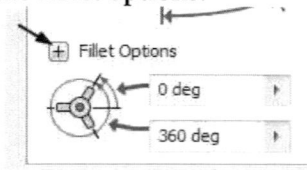

16. Specify the fillet options, as shown below.

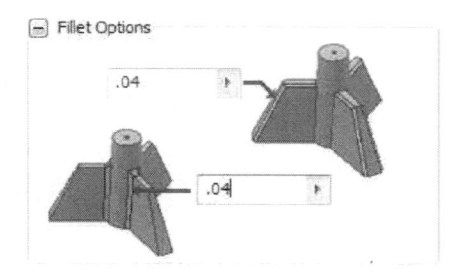

17. Click **OK** to create the bosses with ribs.

Creating the Lip feature

1. Click the **Lip** button on the **Plastic Part** panel of the ribbon; the **Lip** dialog appears.

2. Click the **Lip** button on the dialog.

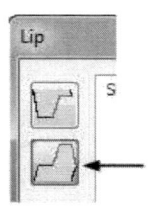

3. Select the outer edge of the bottom face.

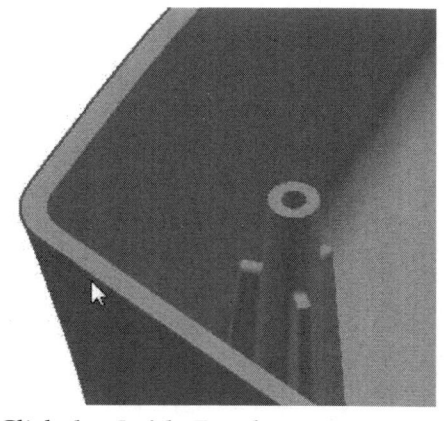

4. Click the **Guide Face** button on the dialog and select the bottom face of the model.

97

Additional Modeling Tools

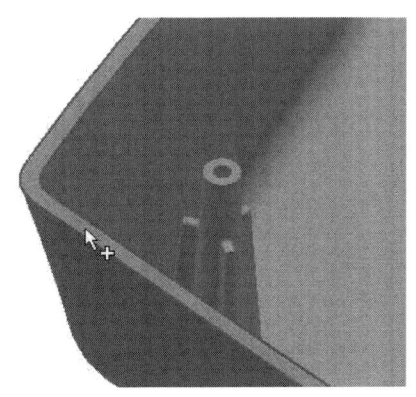

5. Click the **Lip** tab and set the parameters, as shown below.

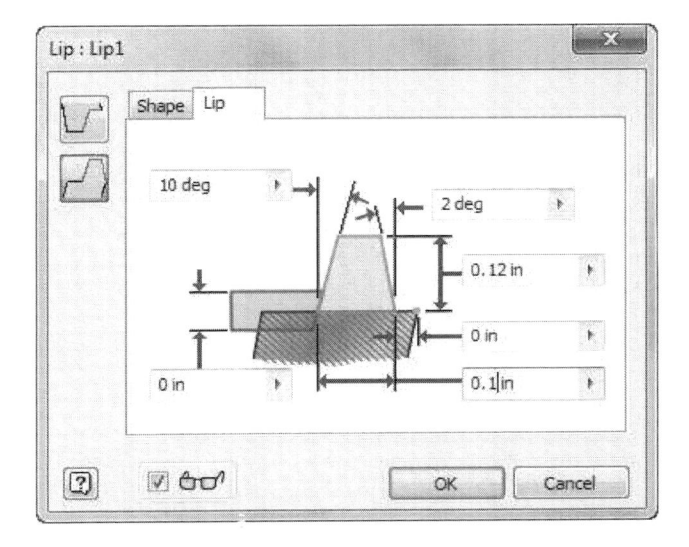

6. Click **OK** to create the lip.

Creating the Grill Feature
1. Create a sketch on the back inclined face.

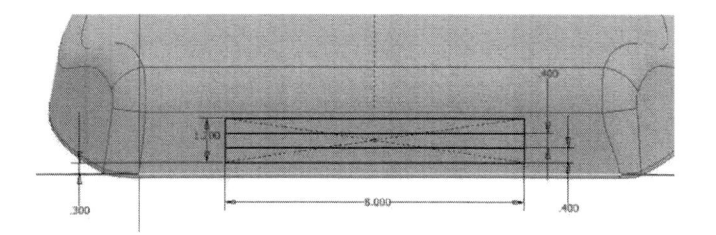

2. Click **Finish Sketch**.

3. Click the **Grill** button on the **Plastic Part** panel.

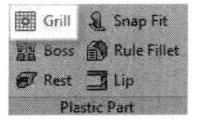

4. Select the rectangle as the boundary and set the **Boundary** parameters, as shown below.

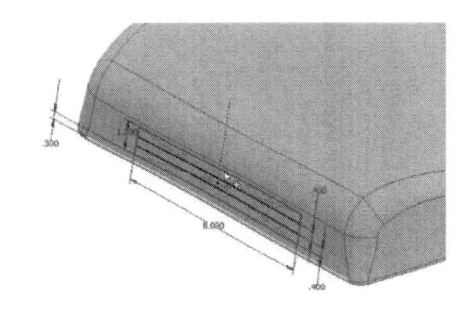

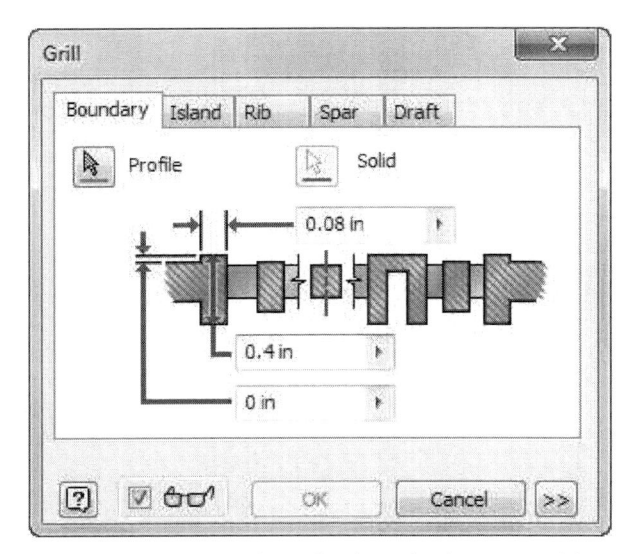

5. Click the **Rib** tab and select the horizontal lines.

6. Set the rib parameters, as shown below.

98

Additional Modeling Tools

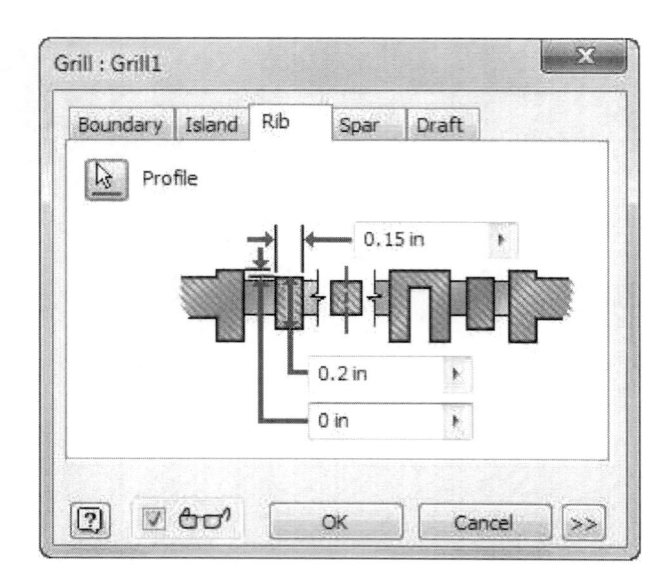

7. Click **OK** to create the grill.

8. Save the model as Plastic Cover.ipt.

Creating Ruled Surface

1. Click **3D Model > Surface > Ruled Surface** on the ribbon and select the bottom edge of the model.

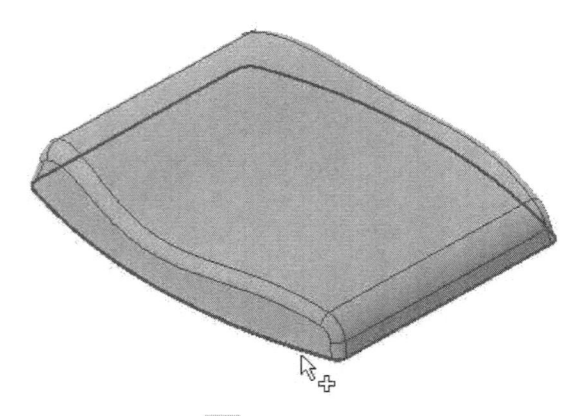

2. Click the **Normal** button on the Ruled Surface dialog.

   The preview of the ruled surface appears normal to the selected edge.

   You can click the **Alternate All Faces** button to change the direction of the ruled surface.

3. Type in 2 in the **Distance** box.

4. Click **OK** to create the ruled surface.

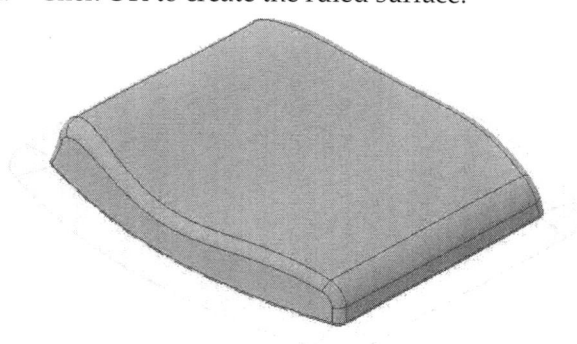

   The ruled surface can be used as a parting split while creating a mold.

5. Close the part file without saving.

Additional Modeling Tools

Sheet Metal Modeling

Chapter 6: Sheet Metal Modeling

This Chapter will show you to:

- Create face feature
- Create Flange
- Create Contour Flange
- Create Corner Seam
- Create Punches
- Create Bend Feature
- Create Corner Rounds
- Flat Pattern

TUTORIAL 1
In this tutorial, you create the sheet metal model shown in figure.

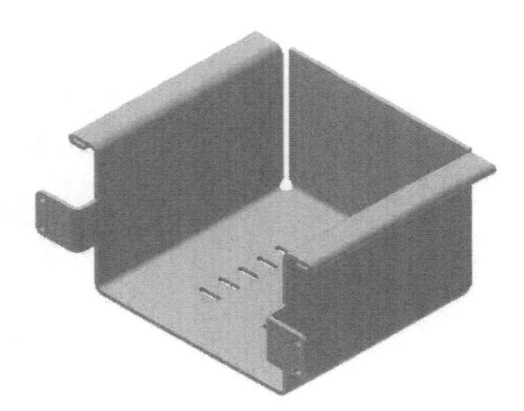

Starting a New Sheet metal File
1. To start a new sheet metal file, click **Get Started Launch > New** on the ribbon.

2. On the **Create New File dialog, click the Sheet Metal.ipt** icon, and then click **Create**.

Setting the Parameters of the Sheet Metal part
1. To set the parameters, click **Sheet Metal > Setup > Sheet Metal Defaults** on the ribbon; the **Sheet Metal Defaults** dialog appears.

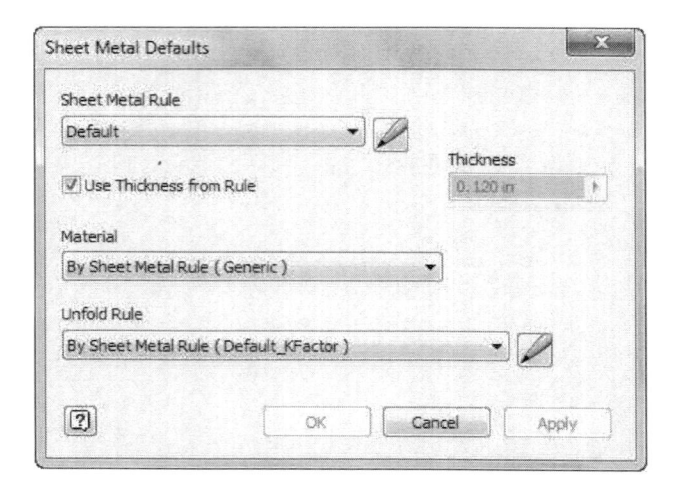

This dialog displays the default preferences of the sheet metal part such as sheet metal rule, thickness, material, and unfold rule. You can change these preferences as per you requirement.

2. To edit the sheet metal rule, click the **Edit Sheet Metal Rule** button on the dialog.

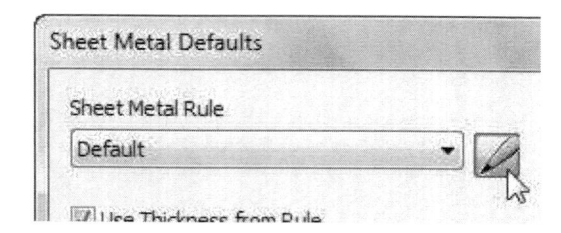

In the **Sheet** tab of the **Style and Standard Editor** dialog, you can set the sheet preferences such as sheet thickness, material, flat pattern bend angle representation, flat pattern punch representation and gap size.

101

Sheet Metal Modeling

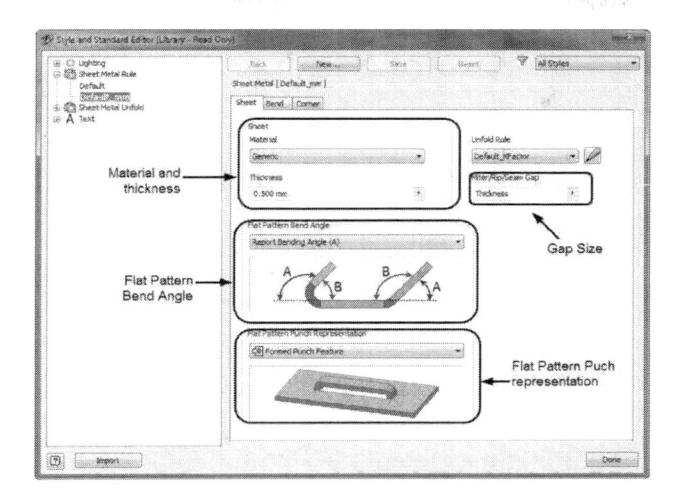

3. In the **Sheet** tab, set the **Thickness** to 0.12 and leave all the default settings.

4. Click the **Bend** tab.

In the **Bend** tab of this dialog, you can set the bend preferences such as bend radius, bend relief shape and size, and bend transition.

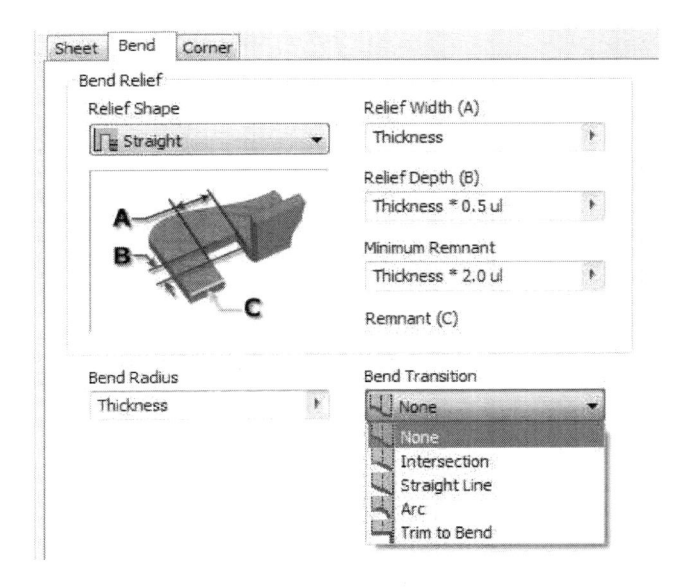

5. Set the **Relief Shape** to **Round**.

6. Click the **Corner** tab.

In the **Corner** tab, you can set the shape and size of the corner relief to be applied at the corners.

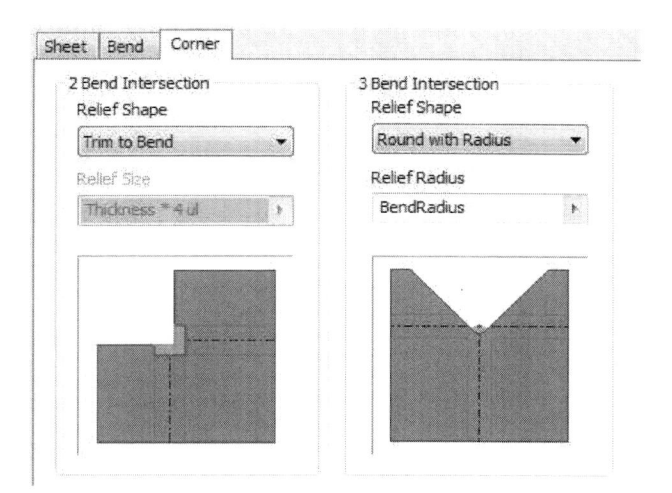

7. After setting the required preferences, click the **Done** button on the dialog, and then click **Yes**.

The **Unfold Rule** defines the folding/unfolding method of the sheet metal part. To modify or set a new Unfold Rule, click the **Edit Unfold Rule** button on the **Sheet Metal Defaults** dialog.

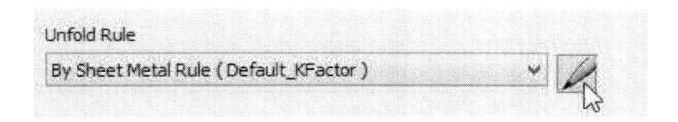

On the **Style and Standard Editor** dialog, select the required **Unfold Method**.

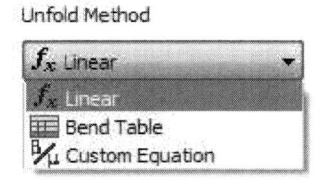

You can define the Unfold rule by selecting the **Linear** method (specifying the K factor), selecting a **Bend Table**, or entering a custom equation. Click **Done** after settings the parameters.

8. Close the **Sheet Metal Defaults** dialog.

Creating the Base Feature

1. Create the sketch on the XZ Plane, as shown in figure.

102

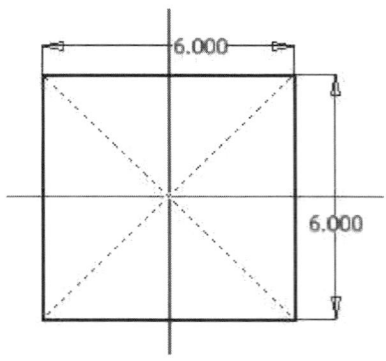

Sheet Metal Modeling

2. Click **Finish Sketch**.

3. To create the base component, click **Sheet Metal > Create > Face** on the ribbon; the **Face** dialog appears.

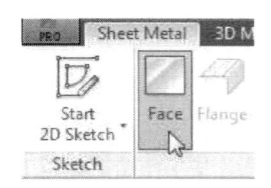

4. Click **OK** to create the tab feature.

Creating the flange

1. To create the flange, click **Sheet Metal > Create > Flange** on the ribbon; the **Flange** dialog appears.

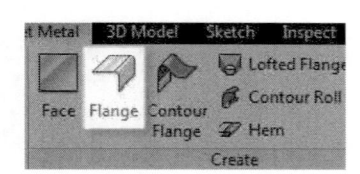

2. Select the edge on the top face, as shown.

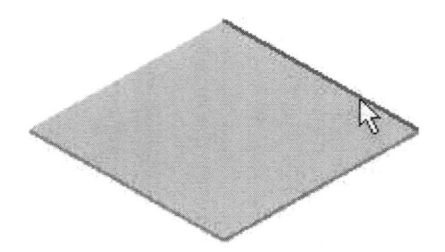

3. Set the **Distance** to 4.

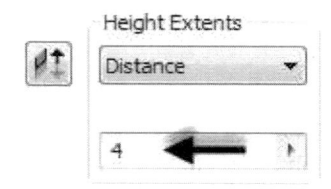

4. Click on the **Bend from the intersection of the two outer faces** icon in the **Height Datum** section. This measures the flange height from the outer face.

5. Under the **Bend Position** section, click the **Inside of the Bend extents** icon.

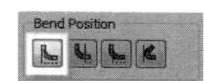

6. Click **OK** to create the flange.

Creating the Contour Flange

1. Draw a sketch on the front face of the flange, as shown in figure.

103

Sheet Metal Modeling

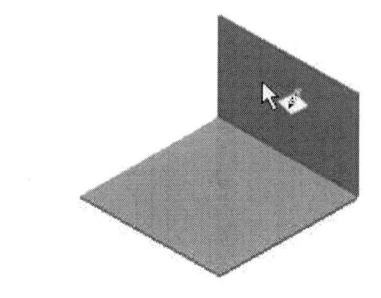

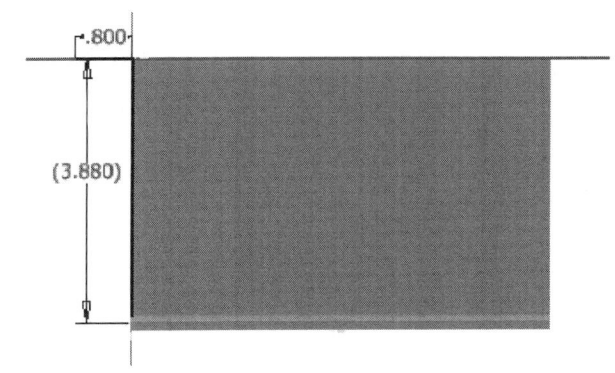

2. Click **Finish Sketch**.

3. To create the contour flange, click **Sheet Metal > Create > Contour Flange** on the ribbon; the **Contour Flange** dialog appears.

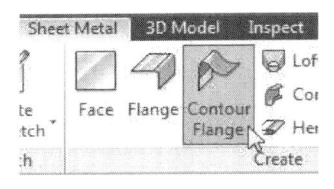

4. Select the sketch from the model.

5. Select the edge on the left side of the top face; the contour flange preview appears.

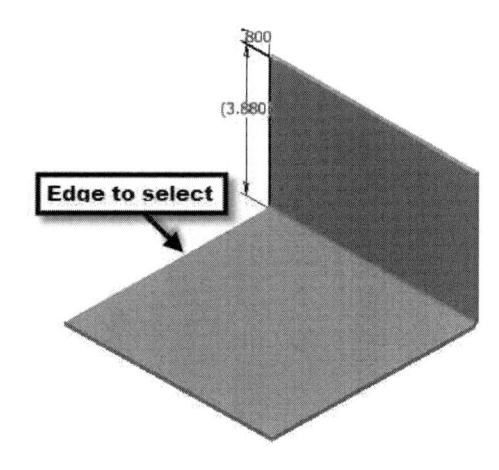

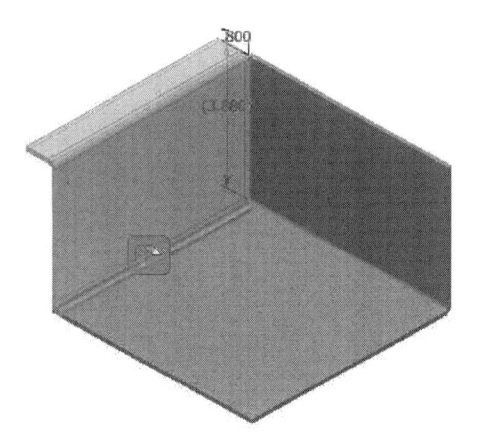

6. Click **>>** located at the bottom of the dialog.

7. Select **Edge** from the **Type** drop-down.

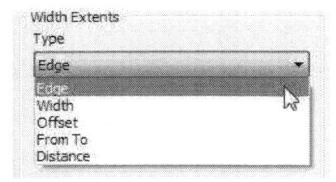

8. Click **OK** to create the contour flange.

104

Sheet Metal Modeling

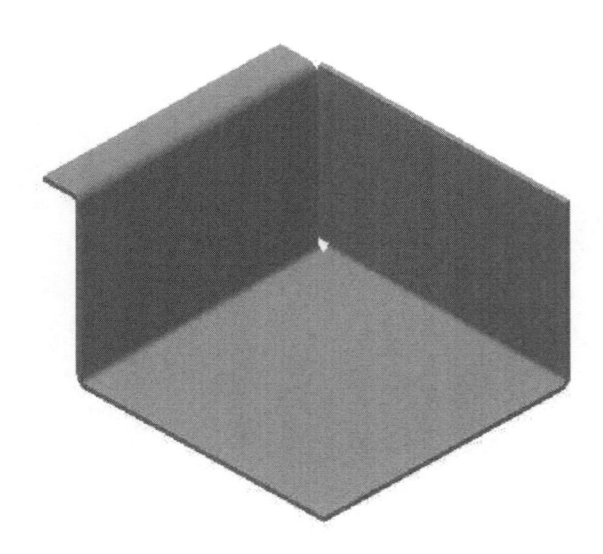

Creating the Corner Seam

1. To create the corner seam, click **Sheet Metal> Modify > Corner Seam** on the ribbon; the **Corner Seam** dialog appears.

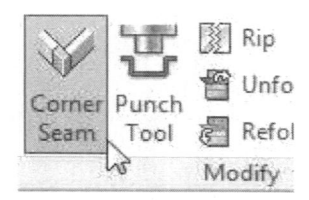

2. Rotate the model.

3. Select the two edges forming the corner.

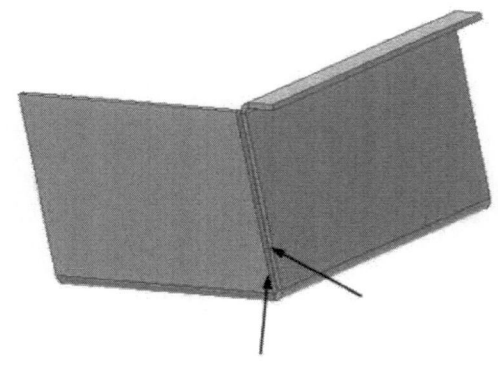

4. Set the parameters in the **Shape** tab of the dialog, as shown.

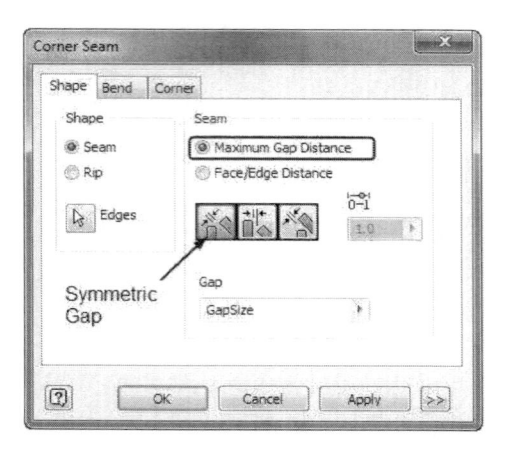

5. Click the **Bend** tab and make sure that the **Default** option is selected in the **Bend Transition** drop-down.

6. Click the **Corner** tab and set the **Relief Shape** to **Round**.

You can also apply other types of relief using the options in the **Relief Shape** drop-down.

7. Click **OK**.

Creating a Sheet Metal Punch iFeature

1. Open a new sheet metal file using the **Sheet Metal.ipt** template.

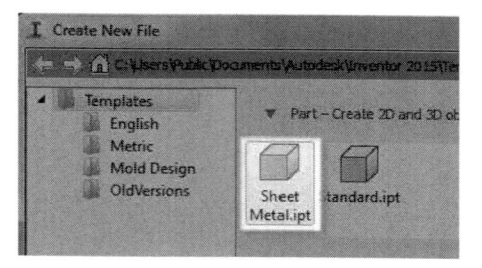

2. Create a sheet metal face of the dimensions 4x4.

105

Sheet Metal Modeling

3. Click **Manage > Parameters > Parameters** f_x on the ribbon; the **Parameters** dialog appears.

4. Select the **User Parameters** row and click the **Add Numeric** button on the dialog. This adds a new row.

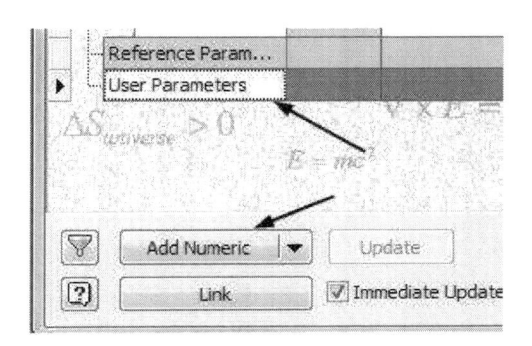

5. Enter **Diameter** in the new row.

6. Set **Unit Type** to **in** and type-in 0.04 in the **Equation** box.

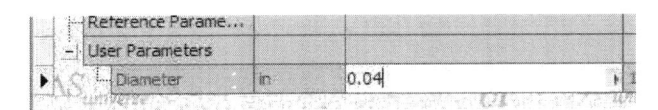

7. Likewise, create a parameter named **Length** and specify its values, as shown below.

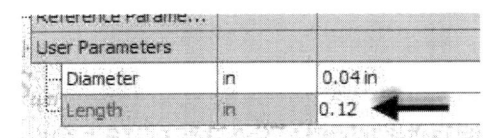

8. Click **Done**.

9. Click **Sheet Metal > Sketch > Start 2D Sketch** on the ribbon.

10. Select the top face of the base feature.

11. Draw a slot, as shown in figure.

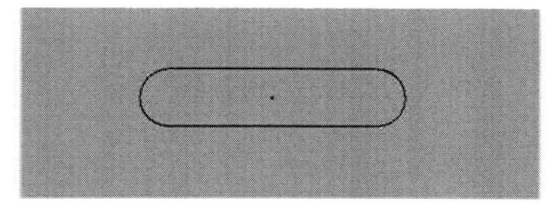

12. Click **Dimension** on the **Constrain** panel and select the round end of the slot.

13. Click to display the **Edit Dimension** box.

14. Click the arrow button on the box and select **List Parameters** from the shortcut menu; the **Parameters** list appears.

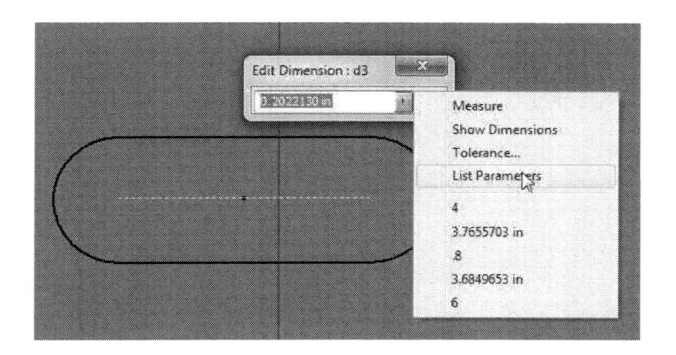

15. Select **Diameter** from the list and click the green check on the **Edit Dimension** box.

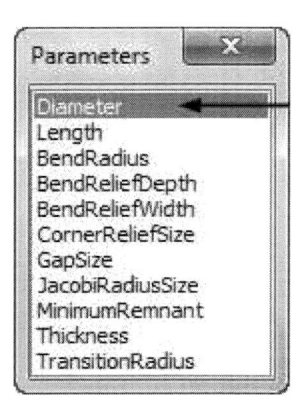

16. Likewise, dimension the horizontal line of the slot and set the parameter to **Length**.

106

Sheet Metal Modeling

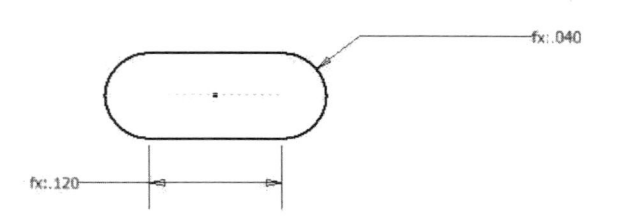

17. Click the **Point** button on the **Create** panel and place it at the center of the slot.

18. Delete any projected edges (yellow lines) from the sketch.

19. Click **Finish Sketch**.

20. Click **Sheet Metal > Modify > Cut** on the ribbon; the **Cut** dialog appears.

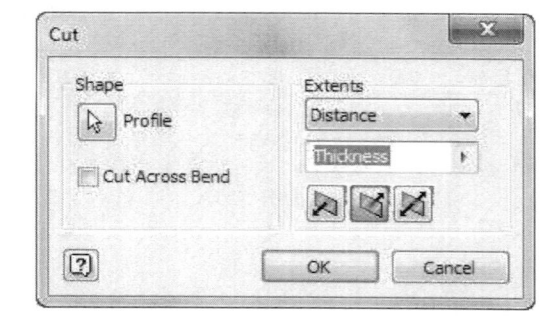

21. Accept the default values and click **OK** to create the cut feature.

22. Click **Manage > Author > Extract iFeature** on the ribbon; the **Extract iFeature** dialog appears.

23. On the dialog, select **Type > Sheet Metal Punch iFeature**.

24. Select the cut feature from the model geometry or from the Browser window. The parameters of the cut feature appear in the **Extract iFeature** dialog.

Next, you must set the **Size Parameters** of the iFeature.

25. Set the **Limit** of the **Diameter** value to **Range**. The **Specify Range** dialog appears.

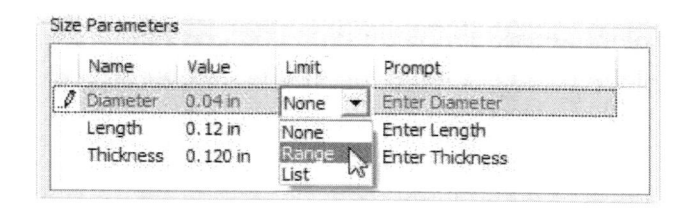

26. Set the values in the **Specify Range** dialog, as shown below and click **OK**.

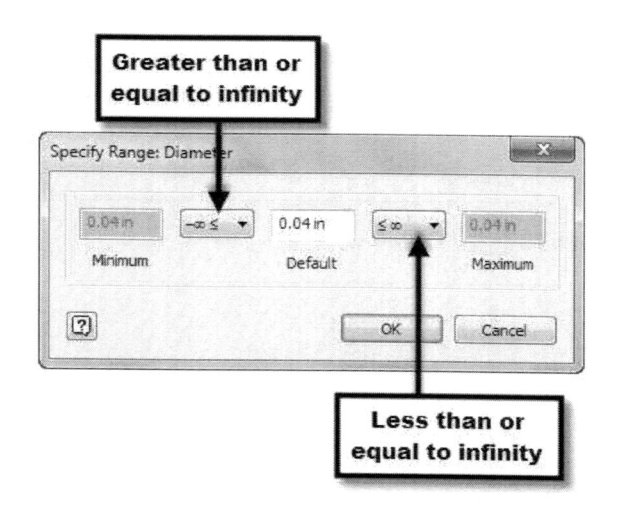

27. Set the **Limit** of the **Length** value to **List**. The **List Values** dialog appears.

28. Click on **Click here to add value** and enter 0.2 as value.

29. Likewise, type-in values in the **List Values**

Sheet Metal Modeling

dialog, as shown below.

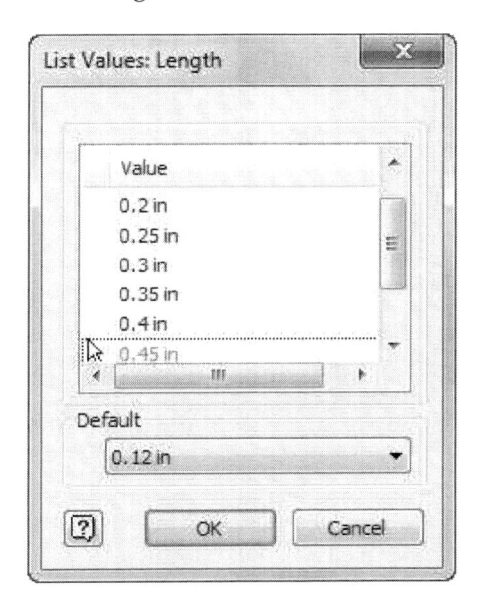

30. Click **OK**.

31. Set the **Limit** of the **Thickness** value to **Range**. The **Specify Range** dialog appears.

32. Set the values in the **Specify Range** dialog, as shown below. Next, click **OK**.

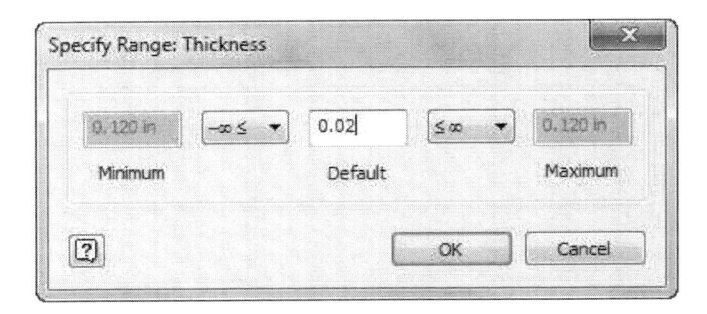

Next, you need to select the center point of the slot. This point will be used while placing the slot.

33. Click the **Select Sketch** button on the **Extract iFeature** dialog.

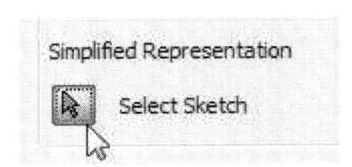

34. Select the sketch of the cut feature from the Browser window.

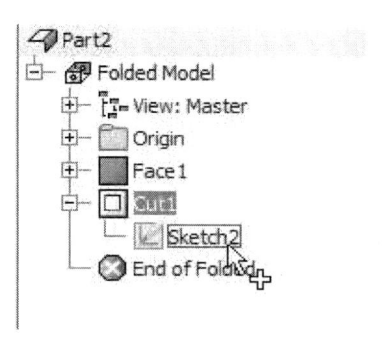

35. Click **Save**; the **Save As** dialog appears.

36. Browse to the **Punches** folder and enter **Custom slot** in the **File name** box.

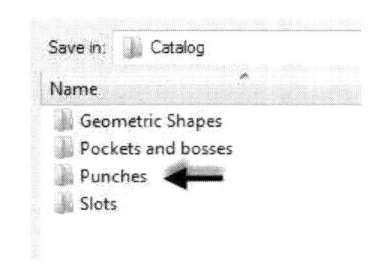

37. Click **Save**.

38. Click **Application Menu > Save**.

39. Save the sheet metal part file as Custom slot.

40. Switch to the sheet metal file of the current tutorial.

Creating a Punched feature

1. Create a sketch on the top face of the base sheet, as shown below.

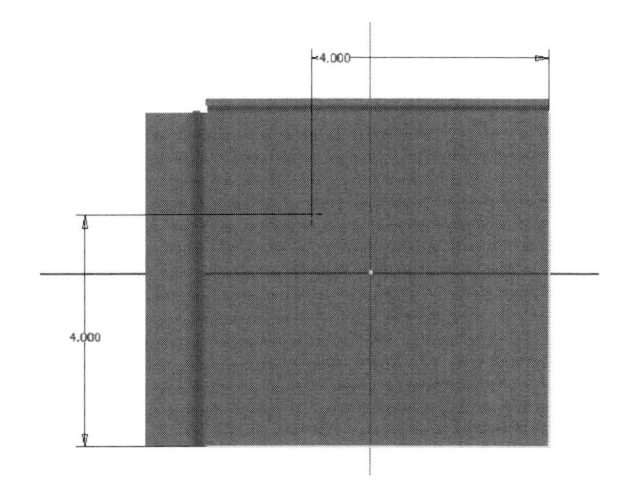

Sheet Metal Modeling

2. Click **Finish Sketch**.

3. To create the punch, click **Sheet Metal > Modify > Punch Tool** on the ribbon; the **PunchTool Directory** dialog appears.

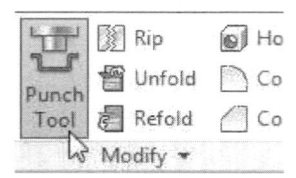

4. Select Custom slot.ide from the dialog and click **Open**; the **PunchTool** dialog appears.

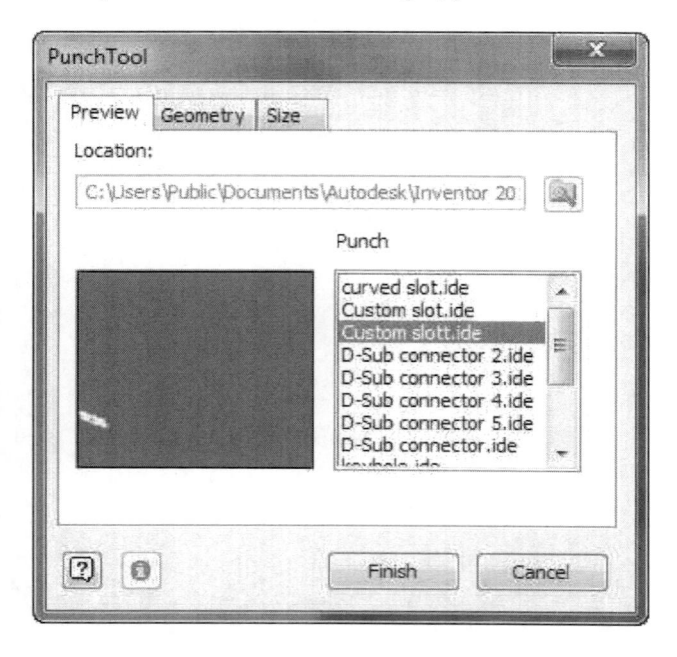

5. Click the **Size** tab on the **PunchTool** dialog.

6. Set **Length** to 0.45 and **Diameter** to 0.1.

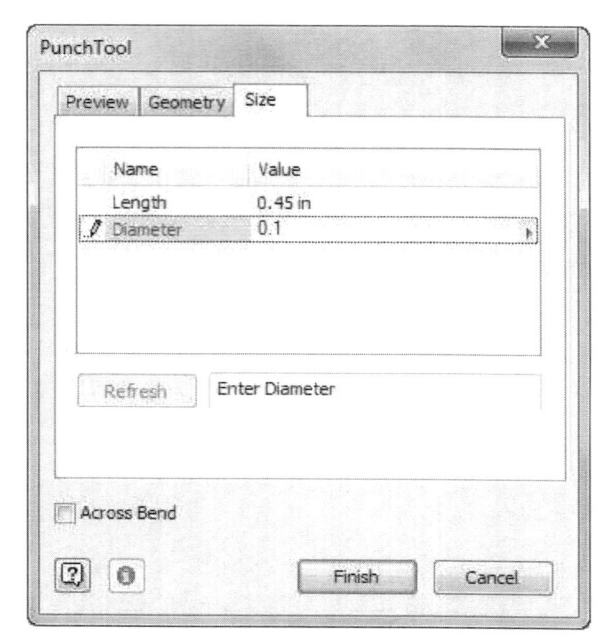

7. Click **Refresh** to preview the slot.

8. Click **Finish** to create the slot.

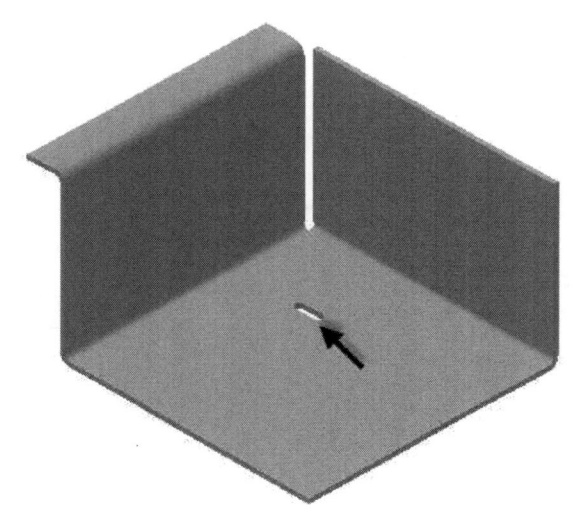

Note: If the slot is not oriented as shown in figure, then click the **Geometry** tab on the **PunchTool** dialog and type-in **90** in the **Angle** box.

Creating the Rectangular Pattern

1. Click **Sheet Metal > Pattern > Rectangular Pattern** on the ribbon. The **Rectangular Pattern** dialog appears.

Sheet Metal Modeling

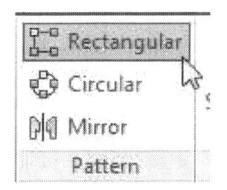

2. Select the slot feature.

*You can also select multiple solid bodies from the graphics window using the **Pattern Solids** option.*

3. Click the **Direction 1** button on the dialog.

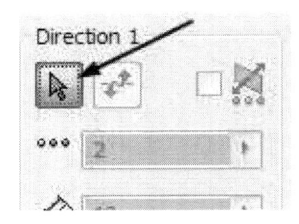

4. Select the edge of the base feature, as shown below.

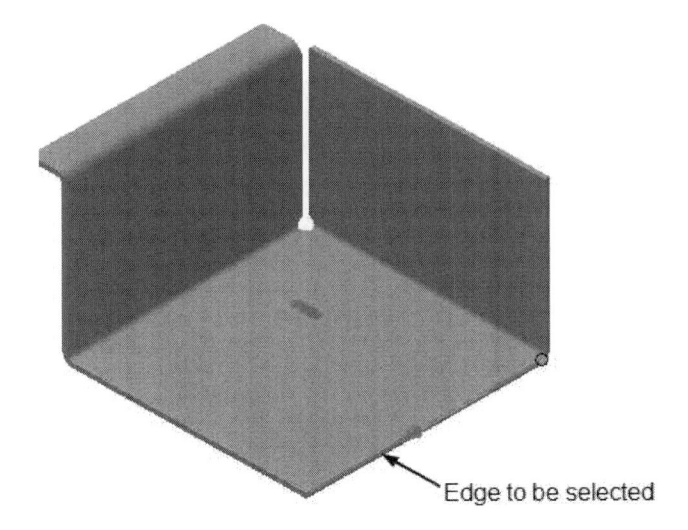

    Edge to be selected

5. Select **Spacing** from the drop-down located in the **Direction 1** group.

6. Specify **Column Count** as 5.

7. Specify **Column Span** as 0.6.

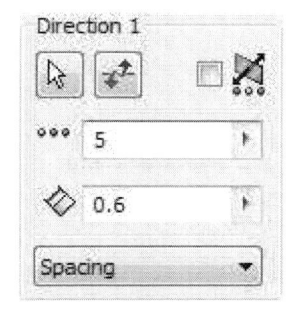

8. Click the **Direction 2** button on the dialog.

9. Select the edge on the base feature, as shown below.

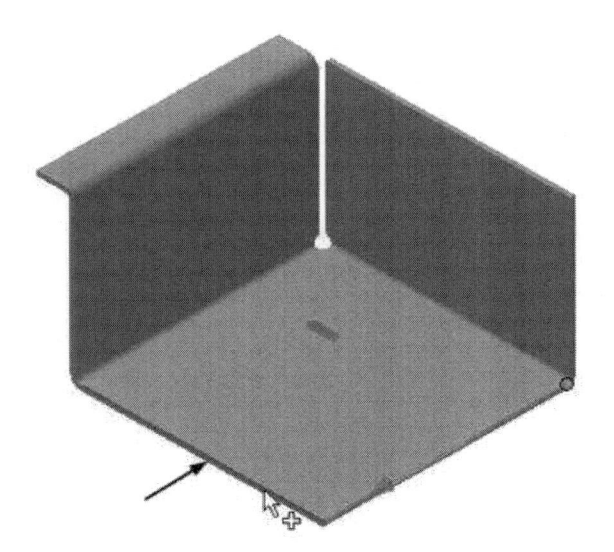

10. Click the **Flip** button to make sure the arrow is pointed toward right.

11. Select **Spacing** from the drop-down located in the **Direction 2** group.

12. Specify **Column Count** as **2**.

13. Specify **Column Span** as 2.

Sheet Metal Modeling

14. Click **OK** to create the pattern.

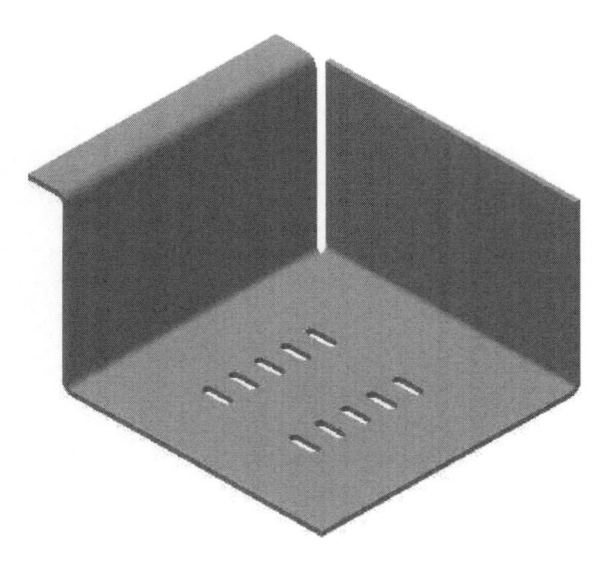

Creating the Bend Feature

1. Create a plane parallel to the front face of the flange feature. The offset distance is 6.3.

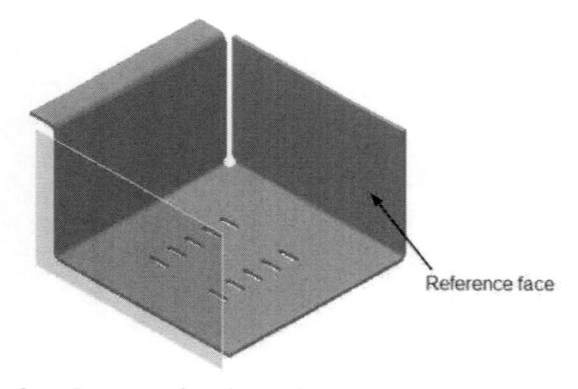

2. Create a sketch on the new work plane.

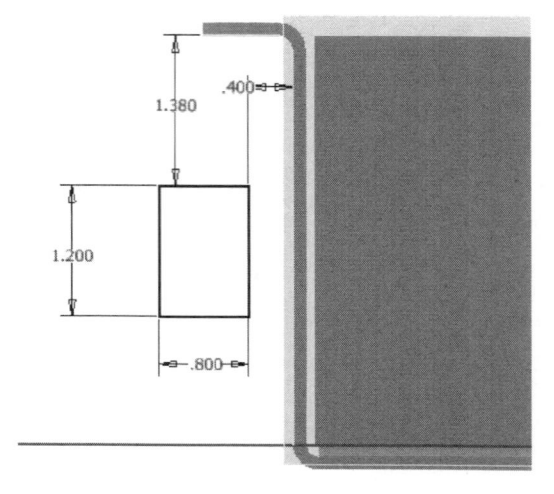

3. Click **Finish Sketch**.

4. Click **Sheet Metal > Create > Face** on the ribbon and create a face feature.

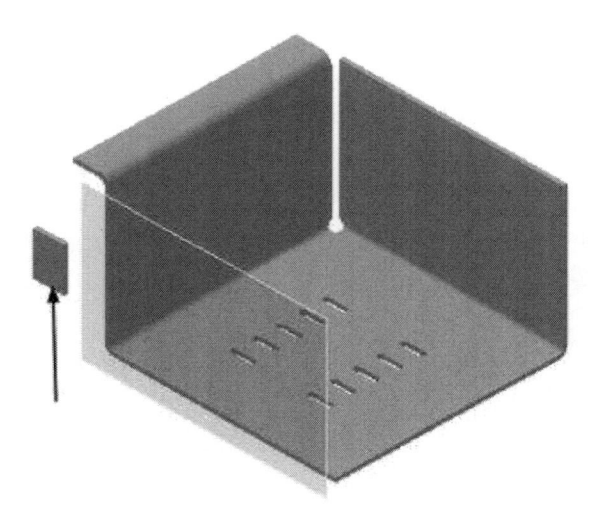

5. Click **Sheet Metal > Create > Bend** on the ribbon. The **Bend** dialog appears.

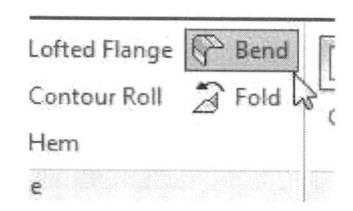

6. Select the edges from the model, as shown below.

111

Sheet Metal Modeling

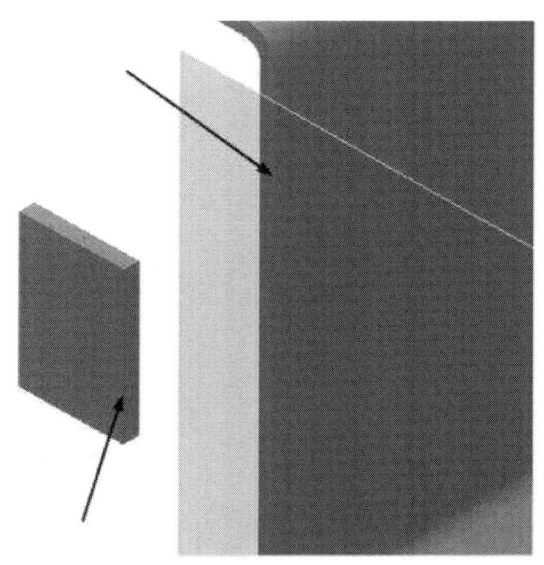

7. Make sure the **Bend Extension** is set to perpendicular.

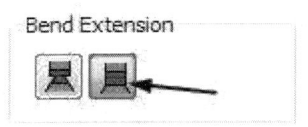

8. Click **OK** to create the bend feature.

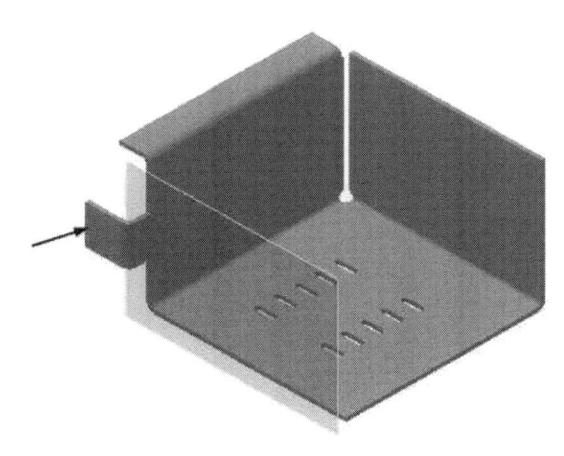

9. Hide the work plane.

Applying a corner round

1. To apply a corner round, click **Sheet Metal > Modify > Corner Round** on the ribbon; the **Corner Round** dialog appears.

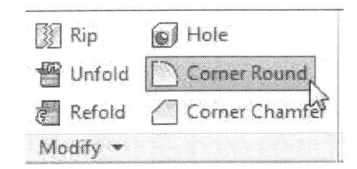

2. Set the **Radius** value to 0.2.

3. Set the **Select Mode** to **Feature**.

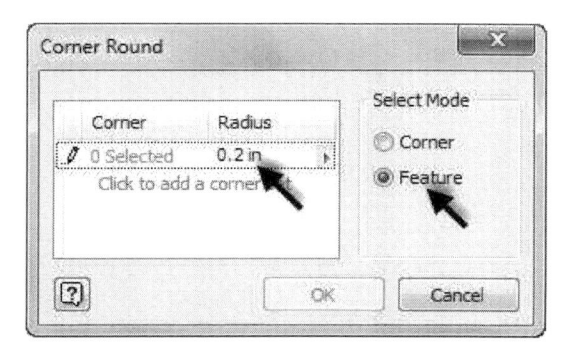

4. Select the face feature from the model.

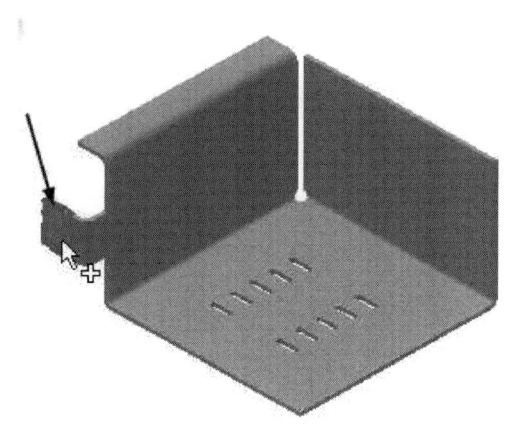

5. Click **OK** to apply the rounds.

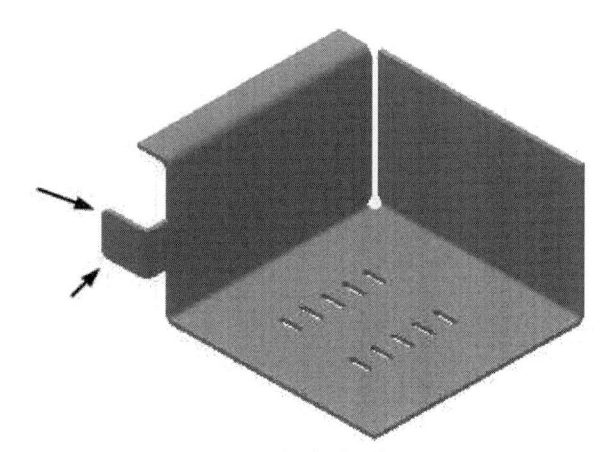

Creating Countersink holes

1. Click **Sheet Metal > Modify > Hole** on the ribbon; the **Hole** dialog appears.

112

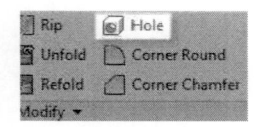

Sheet Metal Modeling

2. Set the **Placement** method to **Concentric**.

3. Set the hole type to **Countersink**.

4. Set the other parameters on the dialog, as shown below.

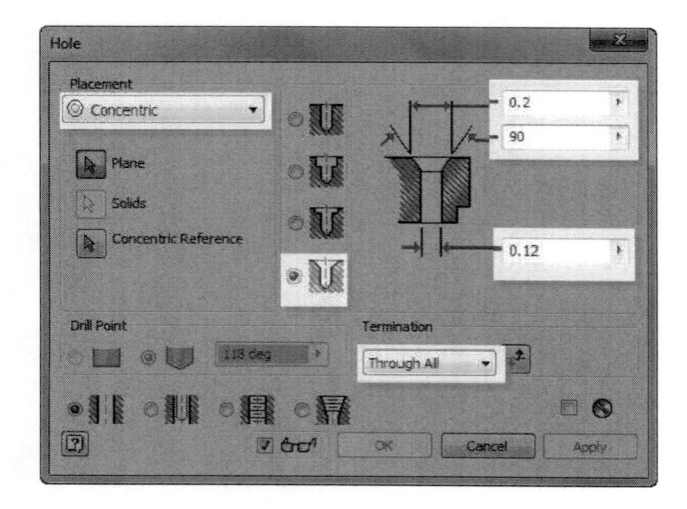

5. Click on the face of the flange, as shown below.

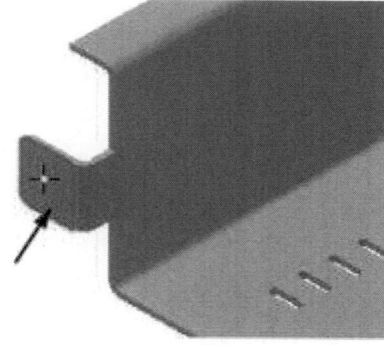

6. Select the corner round as the concentric reference.

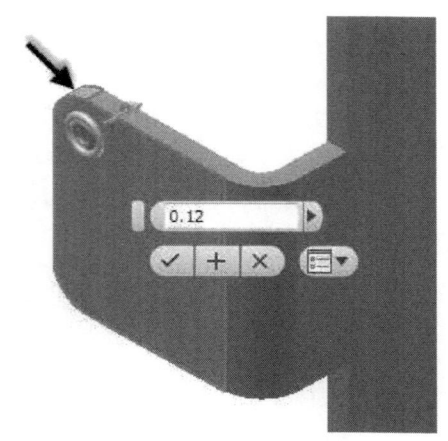

7. Click **Apply**.

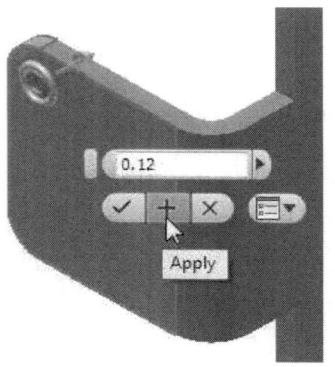

8. Again, click on the flange face and select the other corner round as the concentric reference.

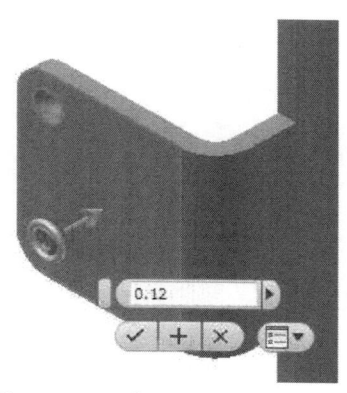

9. Click **OK** to create the countersink.

Creating Hem features

1. To create the hem feature, click **Sheet Metal > Create > Hem** on the ribbon; the **Hem** dialog appears.

113

Sheet Metal Modeling

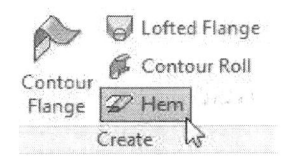

2. Set the **Type** to **Single**.

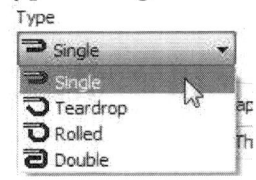

3. Select the edge of the contour flange, as shown below.

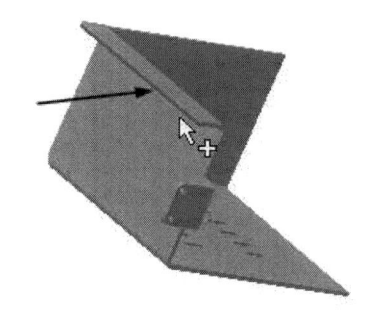

4. Leave the default settings of the dialog and click **OK** to create the hem.

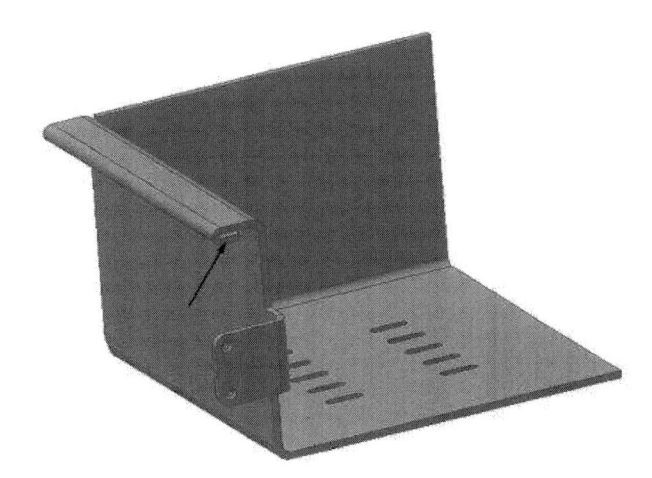

Mirroring the Features

1. Click **Mirror** on the **Pattern** panel; the **Mirror** dialog appears.

2. Click **>>** at the bottom of the dialog and make sure the **Creation Method** is set to **Identical**.

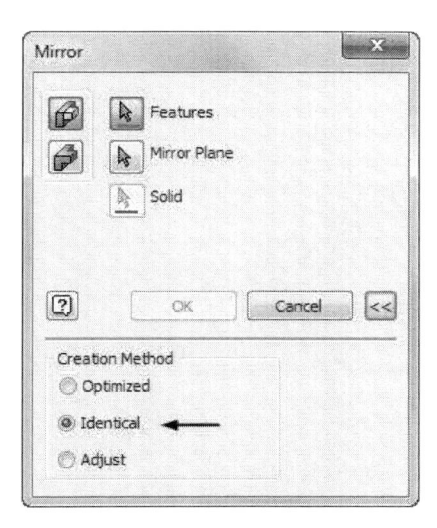

3. Select the features from the Browser window, as shown below.

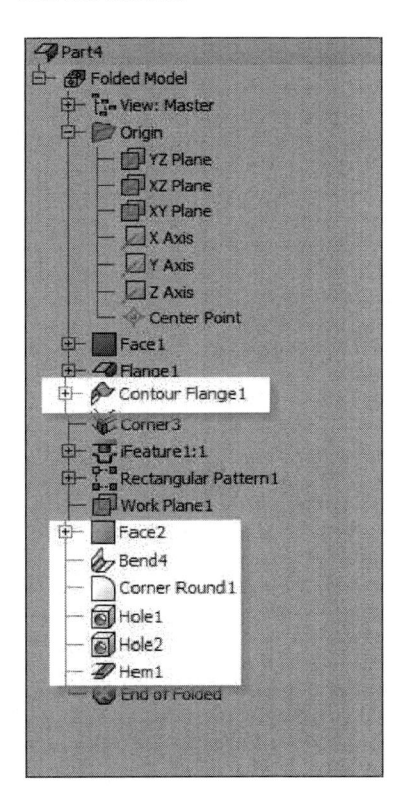

4. Click the **Mirror Plane** button on the dialog and select the YZ Plane from the Browser window.

114

Sheet Metal Modeling

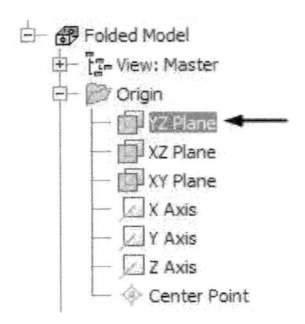

5. Click **OK** to mirror the feature.

6. Create a corner seam between the mirrored counter flange and flange.

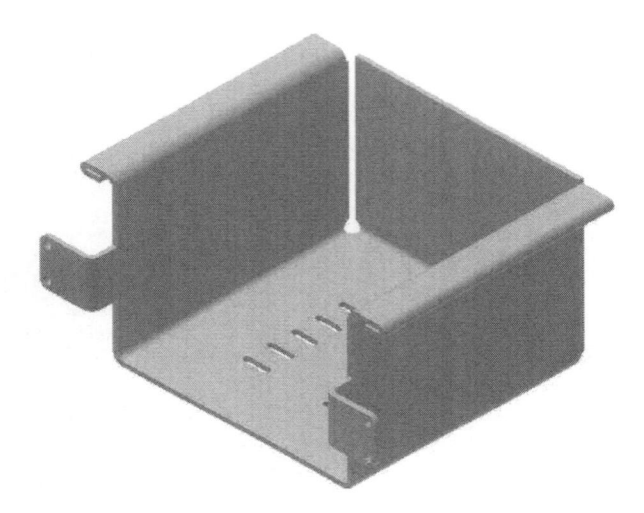

Creating the Flat Pattern
1. To create a flat pattern, click **Sheet Metal > Flat Pattern > Flat Pattern** on the ribbon.

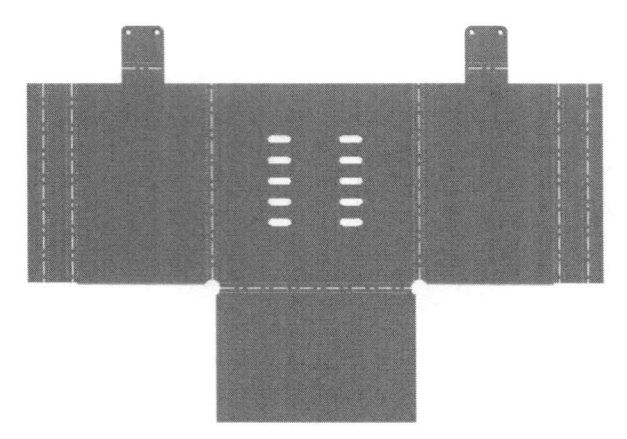

You can set the order in which the bends will be annotation.

2. Click the **Bend Order Annotation** button on the **Manage** panel. The order in which the bends will be annotated is displayed.

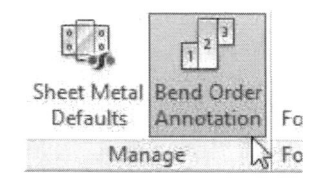

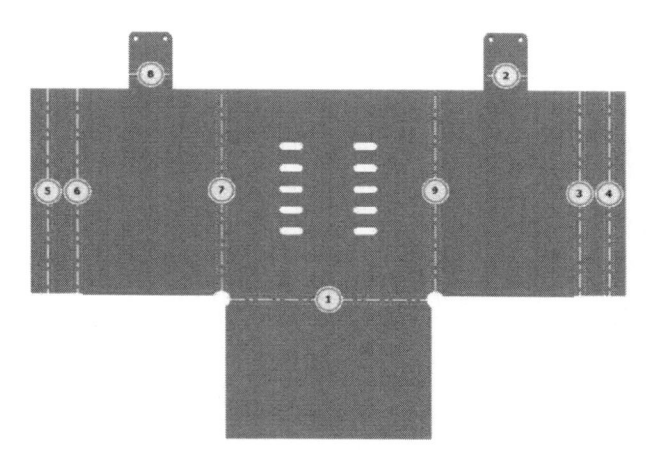

3. To change the order of the bend annotation, click on the balloon displayed on the bend. The **Bend Order Edit** dialog appears.

4. Select the **Bend Number** check box and enter a new number in the box.

115

Sheet Metal Modeling

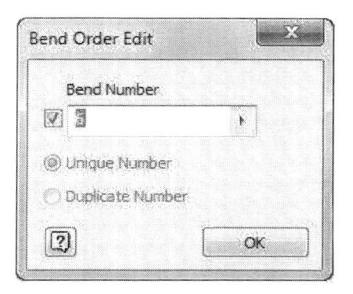

5. Click **OK** to change the order.

6. To switch back to the folded view of the model, click **Go to Folded Part** on the **Folded Part** panel.

7. Save the sheet metal part.

Creating 2D Drawing of the sheet metal part

1. On the Quick Access toolbar, click the **New** button.

2. On the **Create New File** dialog, double-click on **Standard.idw**.

3. Activate the **Base View** tool and insert the Isometric view on the drawing sheet.

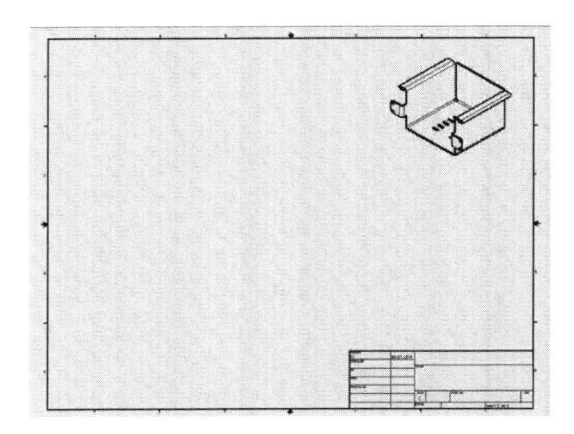

4. Likewise, create the front, and top views of the sheet metal part.

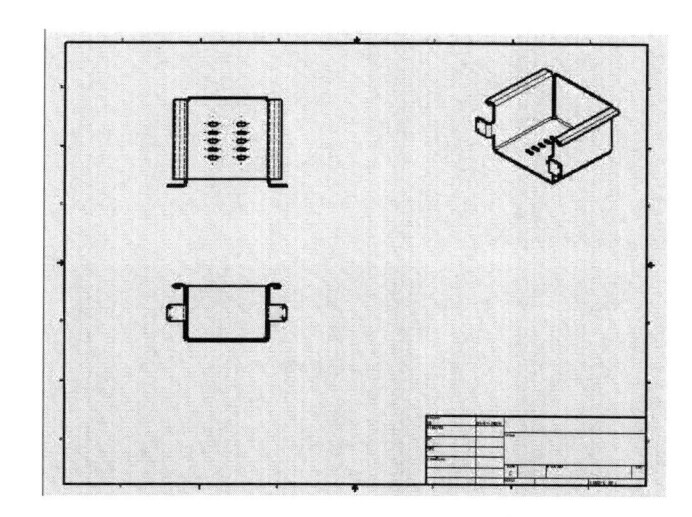

5. Activate the **Base View** tool and select **Sheet Metal View > Flat Pattern** on the **Drawing View** dialog.

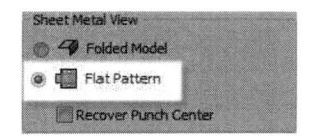

6. Place the flat pattern view below the Isometric view.

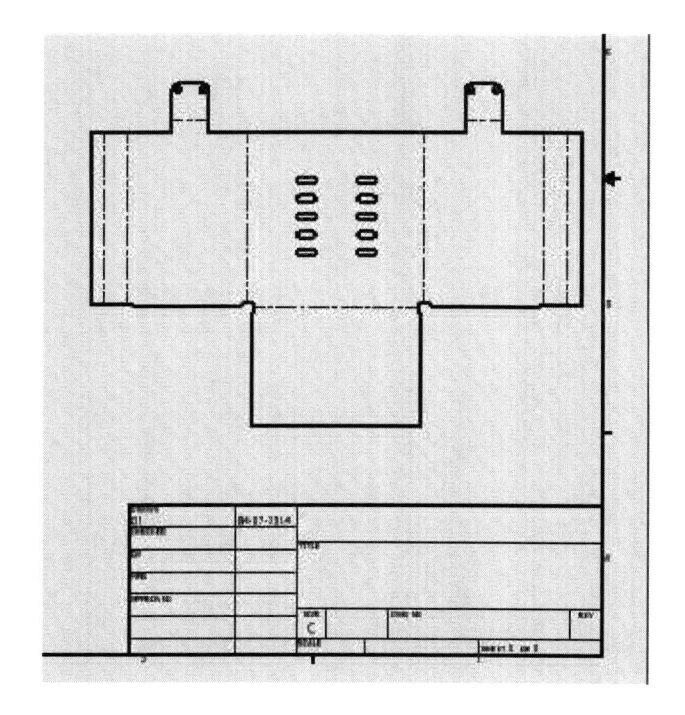

7. To add bend notes to the flat pattern, click **Annotate > Feature Notes > Bend** on the ribbon.

116

Sheet Metal Modeling

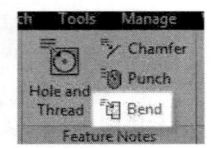

8. Click the horizontal bend line on the flat pattern to add the bend note.

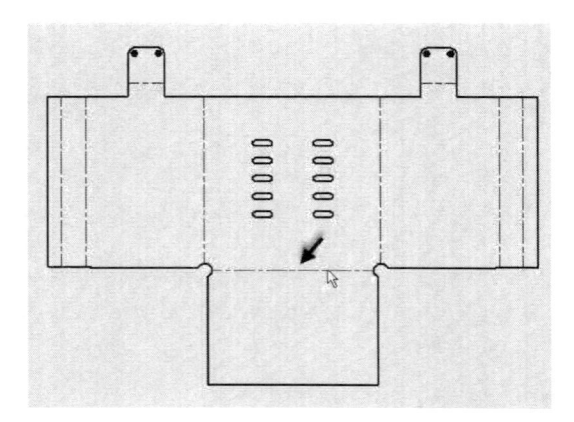

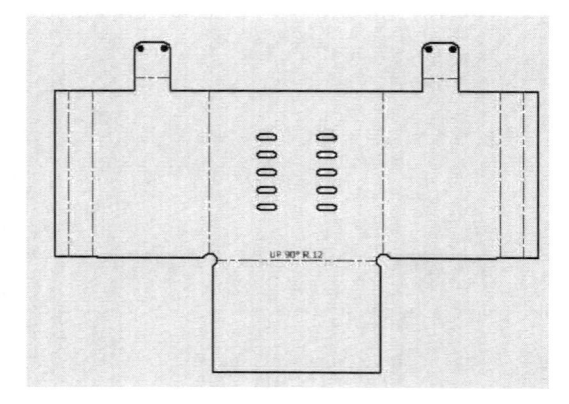

9. Likewise, select other bend lines on the flat pattern. You can also drag a selection box to select all the bend lines from the flat pattern view.

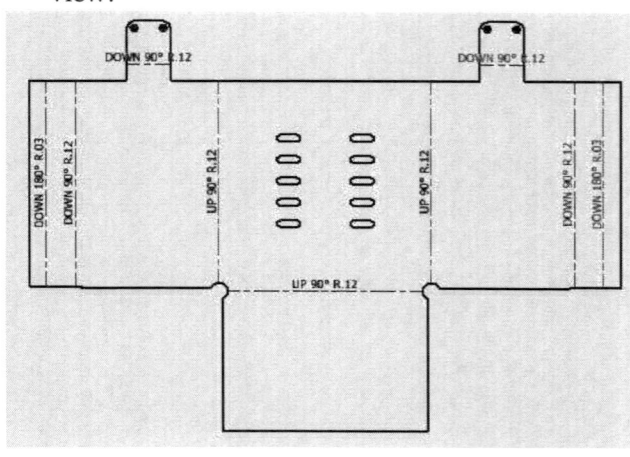

10. To add centerlines to the flat pattern view, click the right mouse button on it and select **Automated Centerlines**.

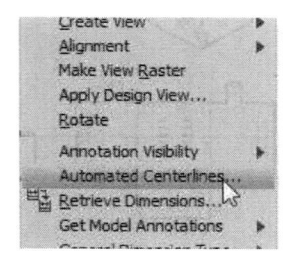

11. On the **Automated Centerlines** dialog, click the **Punches** button under the **Apply To** section.

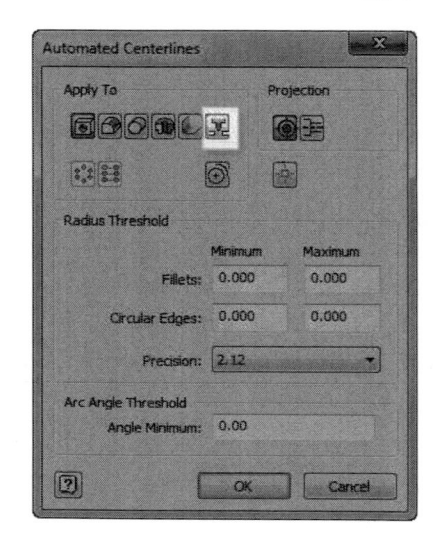

12. Click **OK** to add centerlines to the flat pattern view.

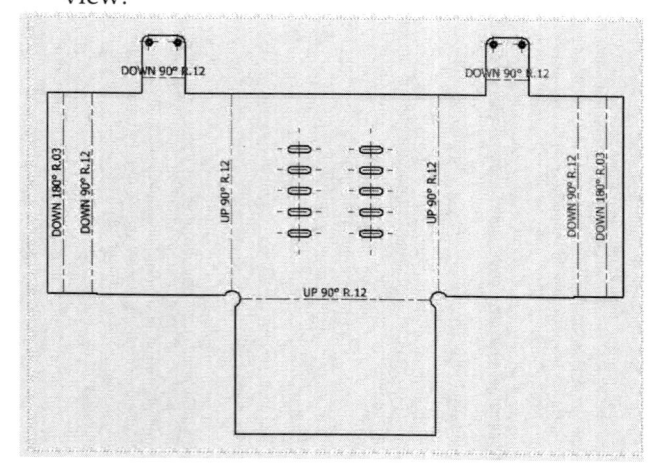

13. Likewise, add centerlines to other views on the drawing sheet.

117

Sheet Metal Modeling

14. To add a punch note, click **Annotate > Feature Notes > Punch** on the ribbon.

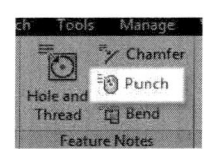

15. Zoom into the flat pattern view and click on the arc of the slot.

16. Move the pointer and click to create annotation.

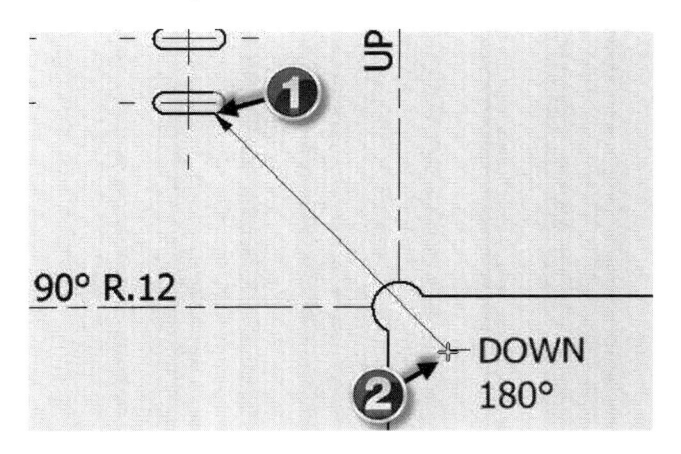

17. Use the **Retrieve Dimension** and **Dimension** tools to add dimensions to drawing.

18. Save and close the drawing and sheet metal part.

Top-Down Assembly and Motion Simulation

Chapter 7: Top-Down Assembly and Motion Simulation

In this chapter, you will learn to

- Create a top-down assembly
- Insert Fasteners using Design Accelerator
- Create assembly joints

TUTORIAL 1
In this tutorial, you will create the model shown in figure. You use top-down assembly approach to create this model.

Creating a New Assembly File
1. To create a new assembly, click **New Assembly** on the welcome screen.

Creating a component in the Assembly
In a top-down assembly approach, you create components of an assembly directly in the assembly by using the **Create** tool.

1. Click **Create** on the **Component** panel. The **Create In-Place Component** dialog appears.

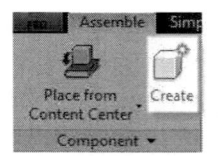

2. Enter **Base** in the **New Component Name** field.

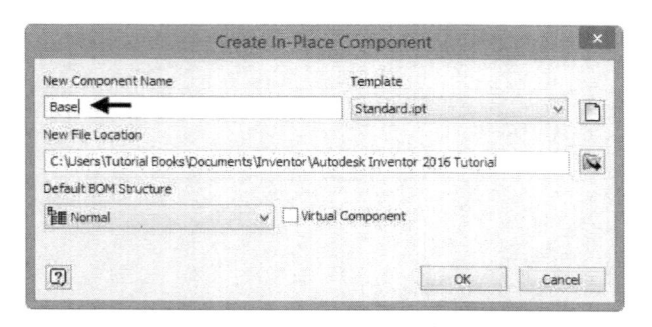

3. In the **Create In-Place Component** dialog, set the **New File Location** to the current project folder.

4. Click the **Browse to New File Location** icon.

5. On the **Save As** dialog, click the **Create New Folder** icon.

6. Type **C07_Tut_01** as the name of the folder.

7. Double-click on the new folder and click Save.

8. Click **OK** on the **Create In-Place Component** dialog.

9. Expand the **Origin** folder in **Browser window** and select the **XZ Plane**. The **3D Model** tab is activated in the ribbon.

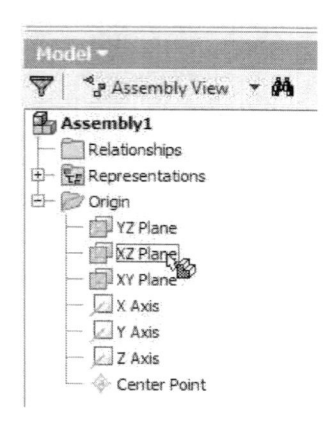

10. Click **Sketch > Start 2D Sketch** on the ribbon.

119

Top-Down Assembly and Motion Simulation

11. Select **XY Plane**.

12. Create a sketch as shown below.

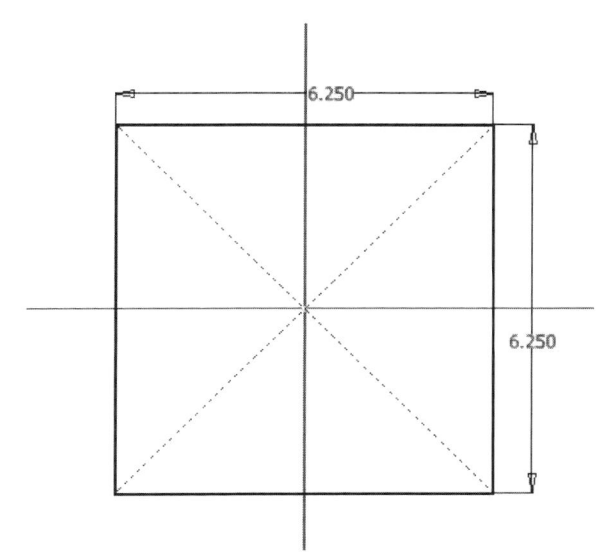

12. Click **Finish Sketch**.

13. Click **3D Model > Create > Extrude** on the ribbon and extrude the sketch up to 1.5 in.

14. Start a sketch on the top face and draw a circle of **2** in diameter.

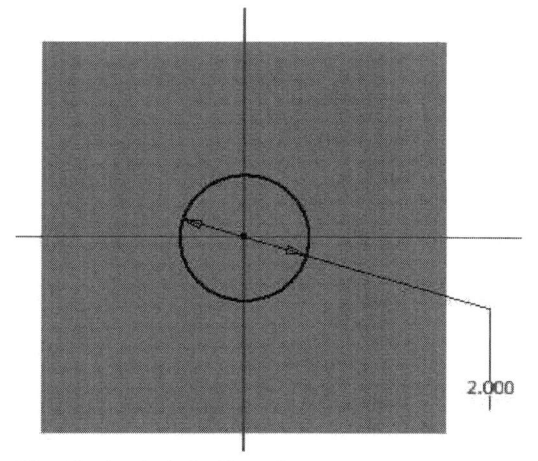

15. Click **Finish Sketch**

16. Extrude the sketch up to 3.75 in distance.

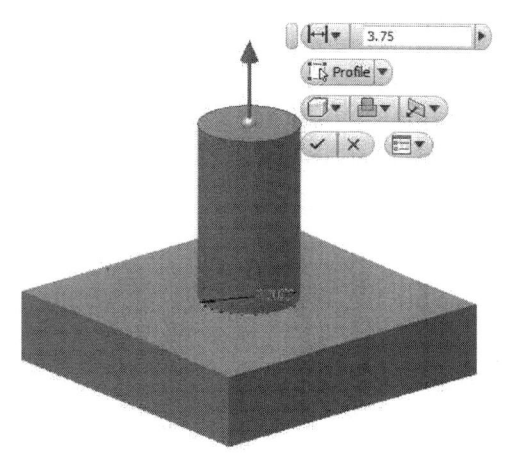

17. Create a counterbore hole on the second feature.

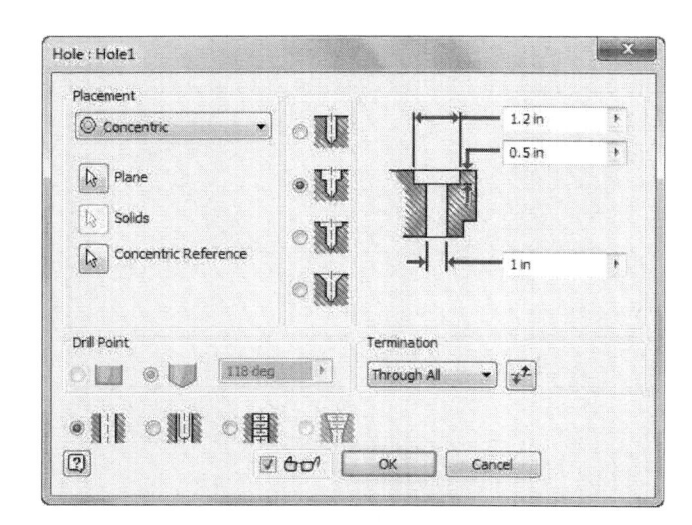

120

Top-Down Assembly and Motion Simulation

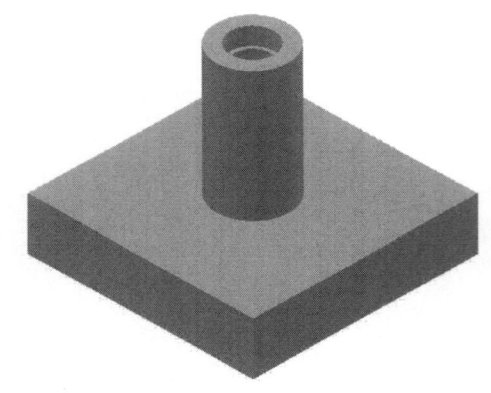

18. Create a through hole of 0.5 diameter on the first feature.

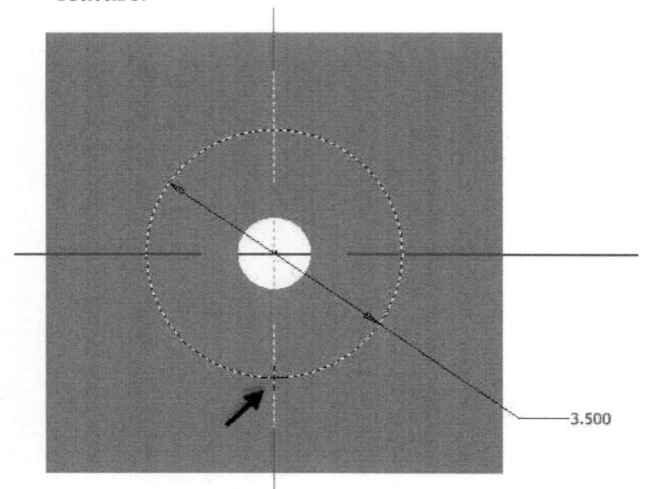

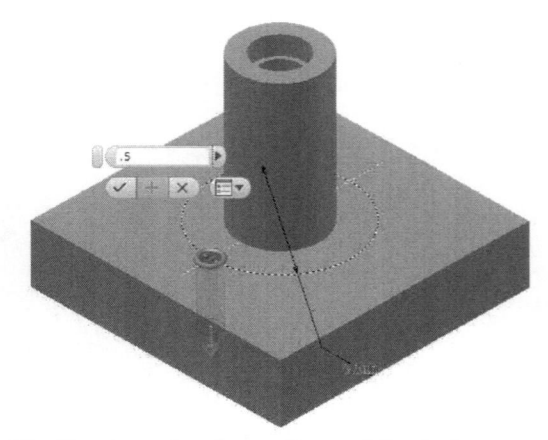

19. Create a circular pattern of the hole.

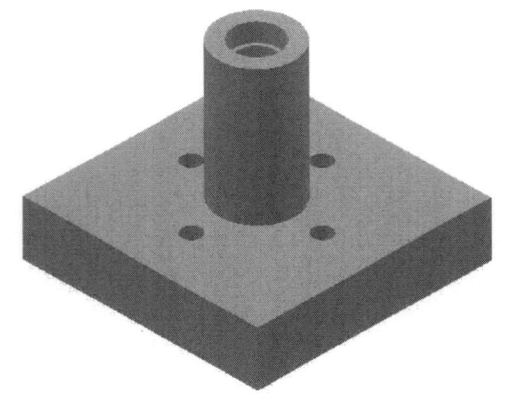

20. Click the **Return** button on the ribbon.

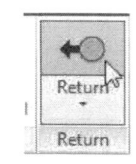

Creating the Second Component of the Assembly

1. Click **Assemble > Component > Create** on the ribbon; the **Create In-Place Component** dialog appears.

2. Enter **Spacer** in the **New Component name** field.

3. Check **Constrain sketch plane to selected face or plane** option.

4. Click **OK**.

5. Select the top face of the Base.

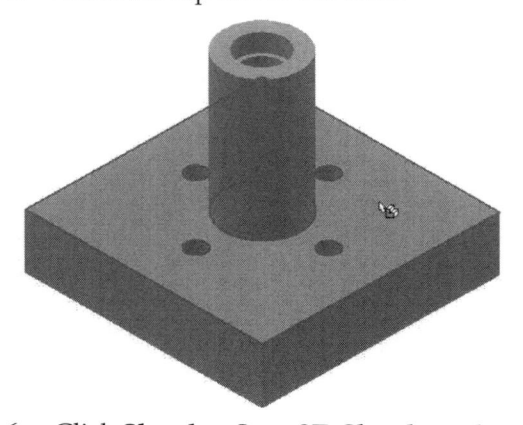

6. Click **Sketch > Start 2D Sketch** on the ribbon.

Top-Down Assembly and Motion Simulation

7. Select top face of the Base.

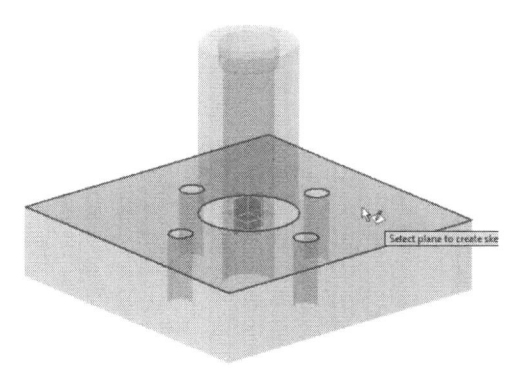

8. On the ribbon, click **Sketch > Create > Project Geometry** and select the circular edges of the Base.

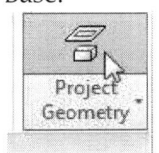

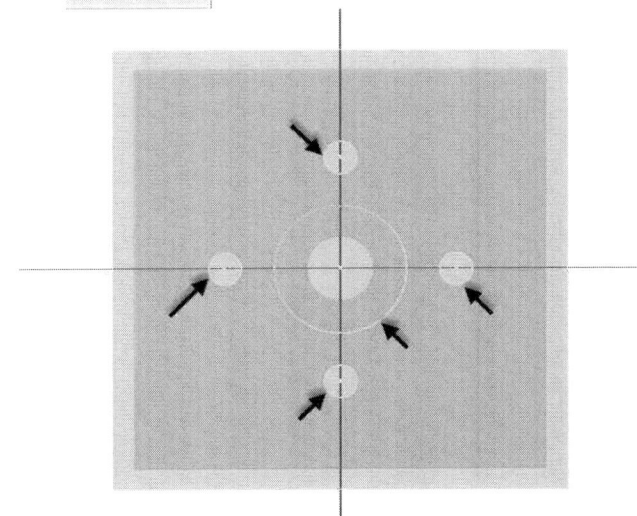

9. Draw a circle of 4.5 in diameter.

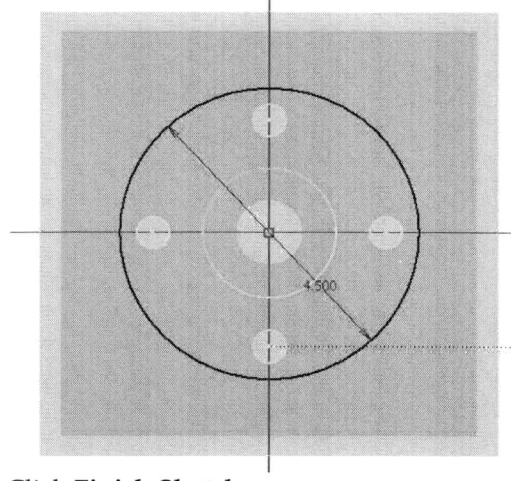

10. Click **Finish Sketch**.

11. Extrude the sketch up to 1.5 in.

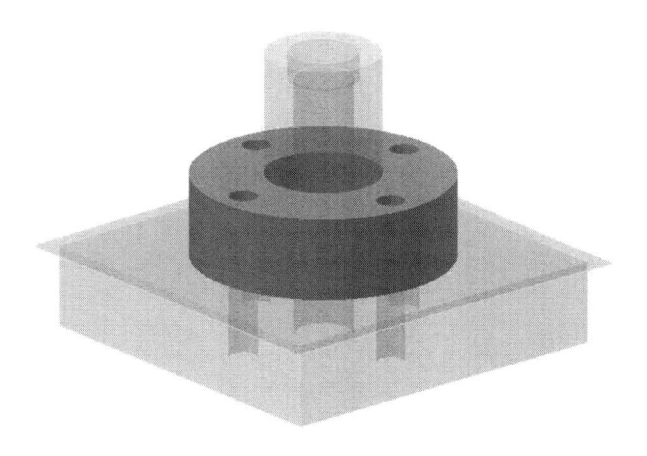

12. Click **Return** on the ribbon.

Creating the third Component of the Assembly

1. Click **Assemble > Component > Create** on the ribbon; the **Create In-Place Component** dialog appears.

2. Enter **Shoulder Screw** in the **New Component name** field.

3. Check **Constrain sketch plane to selected face or plane** option.

4. Click **OK**.

Top-Down Assembly and Motion Simulation

5. Click on the top face of the Base.

6. Start a sketch on the YZ Plane.

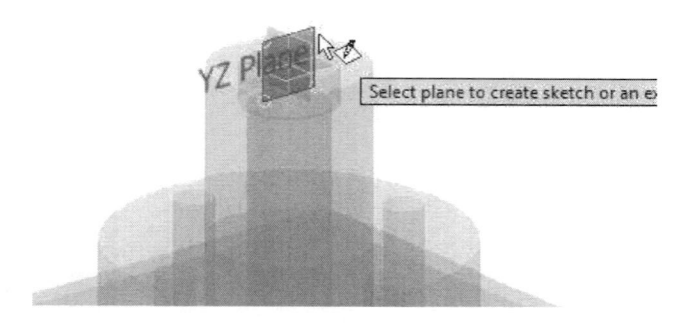

7. Draw a sketch, as shown in figure.

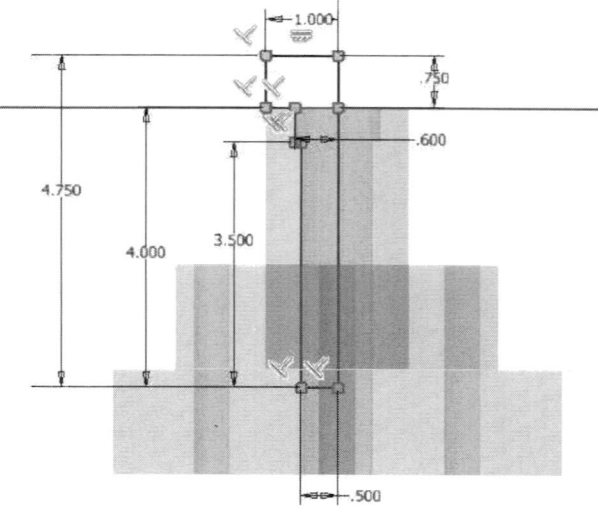

8. Click **Finish Sketch**.

9. Activate the **Revolve** tool and revolve the sketch.

10. Activate the **Chamfer** tool and chamfer the edges, as shown in figure.

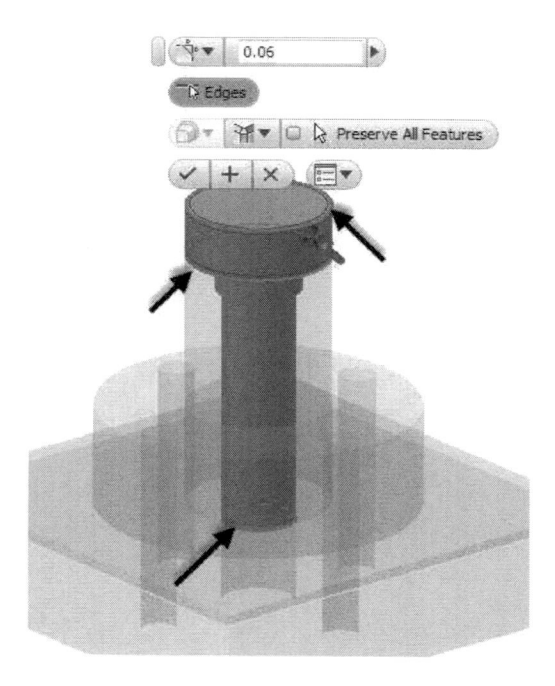

11. Activate the **Fillet** tool and round the edges, as shown in figure.

123

Top-Down Assembly and Motion Simulation

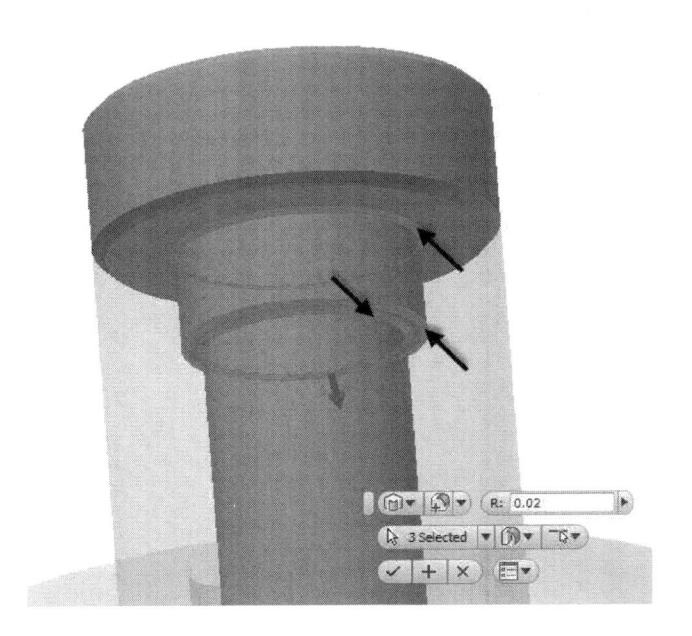

12. Click **Return** on the ribbon.

13. Save the assembly.

Adding Bolt Connections to the assembly

1. On the ribbon, click **Design > Fasten > Bolt Connection**.

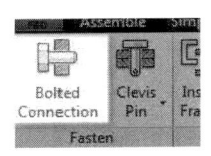

2. On the **Bolted Connection Component Generator** dialog, under the **Design** tab, select **Type > Through All**.

3. Select **Placement > Concentric**.

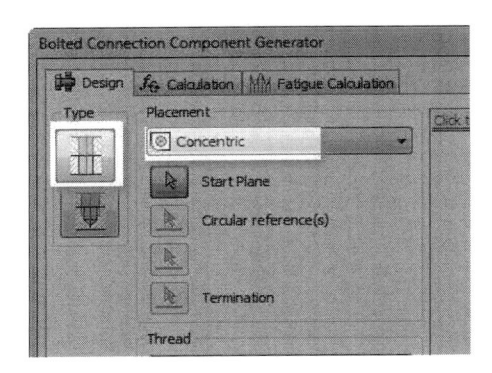

4. Select the top face of the Spacer.

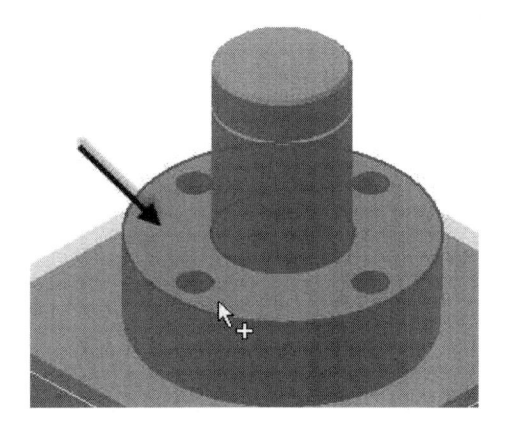

5. Click on the hole to define the circular reference.

6. Rotate the model and click on the bottom face of the base. This defines the termination.

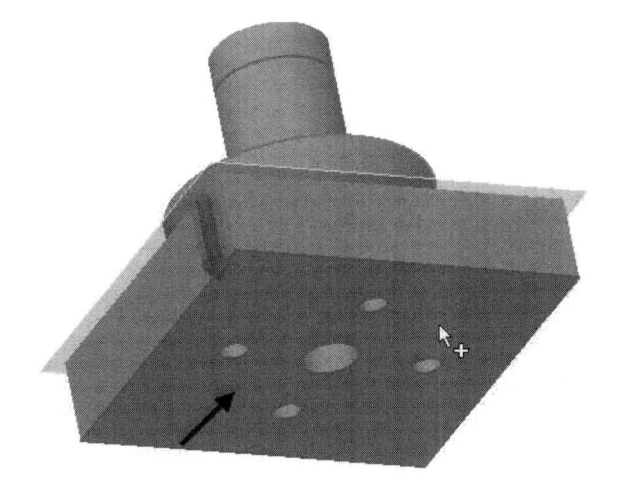

7. On the dialog, set the **Thread** type to **ANSI Unified Screw Threads**.

8. Make sure that the **Diameter** is set to **0.5** in.

Top-Down Assembly and Motion Simulation

9. On the dialog, click **Click to add a fastener**.

10. On the pop up dialog, set the **Standard** to **ANSI** and **Category** to **Hex Head Bolt**.

11. Select **Hex Bolt-Inch**. This adds a hex bolt to the list.

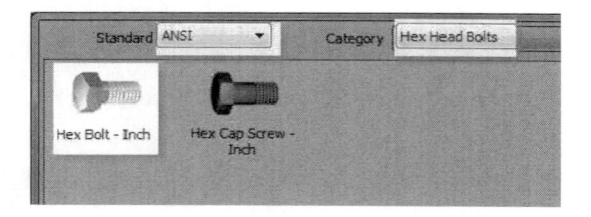

12. On the list, click **Click to add a fastener** below the Hex Bolt.

13. On the pop up dialog, scroll down and select **Plain Washer (Inch)**.

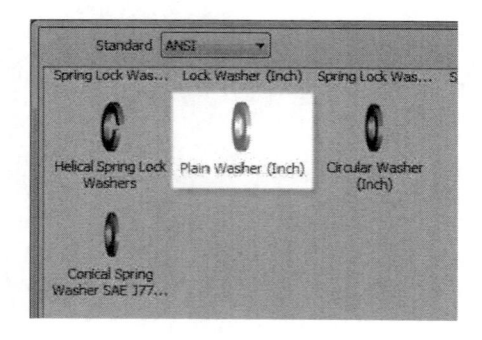

14. Click **Click to add a fastener** at the bottom of the list.

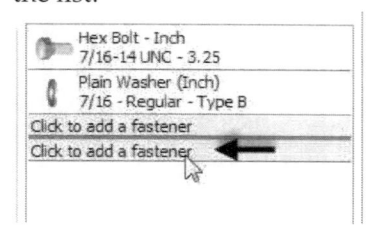

15. On the pop up dialog, scroll down and select **Plain Washer (Inch)**.

16. Click **Click to add a fastener** at the bottom of the list.

17. On the pop up dialog, set the **Category** to **Nuts** and select **Hex Nut -Inch**.

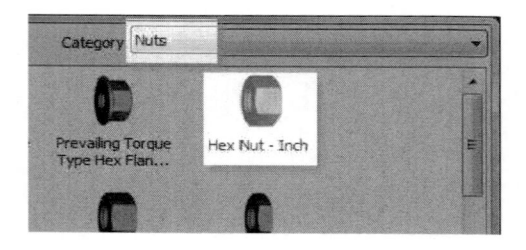

18. Click **OK** twice to add a bolt connection subassembly.

Patterning components in an assembly

1. On the ribbon, click **Assemble > Pattern > Pattern**.

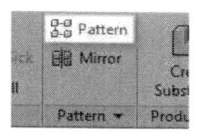

2. Select the **Bolt connection** from the Browser window.

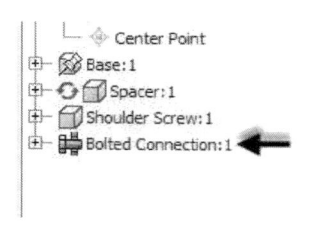

3. On the **Pattern Component** dialog, click the **Circular** tab and select the **Axis Direction** button.

125

Top-Down Assembly and Motion Simulation

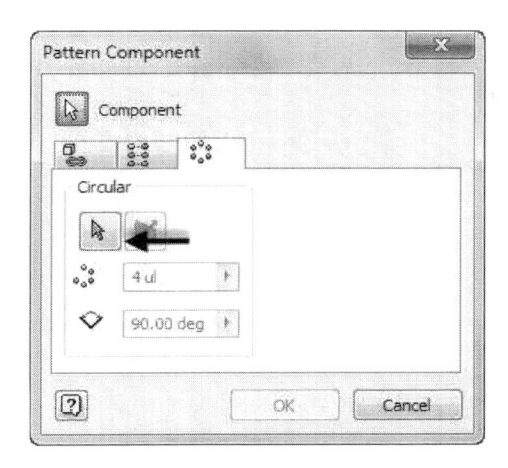

4. Click on the large cylindrical face of the Spacer to define the axis of the circular pattern.

5. On the dialog, type-in 4 and 90 in the **Circular Count** and **Circular Angle** boxes, respectively.

6. Click **OK** to pattern the bolt connection.

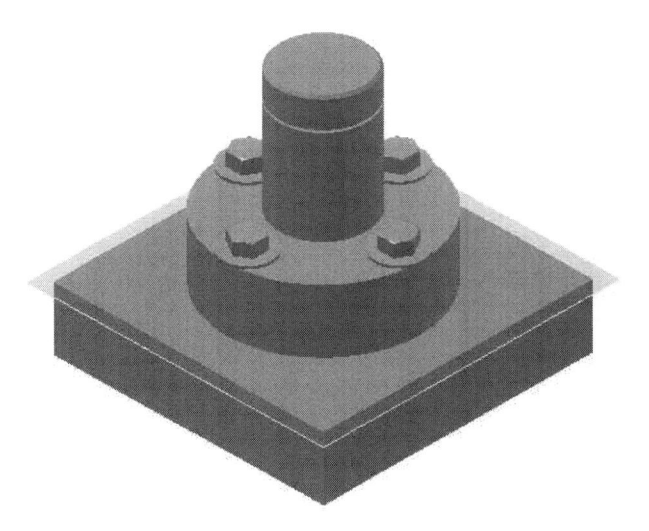

Applying the constraint to the components

1. On the ribbon, click **View > Visibility > Degrees of Freedom**.

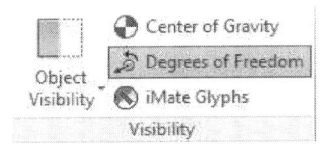

2. On the ribbon, click **Assemble > Relationships > Constrain**.

3. On the dialog, click the **Mate** icon and click on the cylindrical faces of the Spacer and Base.

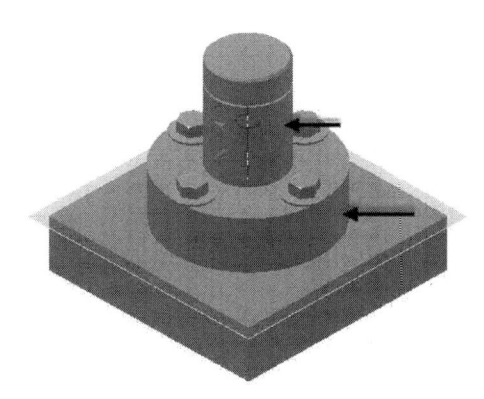

4. Click **Apply**.

5. Click on the cylindrical faces of the Shoulder Screw and Base.

Top-Down Assembly and Motion Simulation

6. Click **Apply**.

7. On the dialog, select **Flush** from the **Solution** section.

8. In the Browser Window, expand the **Origin** folder and select XY Plane.

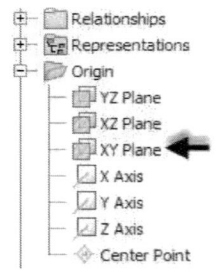

9. Expand the **Origin** folder of the Shoulder Screw and select XZ Plane.

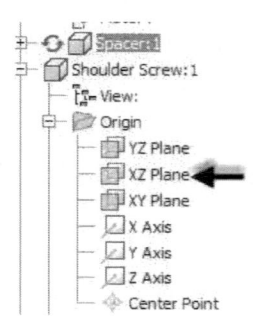

10. Click **OK** to fully-constrain the assembly.

11. Save the assembly and all its parts.

TUTORIAL 2

In this tutorial, you create a slider crank mechanism by applying Joints.

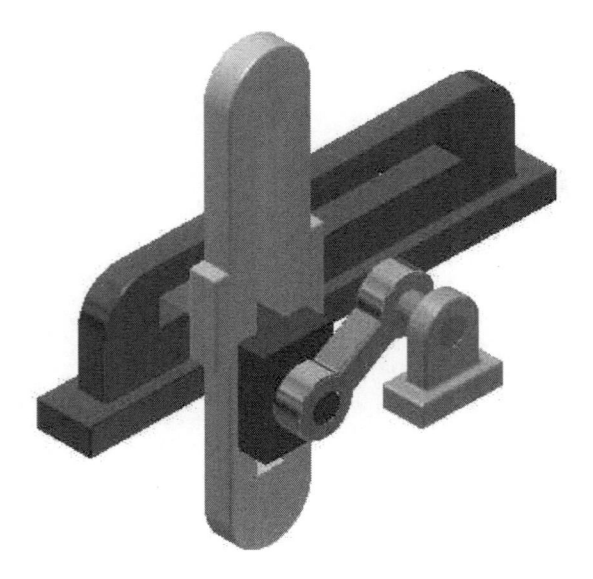

1. Create the **Slider Crank Assembly** folder inside the project folder.

2. Download the part files of the assembly from the companion website. Next, save the files in the **Slider Crank Assembly** folder.

3. Start a new assembly file using the **Standard.iam** template.

4. Click **Assemble > Component > Place** on the ribbon.

5. Browse to the **Slider Crank Assembly** folder and double-click on **Base**.

6. Right-click and select **Place Grounded at Origin**.

7. Right click and select **OK**.

Top-Down Assembly and Motion Simulation

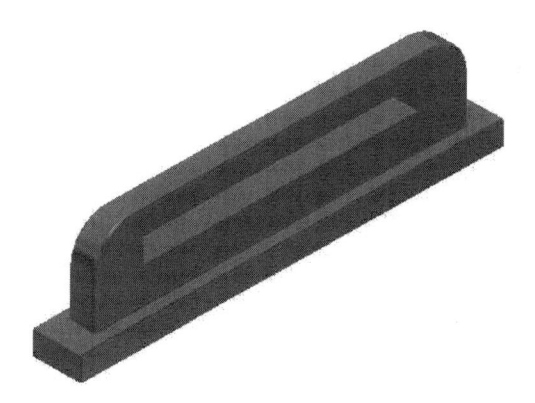

8. Click **Assemble > Component > Place** on the ribbon.

9. Browse to the **Slider Crank Assembly** folder and select all the parts except the **Base**.

10. Click **Open** and click in the graphics window to place the parts.

11. Press **Esc** key.

12. Click and drag the parts, if they are coinciding with each other.

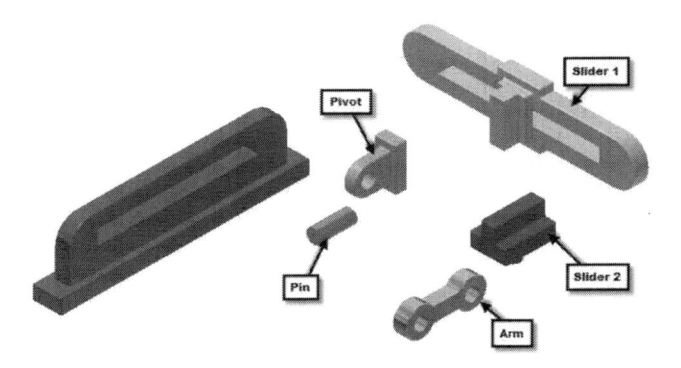

Creating the Slider Joint

1. Click **Assemble > Relationships > Joint** on the ribbon; the **Place Joint** dialog appears.

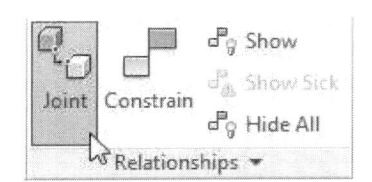

2. Set the **Type** to **Slider**.

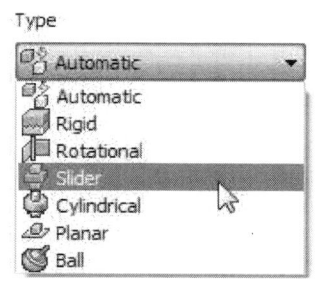

3. Select the face on the Slider1, as shown below.

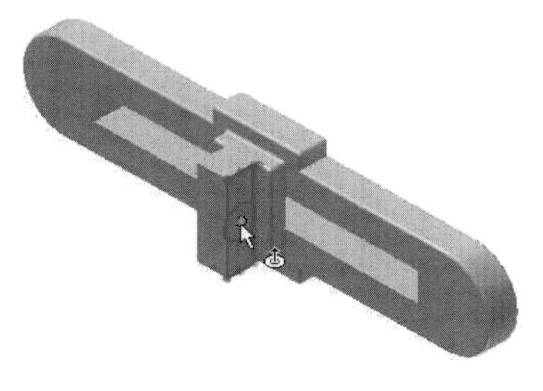

4. Select the face on the Base, as shown below; the two faces are aligned.

5. On the dialog, click the **Flip Component** button.

128

Top-Down Assembly and Motion Simulation

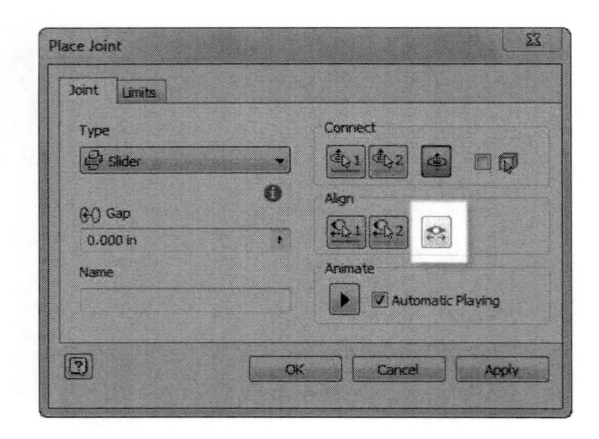

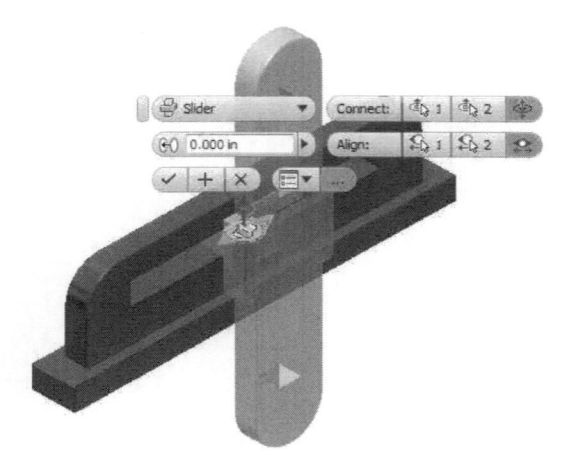

Make sure that the arrow of the joint is along the Y-axis.

5. Click the **Limits** tab on the **Place Joints** dialog.

6. Check the **Start** and **End** options under the **Linear** group.

7. Set the **Start** value to 3.15 in and **End** to -3.15 in.

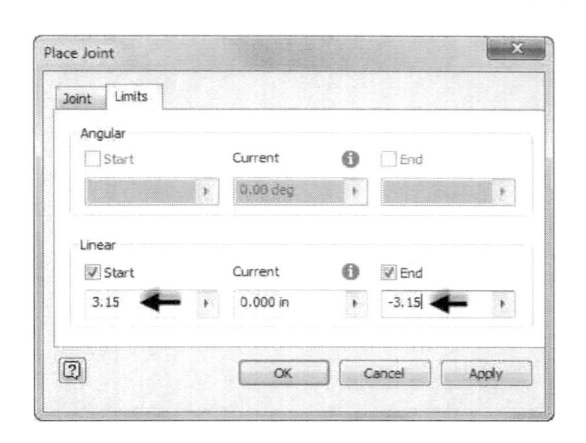

8. Click **OK**.

9. Select the Slider1 and drag the pointer; the Slider1 slides in the slot of the Base.

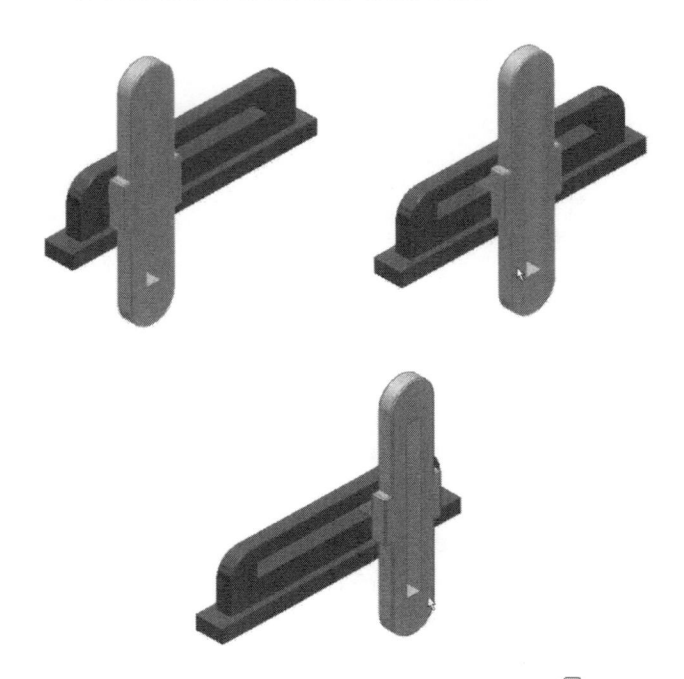

10. Click **Assemble > Relationships > Joint** on the ribbon.

11. On the dialog, set the **Type** to **Slider**.

12. Select the face on the Slider2, as shown below.

13. Select the face on the Slider1, as shown below.

129

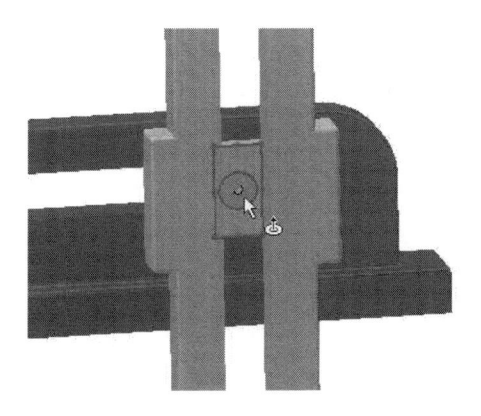

Top-Down Assembly and Motion Simulation

14. Click the **First alignment** button on the dialog.

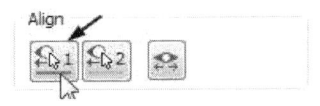

15. Select the edge on the Slider2, as shown below.

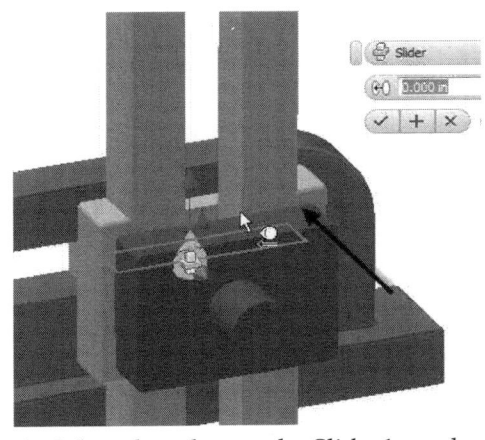

16. Select the edge on the Slider1, as shown below.

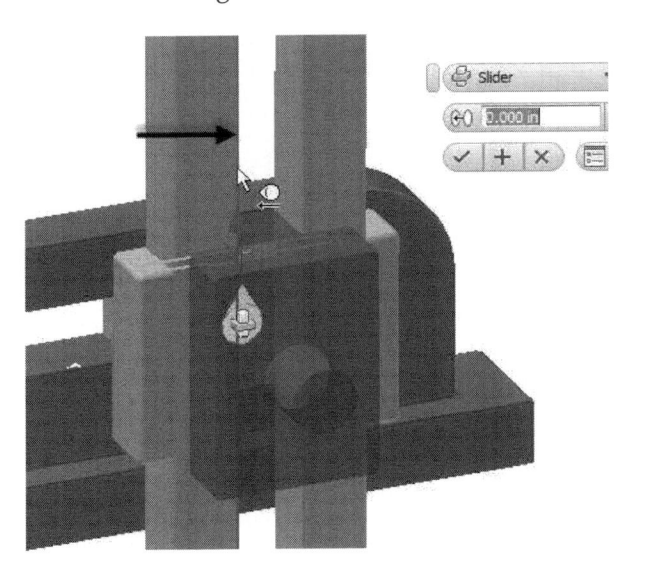

17. Click **OK**.

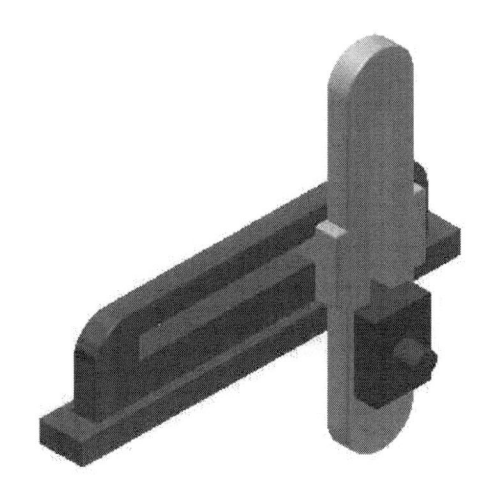

Creating the Rotational Joint

1. Click **Assemble > Relationships > Joint** on the ribbon.

2. Set **Type** to **Rotational**.

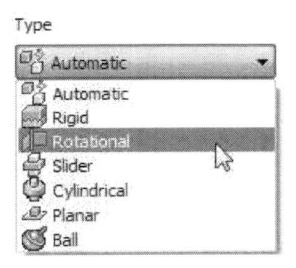

3. Select the circular edge of the arm, as shown below.

4. Select the circular edge of the Slider2.

130

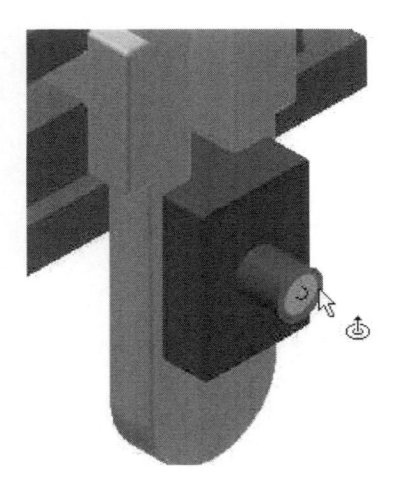

Top-Down Assembly and Motion Simulation

5. Click **OK**.

Creating the Rigid Joint

1. Click **Assemble > Relationships > Joint** on the ribbon.

2. Set the **Type** to **Rigid**.

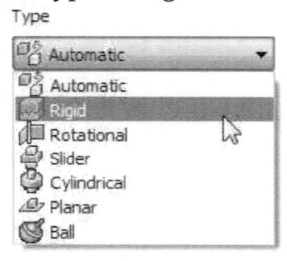

3. Select the top face on the pin.

4. Select the circular edge on the back face of the arm.

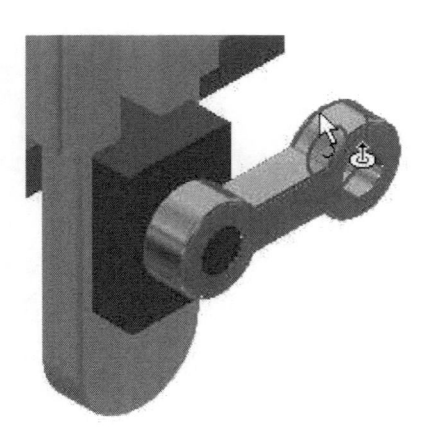

5. Click the **Flip Component** button under the **Connect** group.

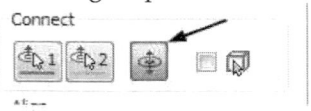

6. Click **OK**.

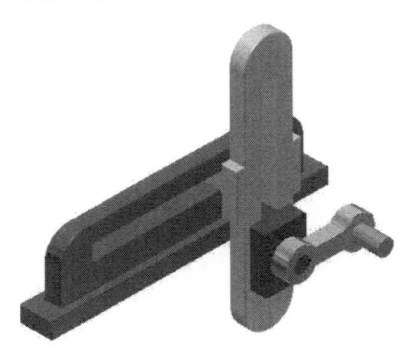

7. Create another rotational joint between the Pin and the Pivot.

Next, you need to constrain the Pivot by applying constraints.

8. Click the **Assemble** button on the **Relationships** panel.

131

Top-Down Assembly and Motion Simulation

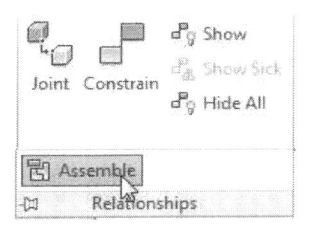

10. Select the bottom face of the Pivot, and then select the bottom face of the Base.

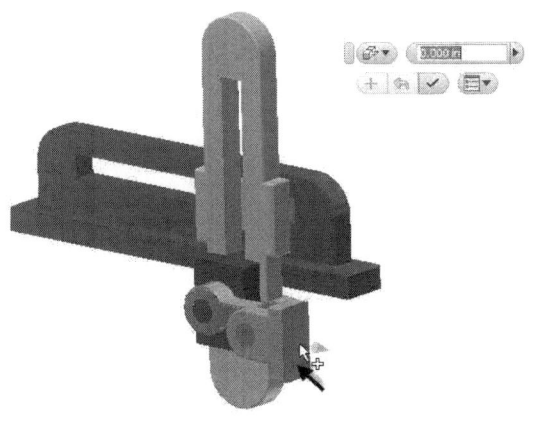

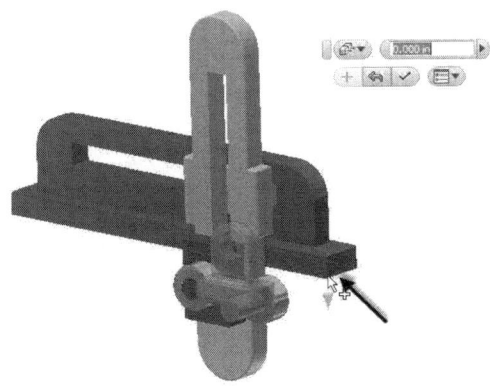

11. Click **Apply** (plus symbol on the mini toolbar).

12. Select the **XZ Plane** of the Pivot and **XY Plane** of the Base from the **Browser window**.

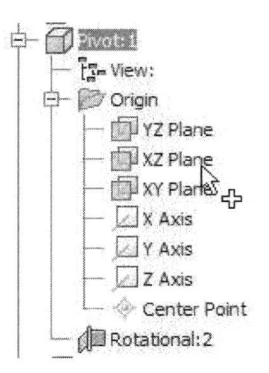

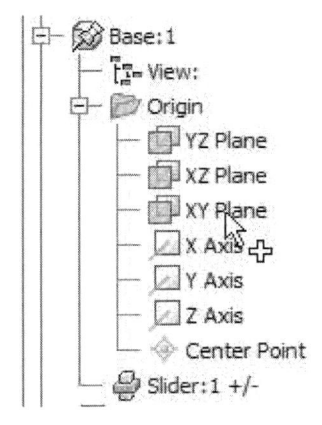

13. Click **OK** (check mark on the mini toolbar).

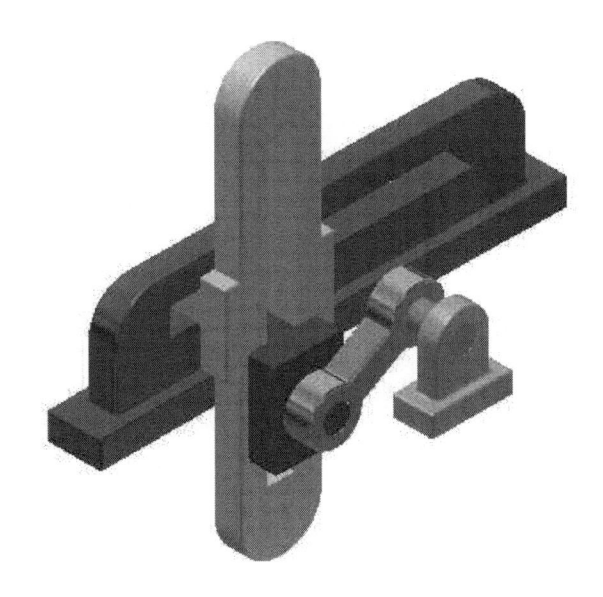

Driving the joints

1. In the Browser window, expand Pivot and click the right mouse button on the **Rotational** joint.

2. Select **Drive** from the shortcut menu.

132

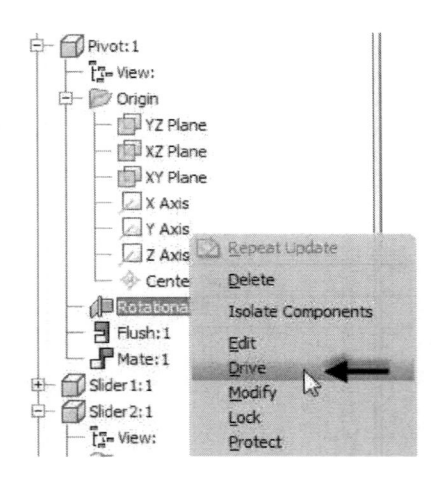

Top-Down Assembly and Motion Simulation

simulate the motion of the slider crank assembly.

7. Click **OK** to close the dialog.

8. Save and close the assembly and its parts.

3. On the **Drive** dialog, type-in 0 and 360 in the **Start** and **End** boxes, respectively.

4. Expand the dialog by clicking the double-arrow button located at the bottom. On the expanded dialog, you can define the settings such as drive adaptivity, collision detection, increment, repetition, and so on.

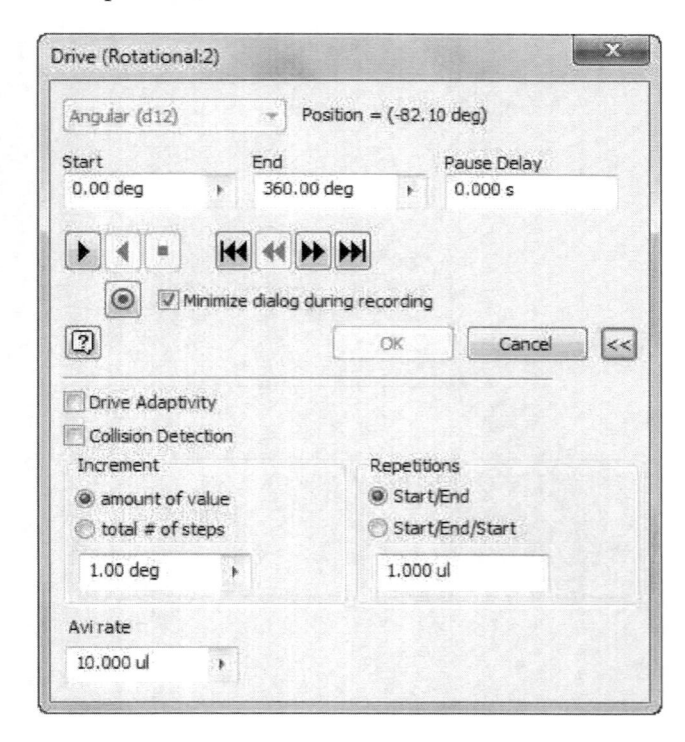

5. Click the **Record** button on the dialog. Specify the name and location of the video file. Click **Save** and **OK**.

6. On the dialog, click the **Forward** button to

133

Dimensions and Annotations

Chapter 8: Dimensions and Annotations

In this chapter, you will learn to

- Create Centerlines and Centered Pattern
- Edit Hatch Pattern
- Apply Dimensions
- Place Hole callouts
- Place Leader Text
- Place Datum Feature
- Place Feature control frame
- Place Surface texture symbol
- Modify Title Block Information

TUTORIAL 1
In this tutorial, you create the drawing shown below.

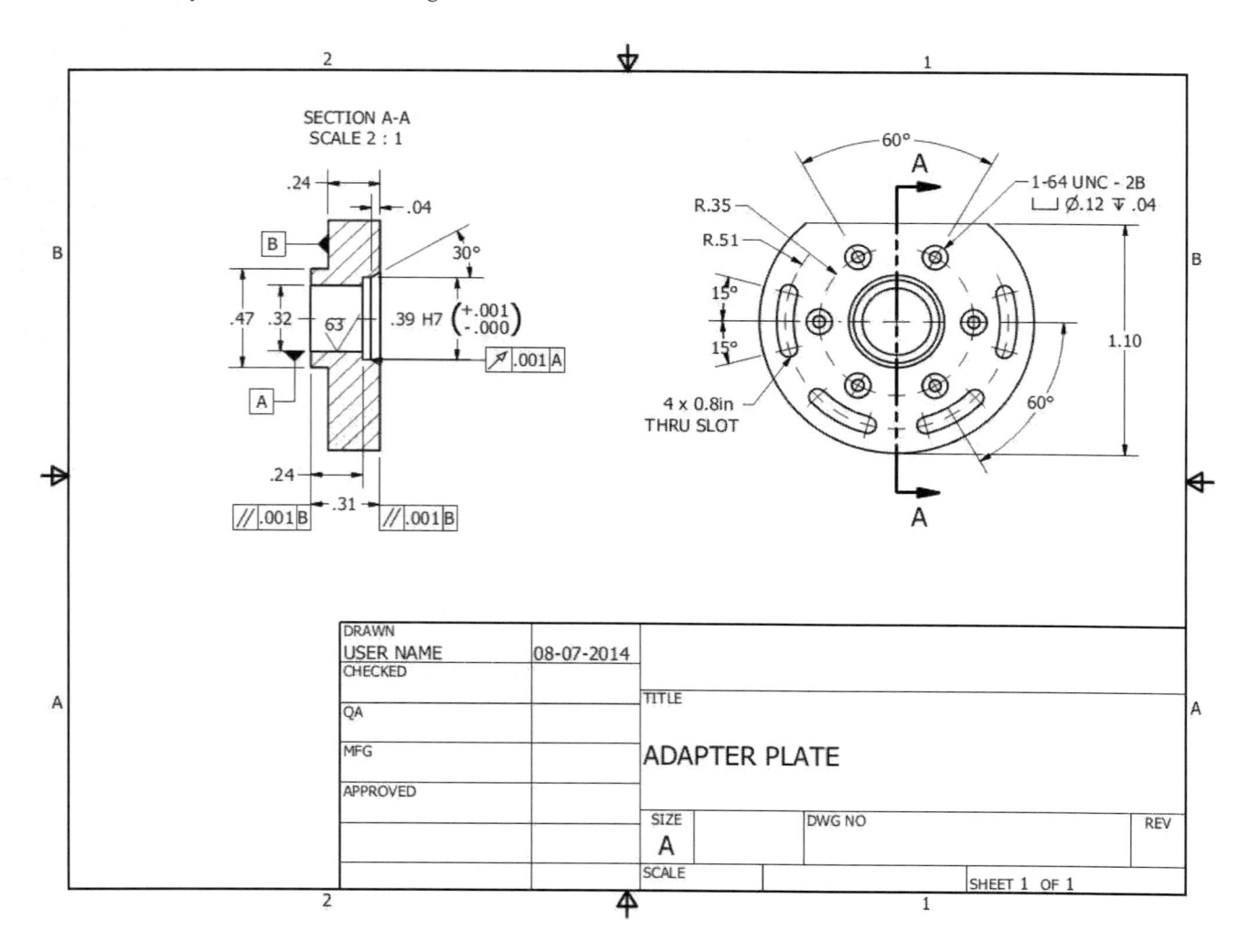

Dimensions and Annotations

1. Open a new drawing file using the **Standard.idw** template.

2. In the Browser Window, click the right mouse on Sheet:1 and select **Edit Sheet**.

3. On the **Edit Sheet** dialog, select **Size > A**, and then click **OK**.

4. Click **Place Views > Create > Base** on the ribbon.

5. Click **Open an existing file** button on the dialog.

6. Browse to the location of the Adapter Plate created in the Tutorial 1 of the Chapter 5. You can also download this file from the companion website and use it.

7. Set the **Scale** to 2:1.

8. Click the Front face on the ViewCube displayed in the drawing sheet.

9. Set the **Style** to **Hidden Line Removed**.

10. Place the front view on the right-side of the drawing sheet.

11. Click **OK** on the dialog.

12. Click **Place Views > Create > Section** on the ribbon.

13. Select the front view.

14. Draw the section line on the front view.

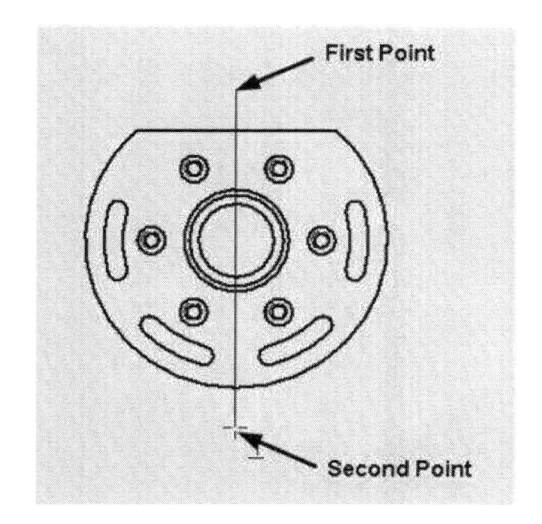

14. Right-click and select **Continue**.

15. Place the section view on the left side.

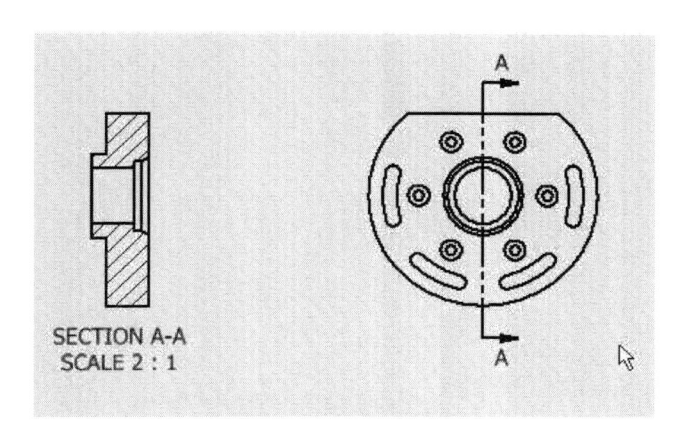

Creating Centerlines and Centered Patterns

1. Click **Annotate > Symbols > Centerline Bisector** on the ribbon.

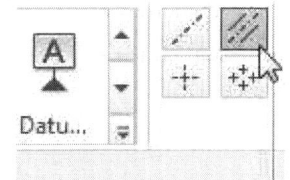

2. Select the parallel lines on the section view, as shown below; the centerline is created.

Dimensions and Annotations

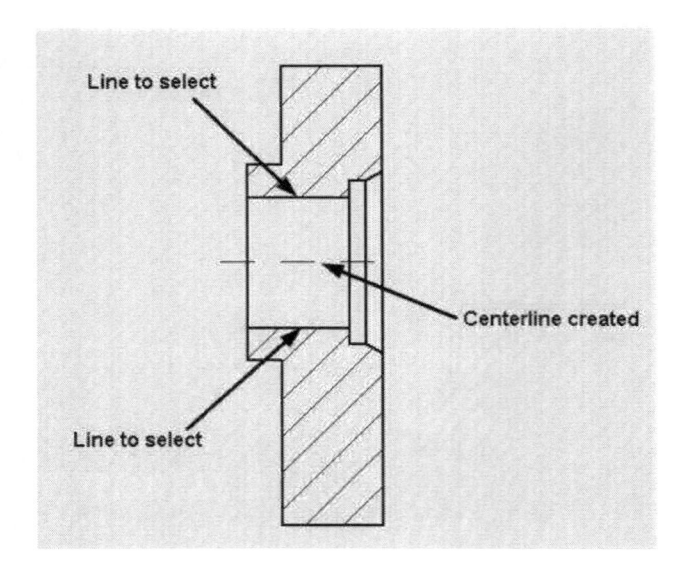

3. Click **Annotate > Symbols > Centered Pattern** on the ribbon.

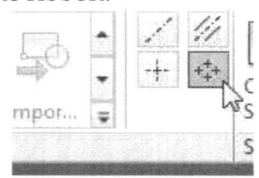

4. Select the circle located at the center.

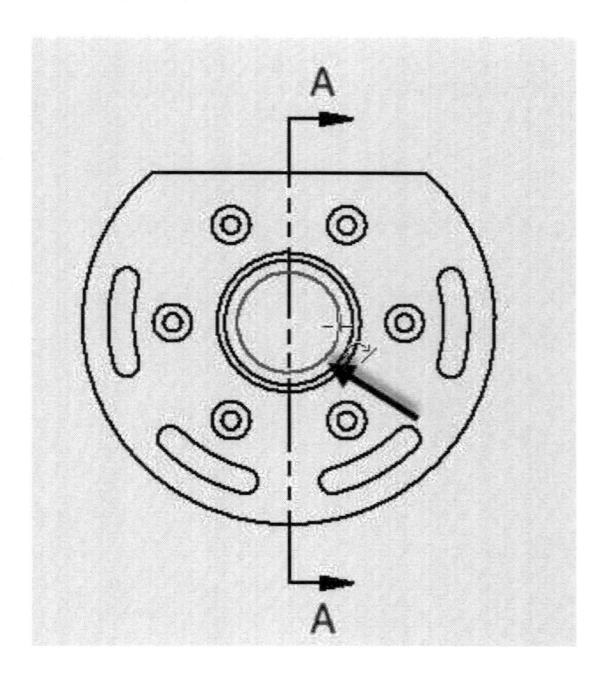

5. Select the center point of anyone of the counterbored holes.

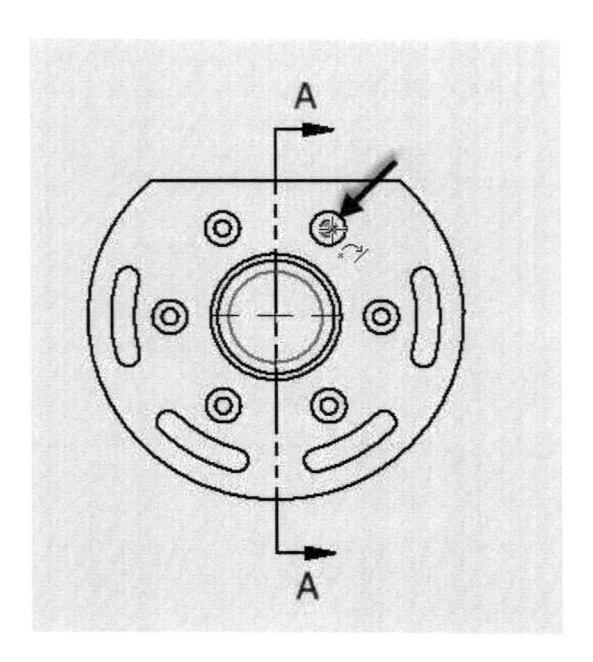

6. Select the center points of other counterbored holes.

7. Click the right mouse button and select **Create**.

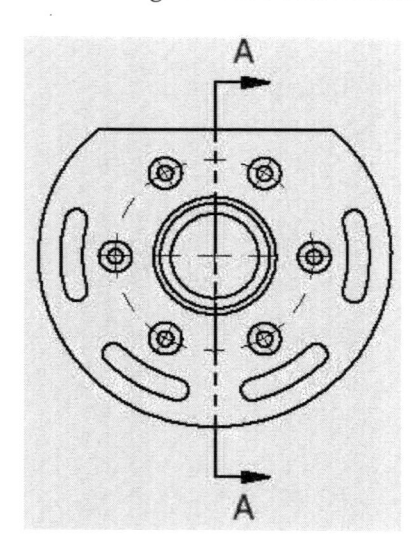

8. Likewise, create another centered pattern on the curved slots. Right-click and select **Create**.

Dimensions and Annotations

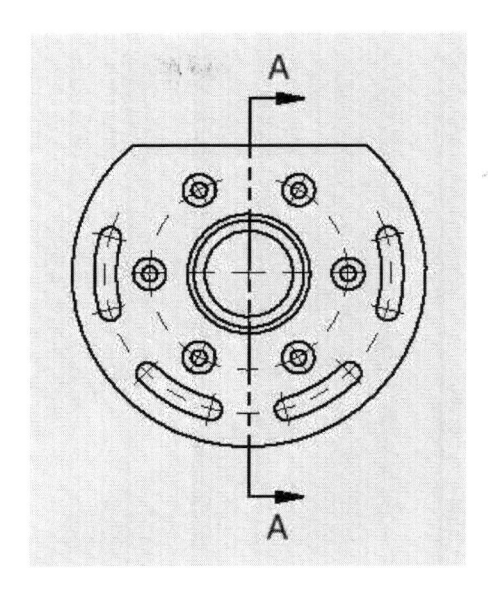

9. Press Esc to deactivate the tool.

Editing the Hatch Pattern
1. Double-click on the hatch pattern of the section view; the **Edit Hatch Pattern** dialog appears.

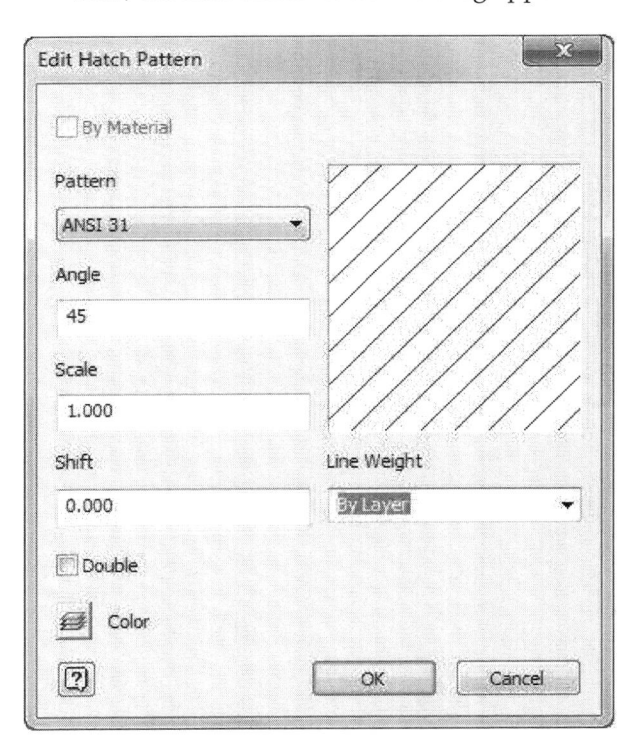

You can select the required hatch pattern from the **Pattern** drop-down. If you select the **Other** option from this drop-down, the **Select Hatch Pattern** dialog appears. You can select a hatch pattern from this dialog or load a user-defined pattern by using the **Load** option. Click **OK** after selecting the required hatch pattern.

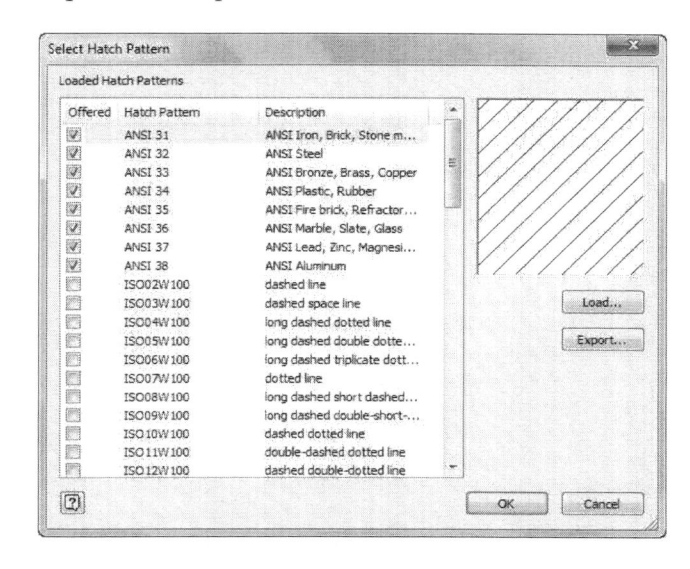

2. Click **OK**.

Applying Dimensions
1. Click **Annotate > Dimension > Dimension** on the ribbon.

2. Select the center line on the slot located at the left.

3. Select the endpoint of the center line of the hole located at the center.

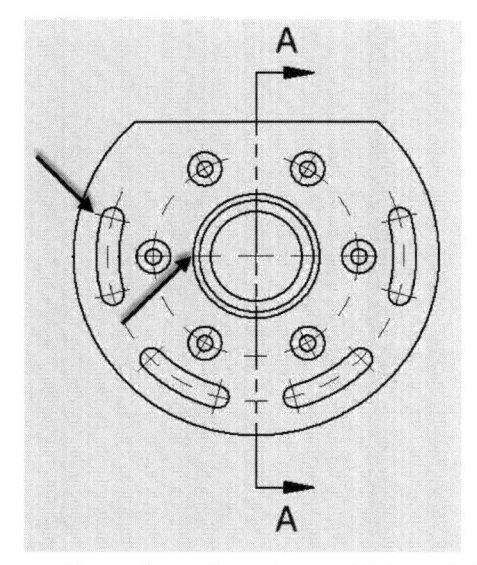

4. Move the pointer toward left and click.

5. Click **OK**.

138

Dimensions and Annotations

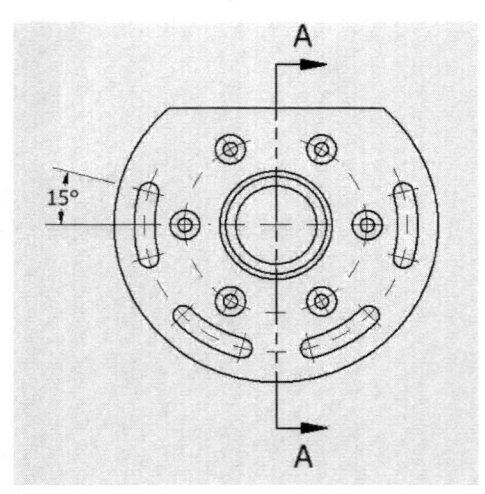

6. Likewise, create another angular dimension, as shown below.

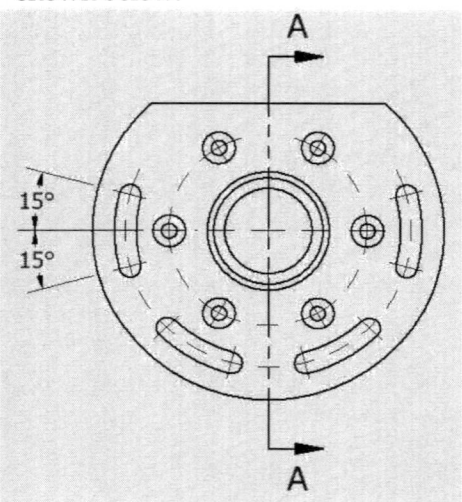

7. Create angular dimensions between the holes, and then between slots.

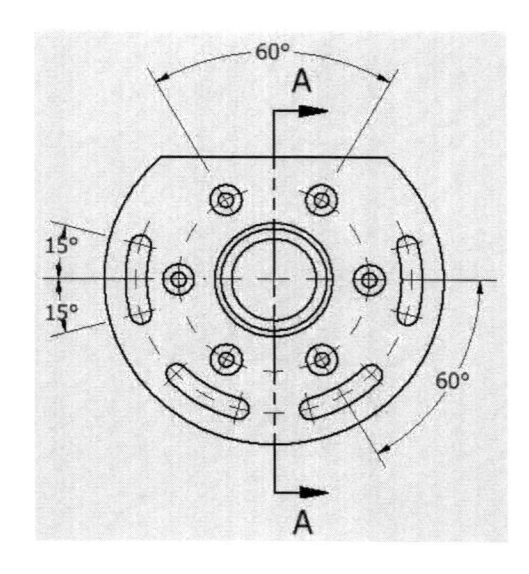

8. Dimension the pitch circle radius of the slots.

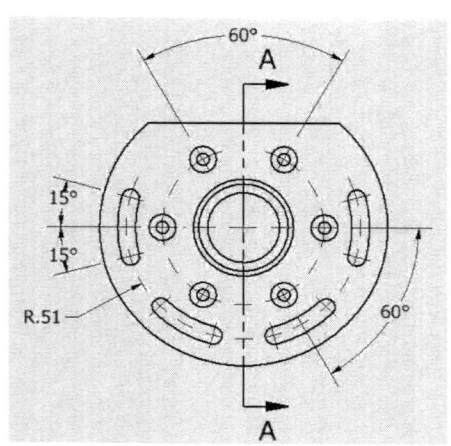

9. With the **Dimension** tool active, select the horizontal line of the front view and the lower quadrant point of the view.

Dimensions and Annotations

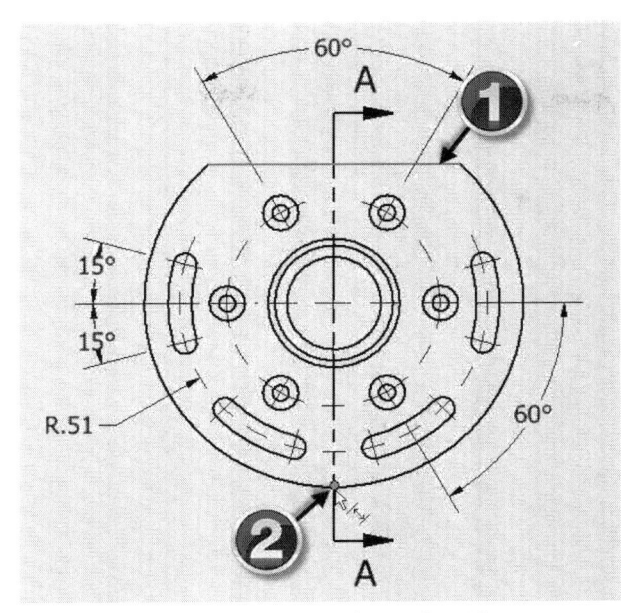

10. Place the dimension on the right side.

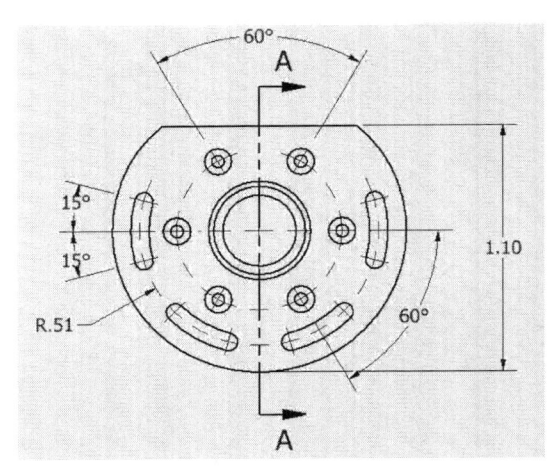

11. Click **Annotate > Feature Notes > Hole and Thread** on the ribbon.

12. Select the counterbore hole and place the hole callout, as shown below.

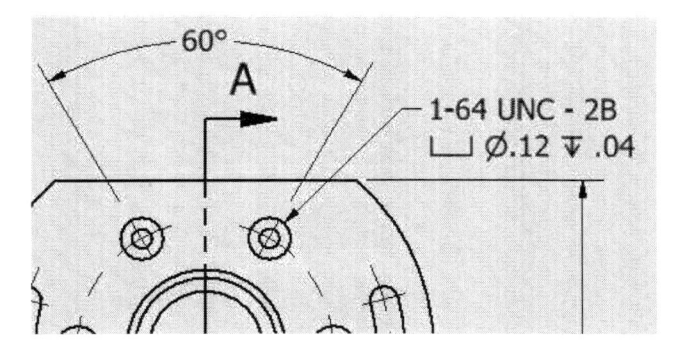

13. Add a pitch circle radius to counter holes.

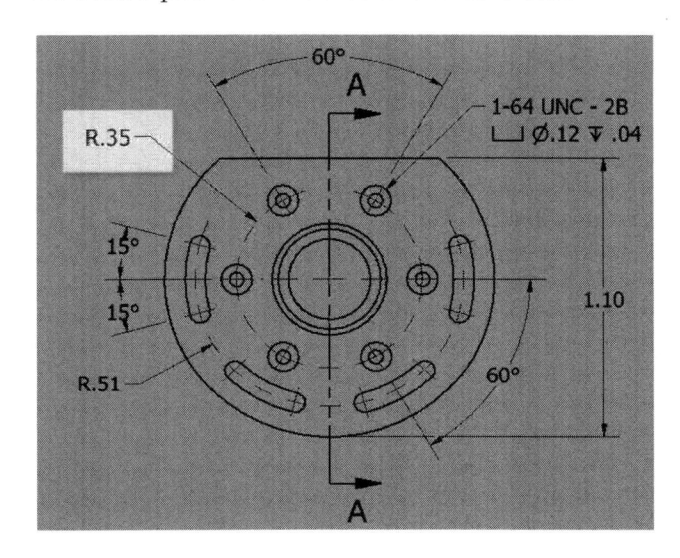

14. Click **Leader Text** on the **Text** panel.

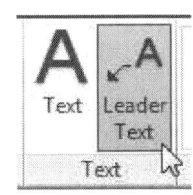

15. Select the slot end, as shown below.

140

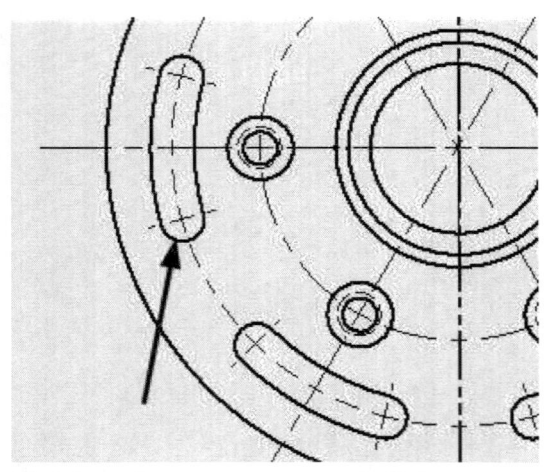

Dimensions and Annotations

16. Move the cursor away and click.

17. Right-click and select **Continue**; the **Format Text** dialog appears.

18. Enter the text shown below.

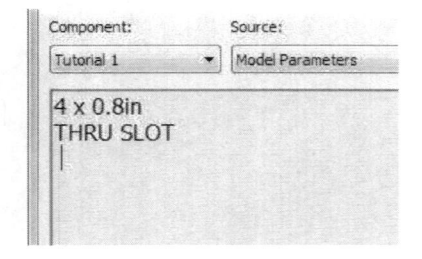

19. Click **OK**. Press Esc key.

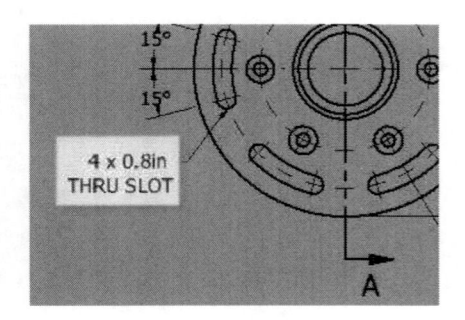

20. Double-click on the section label below the section view.

21. On the **Format Text** dialog, select all the text and set the **Size** to **0.120**. Click **OK**.

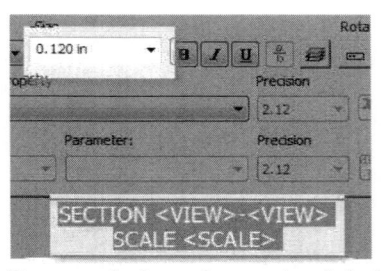

22. Drag and place the section label on the top.

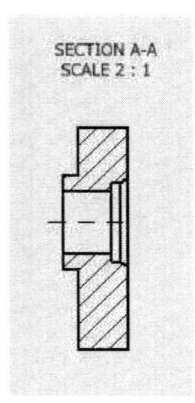

23. Click **Dimension** on the **Dimension** panel.

24. Select the lines, as shown below.

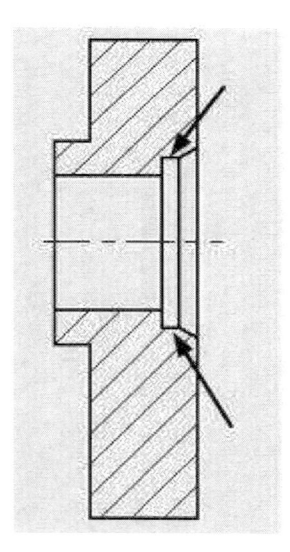

25. Move the pointer toward right and click to place the dimension.

26. On the dialog, click the **Precision and Tolerance** tab.

27. Set the **Tolerance Method** to **Limits/Fits - Show tolerance**.

141

Dimensions and Annotations

28. Select **Hole > H7**.

29. Set the **Primary Unit** value to **3.123**.

30. Set the **Primary Tolerance** value to **3.123**.

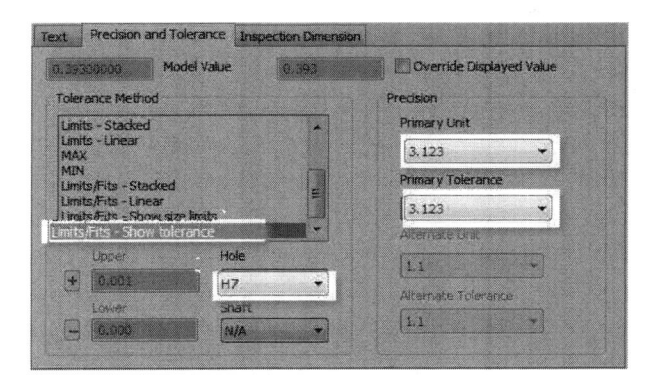

31. Click **OK**.

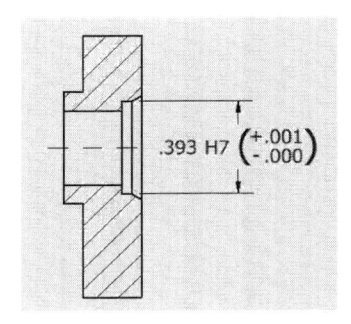

32. Likewise, apply the other dimensions, as shown below. You can also use the **Retrieve Dimensions** tool to create the dimensions.

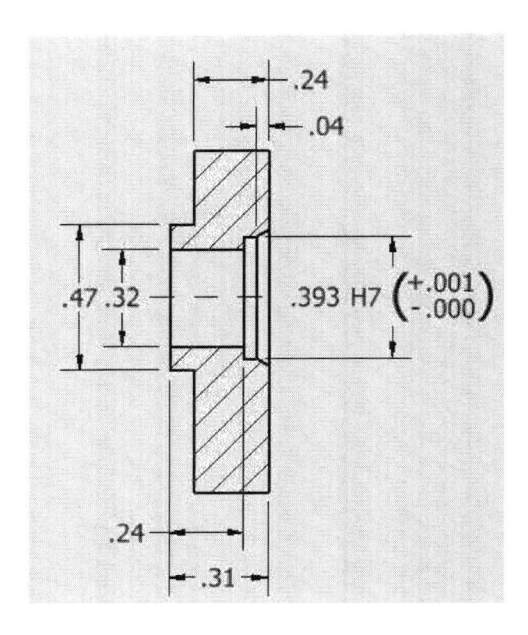

Placing the Datum Feature

1. Click **Annotate > Symbols > Datum Feature** on the ribbon.

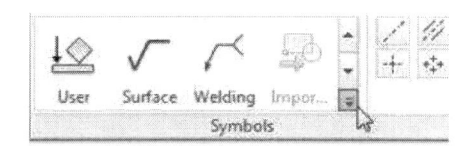

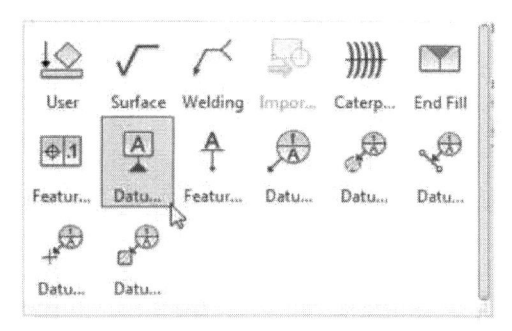

2. Select the extension line of the dimension, as shown below.

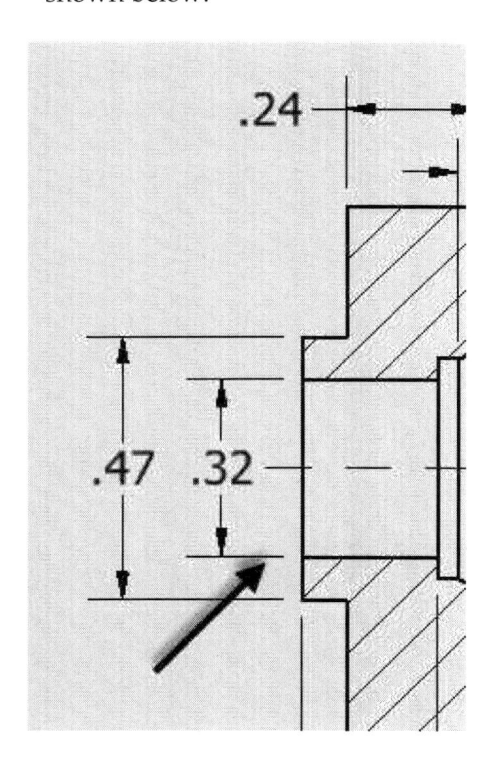

3. Move the cursor downward and click.

4. Move the cursor toward left and click; the **Format Text** dialog appears. Make sure that A is entered in the dialog.

142

Dimensions and Annotations

5. Click **OK**.

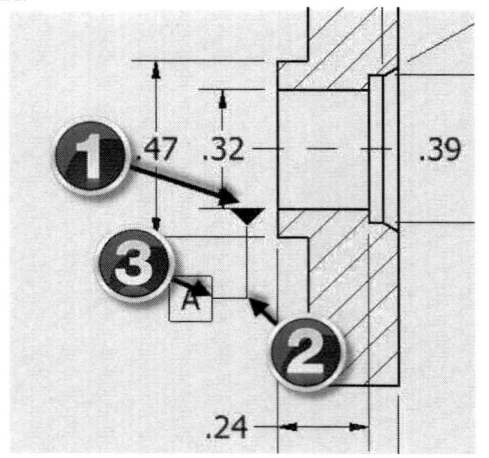

6. Likewise, place a datum feature B, as shown below. Press Esc.

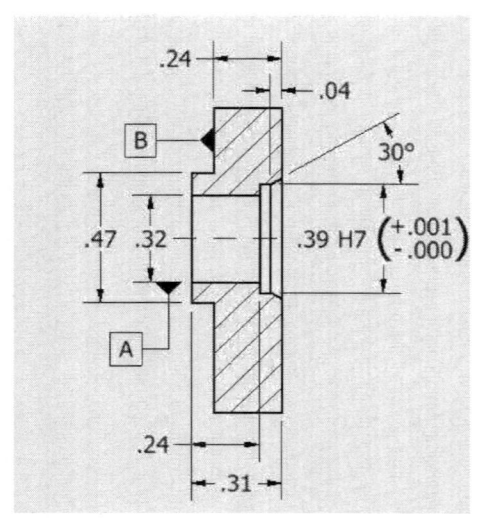

Placing the Feature Control Frame

1. Click **Annotate > Symbols > Feature Control Frame** on the ribbon.

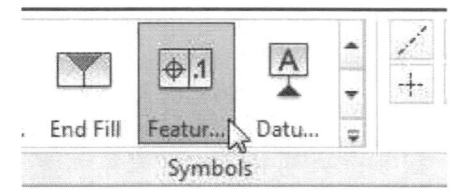

2. Select a point on the line, as shown below.

3. Move the cursor horizontally toward right and click.

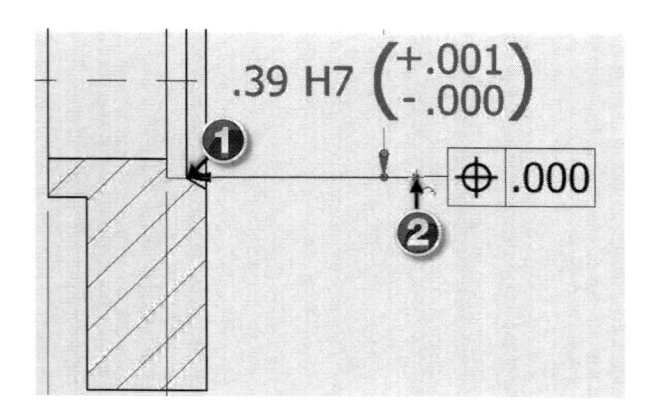

4. Right-click and select **Continue**; the **Feature Control Frame** dialog appears.

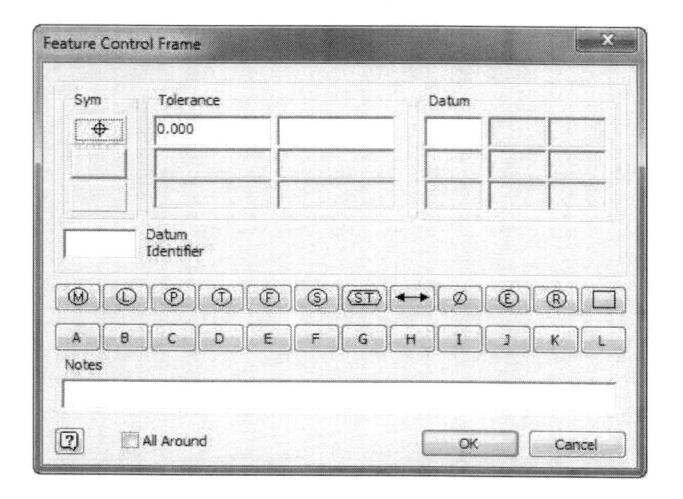

5. On the dialog, click the **Sym** button and select **Circular Run-out**.

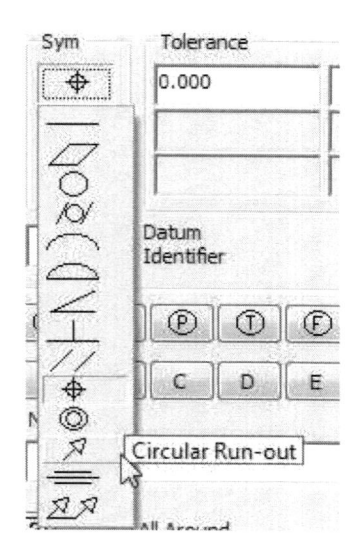

6. Enter 0.001 in the **Tolerance** box and **A** in the **Datum** box.

Dimensions and Annotations

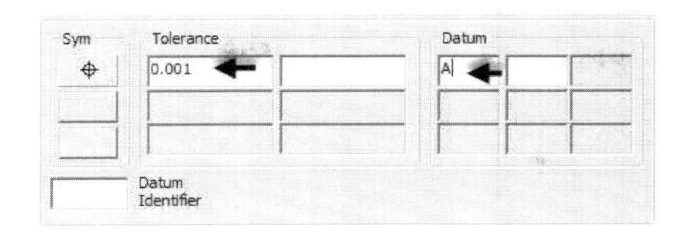

7. Click **OK**.

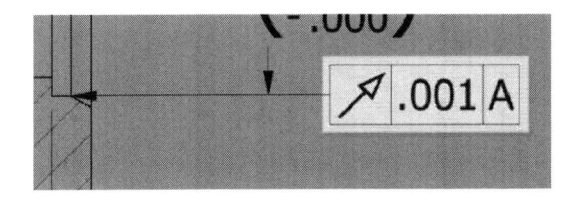

8. Right-click and select **Cancel**.

Placing the Surface Texture Symbols

1. Click **Annotate > Symbols > Surface Texture Symbol** on the ribbon.

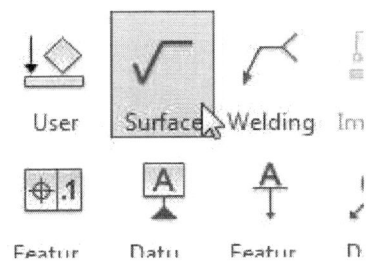

2. Click on the inner cylindrical face of the hole, as shown below.

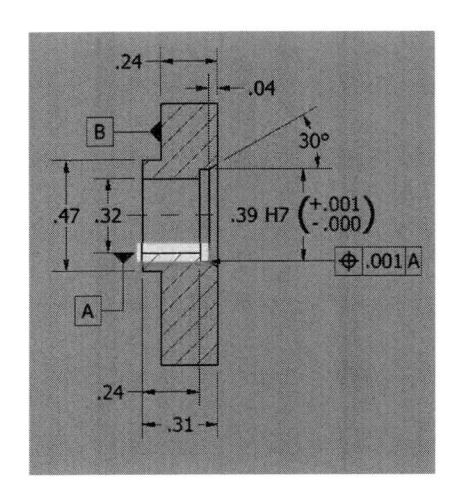

3. Right-click and select **Continue**; the **Surface Texture** dialog appears.

4. Set the **Roughness Average - maximum** value to 63.

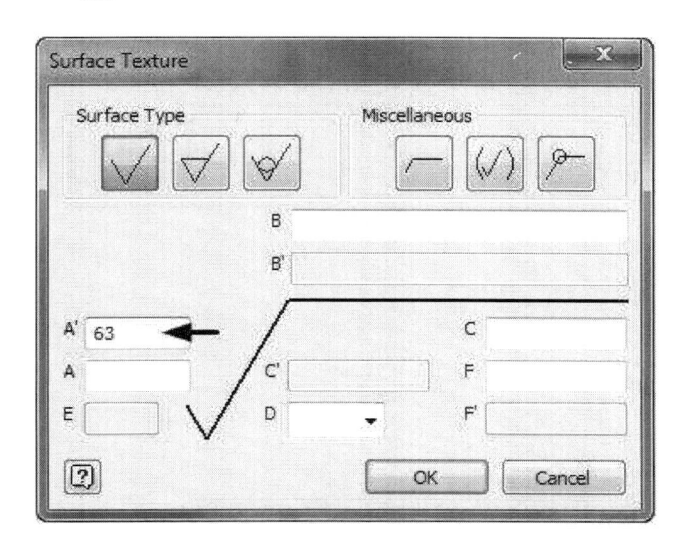

5. Click **OK**.

6. Right-click and select **Cancel**.

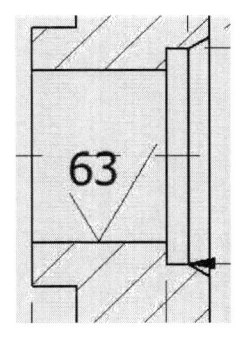

7. Apply the other annotations of the drawing. The final drawing is shown below.

144

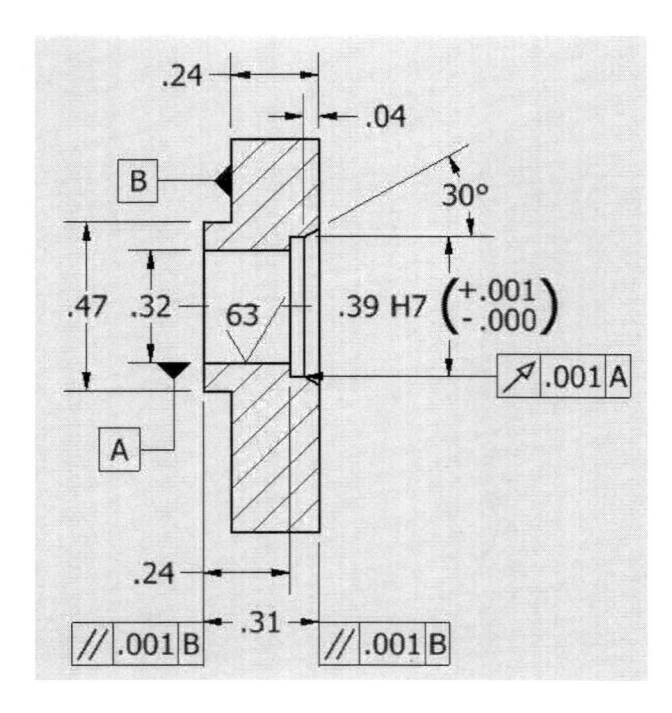

Dimensions and Annotations

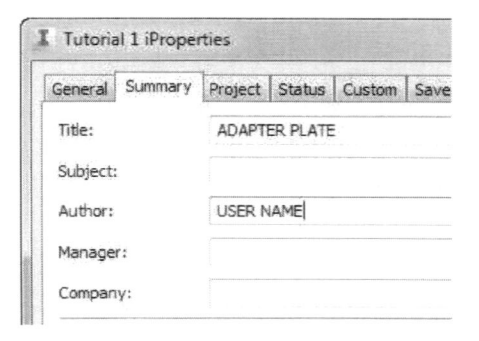

You can also update the Project information, drawing status and other custom information in the respective tabs.

3. Click **OK**.

4. Save the file.

5. To export the file to AutoCAD format, click **Application Menu > Export > Export to DWG**.

6. Click **Save**.

7. Close the file.

Modifying the Title Block Information

1. Right-click on the **Adapter Plate** in the **Browser window**. Select **iProperties** from the shortcut menu.

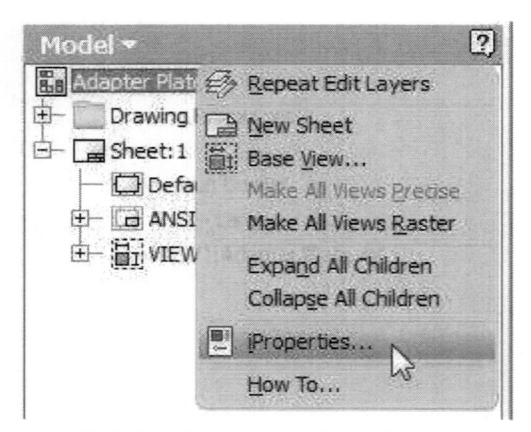

2. Click the **Summary** tab and enter the information, as shown next.

145

Additional Exercises

Additional Exercises

Exercise 1

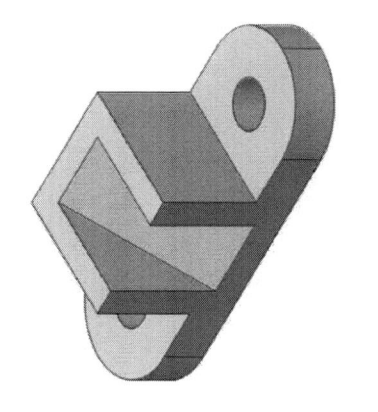

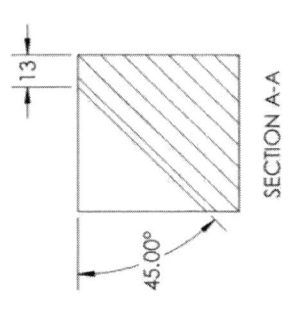

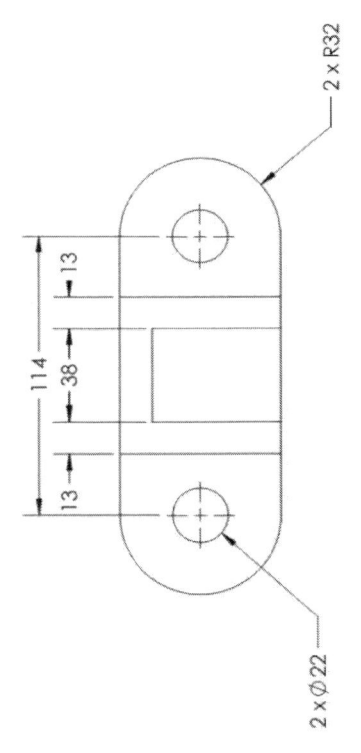

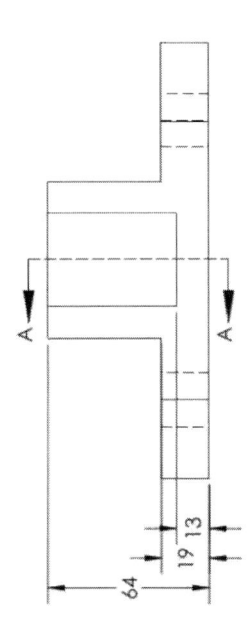

Additional Exercises

Exercise 2

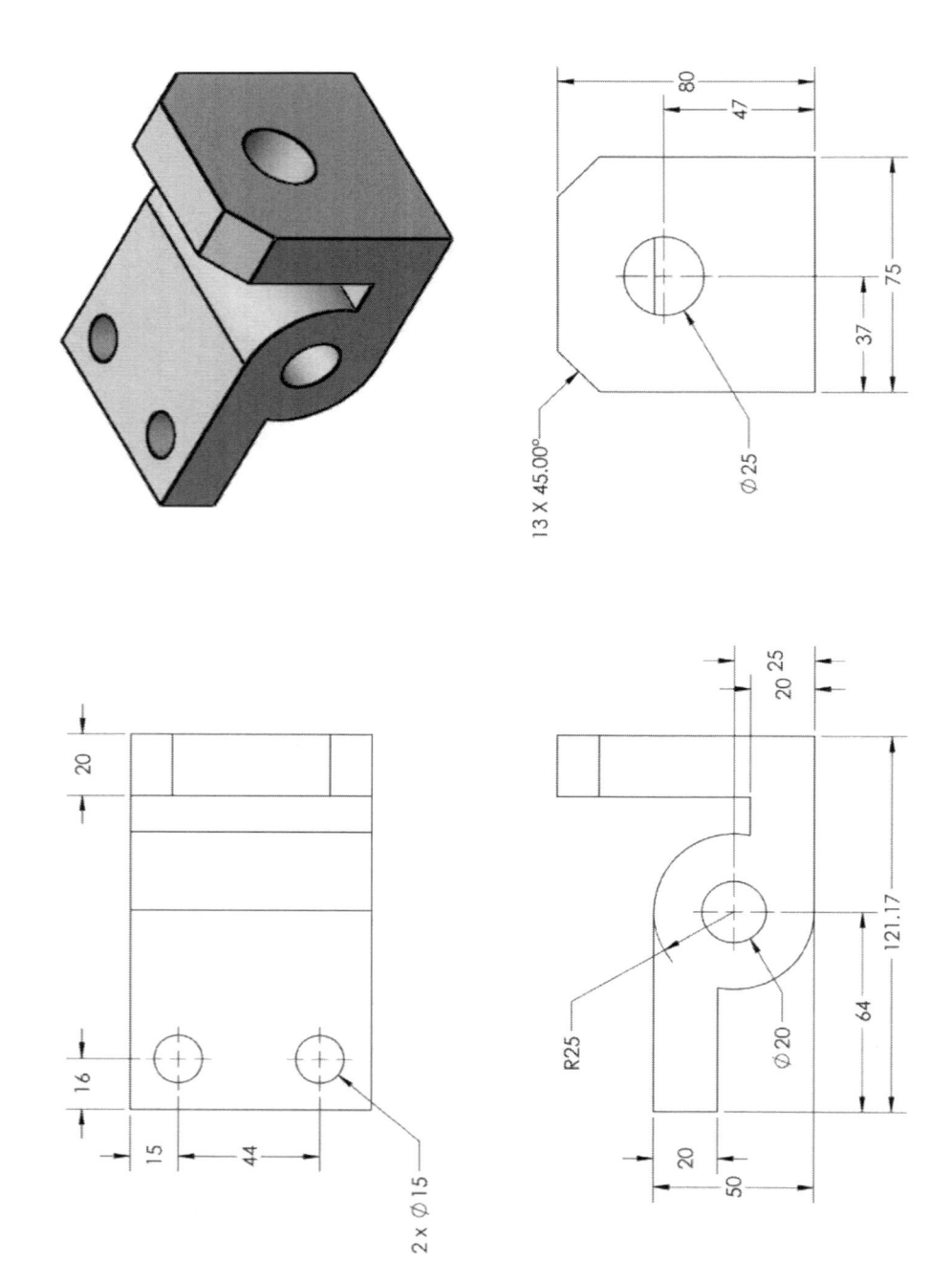

Additional Exercises

Exercise 3

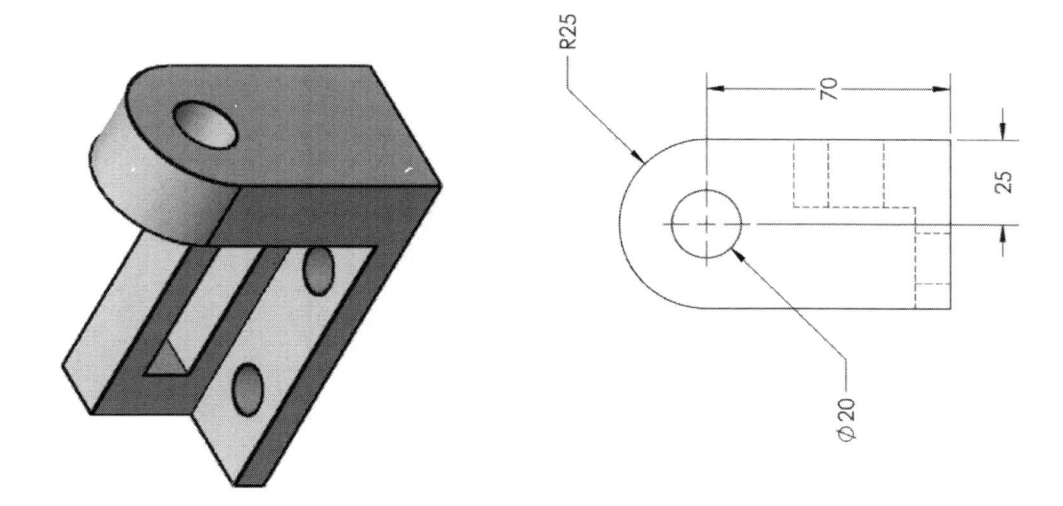

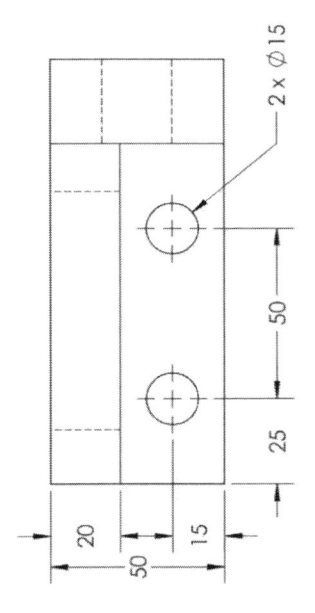

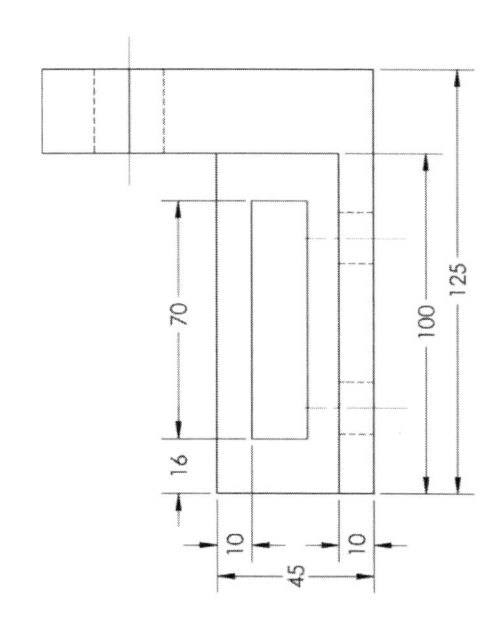

Additional Exercises

Exercise 4

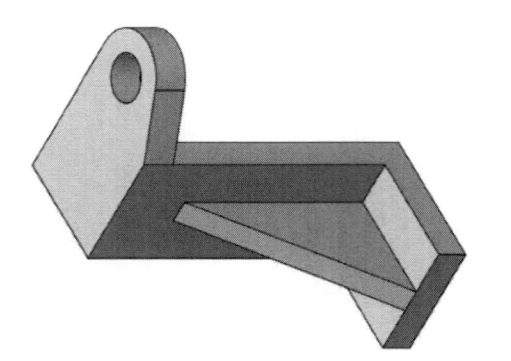

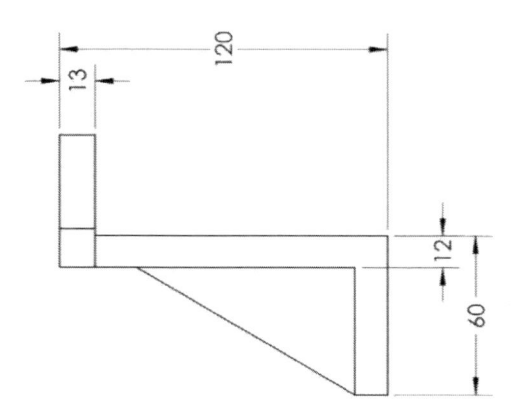

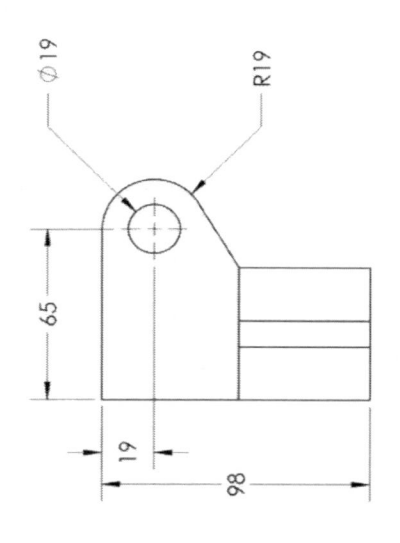

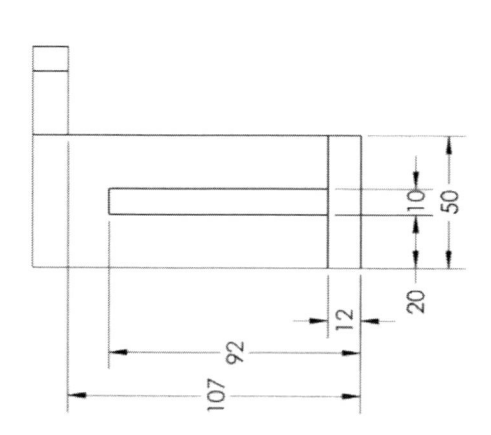

Additional Exercises

Exercise 5

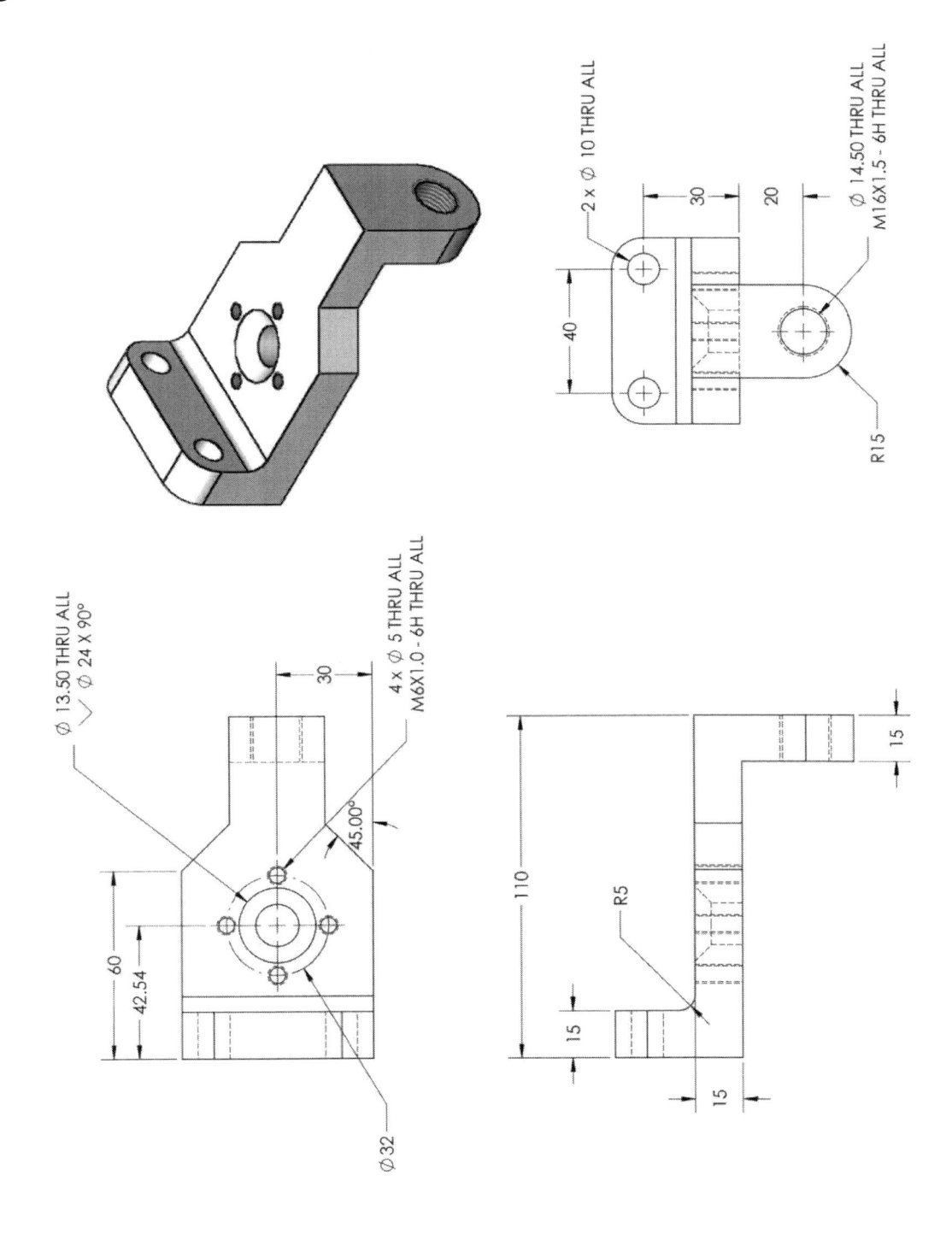

Additional Exercises

Exercise 6

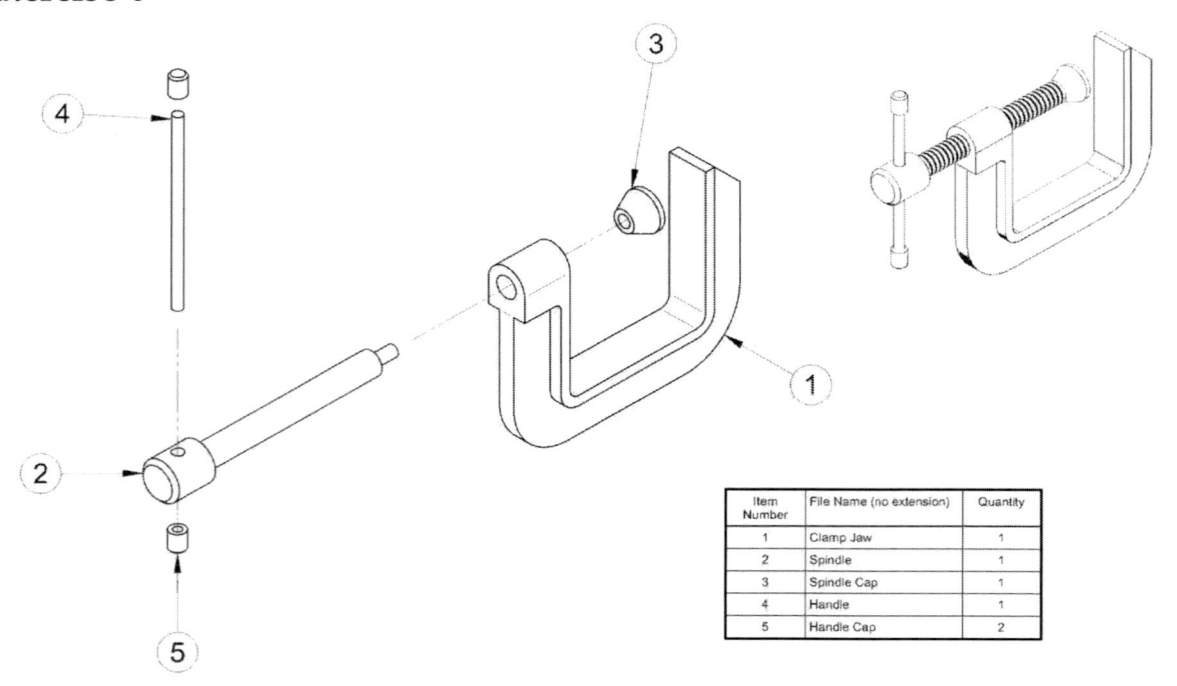

Item Number	File Name (no extension)	Quantity
1	Clamp Jaw	1
2	Spindle	1
3	Spindle Cap	1
4	Handle	1
5	Handle Cap	2

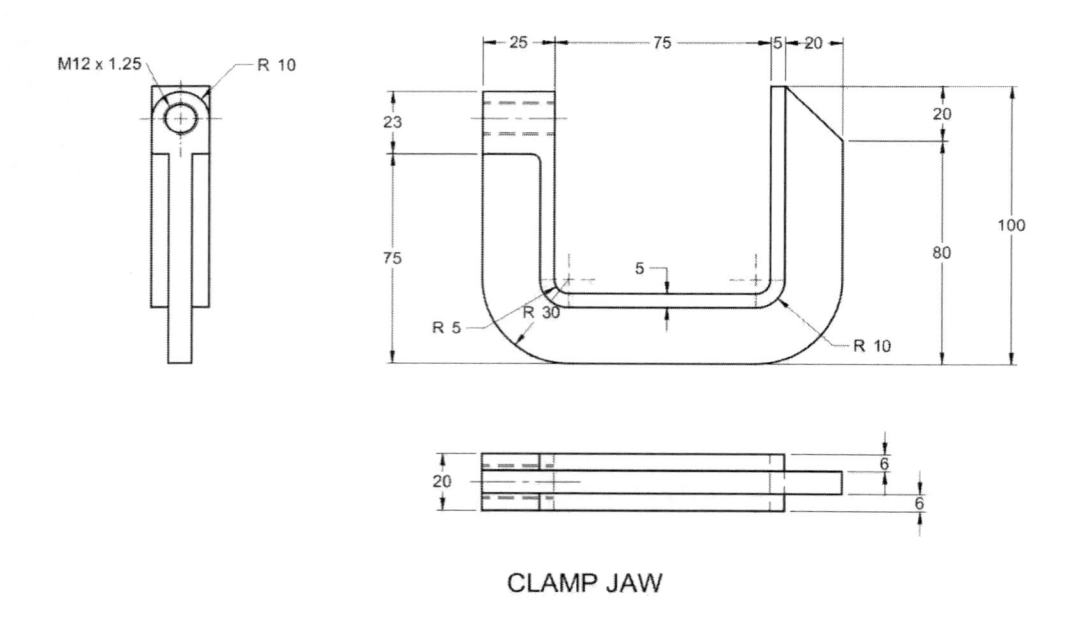

CLAMP JAW

Additional Exercises

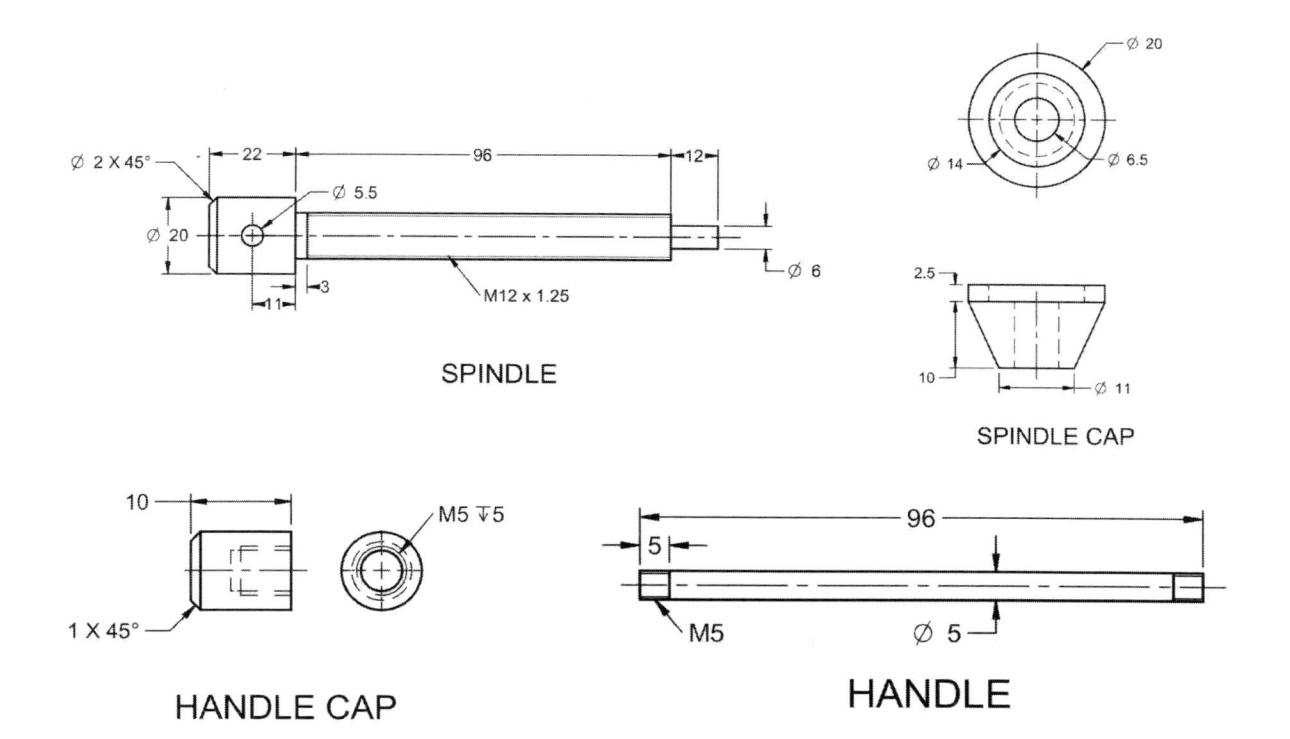

SPINDLE

Ø 2 X 45°, 22, 96, 12, Ø 5.5, Ø 20, 11, 3, M12 x 1.25, Ø 6

SPINDLE CAP

Ø 20, Ø 14, Ø 6.5, 2.5, 10, Ø 11

HANDLE CAP

10, M5 ↧5, 1 X 45°

HANDLE

5, 96, M5, Ø 5

Printed in Great Britain
by Amazon.co.uk, Ltd.,
Marston Gate.